THE
EVERYTHING
BABY'S FIRST YEAR BOOK
2ND EDITION

Dear Reader,

Becoming a parent is exhilarating, exciting, and exhausting, often all at the same time. You are constantly looking for answers and solutions, sometimes to questions you're not even sure how to ask (must be all that lack of sleep!).

Before I had my first baby, I read every book I could find, hoping I would unearth an instruction manual to parenthood that would carry me through at least the first eighteen years of my son's life. But alas, there was none. This book doesn't try to give you this all-inclusive, childhood-to-adulthood guide. Instead, what I hope you find in this book is a combination of practical advice on the basics of childcare; tricks of the trade from other moms who have been in the parenthood trenches and know the real skinny on raising kids; and most of all, support and reinforcement for you, the new parent. I've included my own experiences as a mother of four wonderful kids, only two of whom slept through the night before nine months.

More than anything, I hope this book empowers you to feel good about yourself as a parent. YOU are the expert on your baby, so feel free to take all this advice and accept; adapt; and when appropriate, discard to make it work for your family. Enjoy this first year. It's a precious time that goes by quickly (even when you're so tired, you think you'll never survive it). And congratulations—you're a mom!

Marian Edelman Borden

Welcome to the EVERYTHING® Series!

These handy, accessible books give you all you need to tackle a difficult project, gain a new hobby, comprehend a fascinating topic, prepare for an exam, or even brush up on something you learned back in school but have since forgotten.

You can choose to read an *Everything®* book from cover to cover or just pick out the information you want from our four useful boxes: e-questions, e-facts, e-alerts, and e-ssentials.

We give you everything you need to know on the subject, but throw in a lot of fun stuff along the way, too.

We now have more than 400 *Everything®* books in print, spanning such wide-ranging categories as weddings, pregnancy, cooking, music instruction, foreign language, crafts, pets, New Age, and so much more. When you're done reading them all, you can finally say you know *Everything®*!

QUESTION
Answers to common questions

FACT
Important snippets of information

ALERT
Urgent warnings

ESSENTIAL
Quick handy tips

PUBLISHER Karen Cooper

DIRECTOR OF ACQUISITIONS AND INNOVATION Paula Munier

MANAGING EDITOR, EVERYTHING® SERIES Lisa Laing

COPY CHIEF Casey Ebert

ACQUISITIONS EDITOR Brett Palana-Shanahan

DEVELOPMENT EDITOR Brett Palana-Shanahan

EDITORIAL ASSISTANT Hillary Thompson

EVERYTHING® SERIES COVER DESIGNER Erin Alexander

LAYOUT DESIGNERS Colleen Cunningham, Elisabeth Lariviere, Ashley Vierra, Denise Wallace

THE
EVERYTHING®
BABY'S FIRST YEAR BOOK

2ND EDITION

The advice you need to get you and baby through
the first twelve months

Marian Edelman Borden with Alison D. Schonwald, MD, FAAP

Avon, Massachusetts

*For John, who shared this wonderful parenting
journey with me, with much love and great joy.*

Copyright © 2010, 2002 by F+W Media, Inc.
All rights reserved.
This book, or parts thereof, may not be reproduced
in any form without permission from the publisher; exceptions
are made for brief excerpts used in published reviews.

An Everything® Series Book.
Everything® and everything.com® are registered trademarks of F+W Media, Inc.

Published by Adams Media, a division of F+W Media, Inc.
57 Littlefield Street, Avon, MA 02322 U.S.A.
www.adamsmedia.com

ISBN 10: 1-60550-368-1
ISBN 13: 978-1-60550-368-4

Printed in the United States of America.

10 9 8 7 6 5 4 3 2 1

Library of Congress Cataloging-in-Publication Data
is available from the publisher.

Illustrations by Eulala Conner.

*This book is available at quantity discounts for bulk purchases.
For information, please call 1-800-289-0963.*

Contents

Acknowledgments

Many, many thanks to the professionals, friends, family, and editors who helped in preparing this book:

Alison D. Schonwald, MD, FAAP, who carefully reviewed the manuscript for accuracy.

Pam Bruschi, BS, RN, who patiently answered countless questions with great insight and good humor. Pam is also the mother of four fantastic kids, so she speaks from professional and personal experience.

The wonderful mothers and fathers who shared their experiences and advice about that first year of parenting.

My own children, Charles, Sam, Dan, and Maggie, who have enriched my life and taught me far more than I could ever hope to teach them.

My husband, John, who shares this parenting adventure with love, enthusiasm, wisdom, patience, and a delightful (and much needed) sense of humor.

My parents, Evelyn and Carol Edelman, and in-laws, Edith and Melvin Borden, who were remarkable role models for good parenting.

My editor, Brett Palana-Shanahan, who has been incredibly supportive and thoughtful throughout this project.

My agent, Bob Diforio, who suggested me for this project.

You've all made this book stronger, smarter, and more fun. Any errors are mine.

Introduction

AS YOU NAVIGATE THE speed bumps of parenting an infant, you'll probably feel the need for some direction along the way. In *The Everything® Baby's First Year Book*, you will find the landmarks and mile markers that let you know you and your baby are both where you need to be.

This collection of wisdom from experienced mothers—first time moms, moms of many, vegetarian moms, bottle-feeding moms, and even nervous moms—will do more than help you through the challenges. It will reassure you that you—yes, you—have the resources to be a great mom yourself, and that you can and should have a wonderful time doing it.

Midwives, nurses, doulas, and pediatricians have contributed their expertise to these pages as well. Professional recommendations, information on what is "normal," and a breadth of exposure will support and validate the suggestions to come. It's one thing to consider a mom's opinion; it's quite another when that opinion is seconded by people who know.

Read on! You will find advice that is thoughtful, practical, and simple: from how to survive the first few days back home (accept all offers of help!) to what to do once your baby's mobile (brace yourself). You'll find realistic suggestions on returning to work and finding the right child care. You'll find tips on ways to bathe and feed your baby, and methods for getting him to sleep. As you're going through the suggestions, remember: "tried and true" doesn't happen without "trial and error" and no one trick works for everyone.

Some of the standard soothers and entertainers discussed, such as lullabies and nursery rhymes, are made easier because the words are contained in these pages, but you can also try one of the other suggestions for a little variety. You'll discover that even something as simple as Cheerios can keep your baby amused just long enough for you to finish your meal.

Journal pages for your baby's development—and your own—are included, too. To keep things organized, track his first foods, vaccinations, and even colds and illnesses. Track your progress, as well. Jot some notes on the first time you left the baby for a weekend or how you feel about going back to work.

You see, more than anything, *The Everything® Baby's First Year Book* is about you. It's about when to worry, and when to stay calm. It's about how to relax—and even spoil yourself on occasion!—and how important it is to take care of yourself, physically and emotionally.

You'll learn what you can ask for in the hospital and how to get geared up with the best baby essentials. How do you get out of the house with a new baby? Where do you go? When is it okay to start exercising? The included exercise primer will help you get yourself back in shape, and exercise is as good for the spirit as it is for the body. For extra motivation, you can even do some of the exercises with your baby!

As you prepare for (and adjust to) your new arrival, you'll find this book both useful and helpful. It's a guide and a workbook, but it's also a companion—something to help you along and remind you that you're not alone, that many heads are often better than one. It's something to remind you that there is no year like the first year—enjoy it!

CHAPTER 1

You're a Mom!

Yesterday you were pregnant; today you are a mother. Everything has changed. Yesterday you were wondering if your baby was ever going to come out, if your labor would ever end. Now your baby is lying in your arms or in her tiny bed, and you're wondering just how much it will hurt when you finally work up the courage to stagger to the bathroom.

The First Parenting Myth: "You'll Know"

You've probably spent very little time alone with your new baby. At the moment when the nurse or the midwife or your partner left the room, you also realized that along with the brand-new title of "mother" came the expectation that you were supposed to know, well, everything. You're supposed to know how to fasten a diaper so it doesn't scratch the baby's leg or cover her umbilical cord. You're supposed to know how to breastfeed her when you've never done it before. You're supposed to know how to comfort her when you're not sure why she's crying. You're supposed to know how to bathe, feed, and care for this precious bundle, even if you've never even babysat before.

Right now, let yourself off the hook. There'll be plenty of time for parenting guilt later. Remember: giving birth doesn't mean that you instantly become a parenting expert or that you magically know how to care for a baby. But here's what will happen—you'll learn. You'll ask questions (and you should never be embarrassed to ask); you'll read; and through trial and error you'll learn what works best for *your* baby and *you*.

Some things you'll figure out with the help of your mother, your doctor, or the women in the grocery store. All of these people will be sure to give you all sorts of advice, some of it even useful. Some things you'll find out from the new friends you'll make as you struggle through the early days of motherhood. Some things you'll figure out for yourself—and you'll soon share your tips with your friends. Many of the answers you'll need are in this book, written after much research, consultation with professionals and other moms, and reviewed by medical experts.

In this chapter we'll examine what's happening to you and your baby in the first hours and days after birth. Welcome to Parenthood.

Baby, the Extraterrestrial

A newborn who had a rough—or even a typical—birth does not look like a pink, chubby-cheeked Gerber baby. Don't worry if your first thought is that your baby looks like something from another planet. Give him a little time for the effects of traveling down the birth canal to wear off. Here's what's happening in the first few hours after delivery:

Apgar Scores

Within five minutes after being born, your baby will have his first check-ups. In the delivery room, the doctor will give a quick evaluation of your newborn at one minute after birth, and then at five minutes after birth. This is an Apgar score, a professional evaluation of a newborn's physical condition. It tells the medical team if the baby needs any immediate medical or emergency care. It measures the baby's heart rate (pulse), breathing, grimace (responsiveness), activity (muscle tone), and appearance (skin coloration). The medical team assigns a score of 0, 1, or 2 for each of these five categories, with 10 being a perfect score.

Remember: the Apgar test was designed to give your medical team a quick assessment of your baby's overall physical condition to determine if he needs immediate medical attention. It doesn't predict your baby's long-term health. Few babies score a perfect 10, and many perfectly healthy babies have low scores at birth. You often see lower scores after a long labor and delivery, after a high-risk pregnancy, after a cesarean section, and in premature infants. If you have any concerns, talk to your doctors.

Appearances Can Be Deceiving

Coming through the birth canal can be tough on baby and mom. Your baby may have:

- Head molding (misshapen or pointy)—it will return to its original shape in about a week or even longer. (The heads of C-section babies tend to be round because they haven't been squeezed coming through the birth canal.)
- A caput (a swelling on the head caused by fluid squeezed into the scalp).
- Swollen eyelids. Eye color at birth may not be permanent (usually set by six to nine months).
- Flattened nose (from the pressure during the delivery).
- Floppy ears (cartilage will harden in the next few months).
- Fine body hair.
- Swollen labia or scrotum, swollen breasts (both boys and girls). The nipples may leak a little milky substance. Girls may have a little white

discharge or blood-tinged vaginal mucus. These characteristics are from the pre-birth extra maternal hormones.

- Peeling skin.
- Bluish hands or feet (due to developing circulatory system—it will improve in the first few days).
- Reddish-purplish skin. Babies of all races and ethnicities are born with reddish-purplish skin, which will change to pinkish-red in a day. It seems pinkish because you're seeing the red blood vessels through his thin skin. Permanent skin color will develop over the next six months.
- Slightly bowed legs (from being curled up in the uterus for months). Will cure itself in a few weeks.

Your Baby's First Tests

All states require newborns to undergo certain tests shortly after birth. While it's unlikely that your child will suffer from any of these disorders, many of these diseases can be devastating if left unchecked and untreated.

- In the first forty-eight hours, a pinprick to your baby's heel will provide the blood needed to test for phenylketonuria (PKU), hypothyroidism, and other disorders. But states differ on the number and types of genetic and metabolic disorders for which they test. You can pay for additional testing, but you may need to make arrangements ahead of time. Talk to your doctor about what tests are part of the routine screen, and which others may be advisable.
- While it is not required in all states, the March of Dimes and the American Academy of Pediatrics recommend that all babies undergo a newborn hearing test (which is noninvasive). Talk to your doctor to see if your baby will be tested and, if not, arrange for this simple test. Should there be a hearing problem, early intervention is key.
- All states require that newborns be treated with antibiotic ointment or eye drops within an hour after birth. This prevents eye infections that may result from bacteria or sexually transmitted diseases that your baby may have been exposed to during labor and delivery.
- Some newborns are deficient in vitamin K, which is necessary for normal blood clotting. Therefore, the American Academy of Pediatrics

recommends administering a single injection of vitamin K to all newborns because of the risk of internal bleeding that might result from any trauma during delivery (for example: while unlikely, forceps pressure or vacuum extraction might cause a brain bleed). There has been some concern about a link between vitamin K injections and childhood cancers. Further research has failed to prove any link, but if you have concerns, talk to your doctor.

- The Centers for Disease Control and Prevention (CDC) recommends that all children receive the first dose of the Hepatitis-B vaccine at birth. This is particularly important for children whose mothers are chronically infected. Three doses of the hepatitis B vaccine are needed for full protection. The second dose is recommended at one to two months and the third between twenty-four weeks and eighteen months. If you do not live in one of the thirty-six states that require newborn Hepatitis-B vaccination, talk to your health care practitioner about when your baby will be vaccinated.

Taking Care of Yourself

What's happening to you in the first couple of hours after birth? You have just been through the most intense, life-changing experience there is. You are stunned, exhausted, amazed, thrilled, frightened, and overwhelmed. On top of all that, you have to recover physically and adjust to this major change as soon as possible, because you have a person depending on you who isn't yet aware that she isn't still part of you.

QUESTION

What can the nurses provide to keep me comfortable?
There are several simple things that nurses will bring if you ask. These include extra pillows or a donut cushion, topical anesthetic, witch hazel or a sitz bath, stool softener, and as much ice as you can handle. You can also ask them for more food or fluids.

You may be one of the 99 percent of new mothers who give birth in a hospital. You will probably stay there two days—longer if you had a

C-section, shorter if you opt to go home early. Your body will go through tremendous hormonal and physical changes in the first few days after you give birth. Here's what's happening:

- Your uterus will begin to shrink. This is called *involution* and it will take four to six weeks before your uterus is back to its prepregnancy size (from about the size of a grapefruit immediately after birth to the size of a lime at your six-week checkup). You may experience after-pains, or contractions that occur as the uterus shrinks after you've given birth. You may feel these pains more intensely when you breast-feed, although not all mothers feel them. Ask your doctor if you can use warm packs to relieve the pain. You can also ask the nurses to massage the fundus, the upper, rounded portion of the uterus, through your abdomen. Ibuprofen also helps.

- You will bleed for several weeks as the uterus heals, specifically from where the placenta attached to the uterine wall. The amount of blood may be more than a heavy period. Use sanitary napkins to absorb the blood. Do not use tampons (which might cause an infection) until after you see your doctor at your six-week checkup. You may see blood clots in the first few days, but check with your doctor if you see them after that. Eventually the blood flow will taper off to what is equivalent to a normal period, and then to spotting. The blood's color will go from bright red to brown to yellow/white-ish. If the blood flow gets heavier or darkens in color, it might mean you're doing too much and should rest. When in doubt, call your doctor. If your bleeding is so heavy that you soak through a sanitary pad every hour for two hours, contact your doctor or midwife as this may be a sign of post-partum hemorrhage.

- You will need to urinate frequently in the first days after giving birth as your body eliminates the extra fluid it stored in the last months of pregnancy. The nurses will keep a close watch on your urine output. Sometimes your bladder may be weakened and overdistended by the large amount of urine produced. Urinary retention can result and require bladder catheterization.

- Whether the doctor performed an episiotomy, a surgical incision through the perineum, or you experienced a small-to-medium-sized tear in that area, your bottom is going to be sore for two to ten days. You may need pain medication. Don't try to be a heroine and tough it out. If you think you need something for the pain: ask. Just remember that narcotic pain-relieving drugs can also cause constipation, so you'll need to eat plenty of fiber and drink lots of fluids. Be sure to remind your doctor if you are breastfeeding so that only safe medications are prescribed.

You will want to ice the area in the first twenty-four hours to reduce swelling. After the first day, switch to heat. Apply hot compresses and sit in sitz baths to draw blood to the area, which promotes healing.

- You may have started to produce colostrum (the first milk) in the last few weeks of pregnancy. The real milk doesn't "come in" until the second, third, or fourth day after giving birth. See Chapter 6 for a full discussion about breastfeeding.

Keep in mind that in those first couple of days your breasts may become engorged and very painful. They may feel hard and knotty. To relieve the engorgement, you should wear a proper-fitting bra (or a nursing bra if you plan to breastfeed). Apply ice, take some pain medication, and manually express some milk to ease the pain.

If you don't plan to breastfeed, wear a tight-fitting bra as soon after delivery as possible. When you shower, avoid hot water on your breasts.

ALERT

The following symptoms could indicate a post-partum complication, which can be life threatening: fever above 100.4°F (orally); blood clot larger than a walnut; bad-smelling discharge; pain when urinating that gets worse as time passes instead of better; pain in calf or thigh without redness; pain or reddened and tender area on breast.

The Cesarean Delivery

A cesarean delivery complicates the postpartum recovery for the simple reason that it is major abdominal surgery. Respect the fact that your body needs to heal. Don't downplay the pain or try to ignore it in an attempt to get your life back to "normal." Take pain medication as you need it and according to what the doctor prescribes.

Just like mothers who have delivered vaginally, your uterus needs to shrink, your bladder may become distended, you may become constipated (surgery may temporarily decrease the motility of the intestines), and your breasts may become engorged.

Although it's painful, moving, even gingerly, is the best way to recover more quickly. If you need pain medication to get up and walk a little, take it. Support your incision by holding a pillow over it. While you may feel like you want to bend forward as you walk, try to stand up straight.

Nurses will be checking for rumblings in your stomach and intestines. A few hours after delivering, take sips of water. If you can tolerate water without vomiting or nausea, you will move to broth and Jell-O; and then finally to semi-soft foods.

Make the Most of Your Hospital Stay

You'll probably be in the hospital for about forty-eight hours if you have a normal delivery. If you have a cesarean, you'll most likely be discharged on the fourth or fifth day after delivery. In either case, you want to use the time in the hospital to get back your strength while you get acquainted with your new baby.

If at all possible, get yourself moved to a private room (most hospitals offer private rooms for a surcharge). Phone calls, visitors, and your baby's wakings will interrupt your sleep often enough; add another mother, her baby, and her guests into the mix, and you're likely to go home more tired than when you entered. Also, your partner will probably not be allowed to stay overnight if you have a roommate.

Grand Central Station

Even if you snag a private room and limit your visiting list, your hospital room can seem like a busy train station. Expect to see your midwife or doctor and nurses, your baby's pediatrician and nurses, a lactation consultant, and aides or volunteers who deliver food. You'll also get impromptu visits from the florist, janitorial staff, and hospital administrators, as well as various repairmen who arrive just as you are falling asleep.

If you've had your baby at home, your midwife will typically stay with you for several hours after the baby is born, taking both your and your baby's vital signs, cleaning up, and making sure you get something to eat. She'll be back again the next day to check you and your baby, make sure breastfeeding is successfully underway, and to assess the home situation—if the house is a wreck and there is no food in the refrigerator she'll probably suggest that you need a little more help.

Whether you have a hospital or home birth, you need to limit the number of visitors and restrict how long they stay. Your hospital room or home should not become everyone's favorite new hangout—no matter how anxious family and friends may be to see the new arrival. You need the rest and you and your baby don't need the germs that visitors may bring.

Include the Siblings

If you have an older child or children who will be visiting you in the hospital, have the new baby taken to the nursery before the older child arrives. Even if the baby is staying in the room with you, this is the time for the baby to stay for a short time in the nursery so that you have an initial one-on-one with your older child.

Your older child needs lots of hugs and reassurance from you. Let her play with the buttons on your bed. Have a small gift for the big brother or sister. Then send the child with your partner to the nursery to get the baby (your child can help push the bassinet down the hall). You might even want to ask the child to help return the baby to the nursery when it's time to leave.

Limit the visitation to no more than an hour, less if your older child is under two—she'll get bored, and you need the rest.

Chow Time

It's hard to think about food during labor, but if you've had a vaginal delivery, odds are that you'll be starving the minute that baby gets out. You've just completed a marathon-type event, and your body has used every calorie available. Hopefully you packed some snack items in your overnight bag. Your partner or family can also bring some food in, but take it easy, even if you're craving something hot and spicy. Your body is still getting back to normal and you don't want to complicate digestion.

Check out the hospital menu. When making your choices your first concern should be calories—you burned many more calories than you took in during labor, briefly putting your body into a state of starvation. The creation of breastmilk also burns calories; you'll use about 500 calories a day more than a woman of your size who is not breastfeeding. So circle at least two items in every category on that menu to cover your caloric bases. Circle anything you think you might possibly want to eat—you're better off having too much rather than too little.

Try to pick a lot of high-protein foods, since your body needs the protein to repair itself. Yogurt, milk, pudding—circle them all, as breastfeeding moms need the equivalent of five glasses of milk a day. Look (and you may have to look hard in some hospitals) for fresh fruits, salads, or vegetables. Constipation is a danger for you because your digestive system slowed down during labor and will take a while to get going again.

Beverages—check all of them, as long as they are decaffeinated. You need to drink at least twelve eight-ounce glasses of fluid daily to replace those lost during labor, keep your stools soft, prevent urinary tract infection, and establish a good milk supply.

Shut-Eye

During your hospital stay your first priority should be getting as much sleep as you possibly can. For the next several months—and possibly years—your nights will not be your own, so sleep now.

Talk to the nurse. Tell her how much sleep you missed during the labor and how tired you are. Ask her to only wake you for your baby's feedings and not to take your temperature. While some nurses won't be able to grant this request because it is against hospital policy, you should still ask. It will help your case if your provider (midwife or doctor) makes the request as well.

First Line of Defense: Hospital Medical Staff

Your nurses are responsible for monitoring your vital signs: your blood pressure, pulse rate, and temperature. Any variation from the norm might indicate the beginnings of an infection or excessive bleeding, and their primary task is to watch out for that. Follow-up care includes making sure other things are proceeding normally, including breastfeeding, the healing of your episiotomy or perineum tear, and the firmness of your uterus (which may need massaging).

The nurses' second most critical task is to make sure that you urinate. They will harass you about urinating at a time when you wish they would just leave you alone. They will get clearly annoyed if you forgetfully urinate and flush the toilet without telling anyone.

The first trip to the bathroom will probably not be something you are looking forward to. It may feel fine, or it may hurt because your urethra was banged up during the birth. You may also find that once you get there you simply can't pee, either from fear of pain or because of damage to your perineum. You may feel like you're on fire. You can help avoid this burning feeling by spraying warm water while you urinate (the hospital will probably give you a bottle for this purpose).

The first bowel movement can also be scary; your muscles relaxed during the birth and you will have to push a lot harder to get a bowel movement out. After giving birth, the idea of doing anything like pushing seems crazy, and pushing against stitches—if you have them—hurts. Ask for a stool softener to take for the first few days—it can't hurt and may help a lot.

In addition to the nurses, your midwife or doctor will be in to check on you, and your pediatrician (or the hospital's pediatrician, if yours is not available or does not see children at that hospital) will check your baby. The pediatrician will make sure that the baby appears healthy physically and that there are no obvious deformities, heart problems, or physical concerns that are easily corrected if detected early. The pediatrician will also be evaluating breastfeeding—how it's going so far, and whether you are nursing frequently enough (regardless of whether your milk is in yet)—and will recommend a lactation consultant if necessary.

Don't Be Shy—Ask!

When you are moved into your postpartum hospital room, you'll probably be handed a bag containing information sheets about everything from baby care to when the baby's first picture will be taken, as well as ice packs, sanitary napkins, and a squirt bottle for cleaning yourself after using the toilet. (Remember, you can also use this "peri-bottle" to spray yourself with warm water while you're urinating if the urine stings.) Forget about the paperwork for now and go for the ice packs—for the next few days, ice is your best friend. Good alternatives to instant ice packs are hospital gloves packed with ice; they seem colder and more flexible. Ask the nurse for one or two, and keep requesting ice refills as they warm up.

ESSENTIAL

You can also ask for a sitz bath to help heal the perineum. You will probably be given a plastic tub that fits into the toilet and is filled with warm water. Bring a book, and settle in for at least fifteen minutes several times a day. In addition to feeling great, sitz baths may remove bacteria, reduce the risk of infection, and increase circulation, which speeds healing. You'll get to take the little tub home.

Premoistened witch hazel pads help with the swelling as well. Get a jar from the nurse and use them to line your sanitary napkin or put them on top of an ice pack. If you're really sore, you can ask for a topical anesthetic and squirt a blob of foam onto the pad. If you're still sore when you get home, try pouring witch hazel on a few of your maternity sanitary pads (get them thoroughly damp, but don't completely soak them) and freeze them. Moms say these super ice packs are awesome for perineal pain. You can also soak square gauze pads in witch hazel and refrigerate them.

Yes, It Hurts

You will hurt. You don't push something as big as a newborn baby out of a passage as narrow as your vagina without incurring some damage. You may have experienced a natural tear or had an episiotomy, and the stitches in your perineum may pull and itch. You may have gotten through with nary a stitch, but have bruised labia. And you may have aches and pains where you never expected them, from your thigh muscles if you labored standing, to your chest muscles if you had a hard time pushing. You may have hemorrhoids.

Are My Insides Falling Out?

The sensation of feeling your insides sag is a surprising one. While you never really noticed before the birth, looking back you may recall that your insides always felt snug. Now they don't. If you've had a cesarean you may worry that your insides could literally fall out, but remember that they are held in place, inside and out, by several layers of stitches and staples.

Hemorrhoids

Hemorrhoids are swollen veins around the rectum that are typically caused by pressure—like carrying and pushing out a baby. Many new moms have hemorrhoids; the good news is that, in most cases, they go away. The bad news is that, while present, they can make having a bowel movement, or even sitting down, extremely uncomfortable. To find relief:

- Avoid constipation. Drink lots of water, walk around, eat fresh fruits and vegetables, and take a stool softener.
- Soak in a warm bath (bathtub or sitz bath).
- Sit on a donut. These blow-up cushions relieve pressure until the hemorrhoids heal; carry the donut with you—it beats standing all the time.
- Use over-the-counter remedies, which include Tucks pads, refrigerated bottled witch hazel, and hydrocortisone cream.

Tailbone

You may feel pain in your tailbone, which can take a pounding during a vaginal birth. It may be bruised, in which case the pains will go away after a month or so, or it may be dislocated. Stretching can also help make your tailbone feel better. Talk to your health care provider if you continue to have pain a few weeks after delivery.

Afterpains

Afterpains are cramps caused by your uterus contracting. They're not usually so bad with your first child, but the strength of them can surprise second-time moms. This is the time to reach for a pain killer, typically acetaminophen (Tylenol), ibuprofen (Motrin or Advil), or a prescription narcotic such as Tylenol with codeine, hydrocodone (Vicodin), or oxycodone (Percodan). Acetaminophen and ibuprofen have few side effects and are generally considered benign. All the narcotics can cause dizziness, nausea, and vomiting. Codeine and Percodan can also increase constipation. If you are breastfeeding, talk with your doctor about your pain-relief options.

Sweating, Itching

You may sweat more than normal as your body sheds the extra fluids it stored during pregnancy. You also may have some unexplainable symptoms—moms have reported itchy rashes that can appear anywhere on the body. (The reason for this is not clear, but it is not uncommon, and the rashes go away on their own.) None of these are anything to worry about.

The Shakes

You may start to shake immediately after delivery, regardless of whether you delivered vaginally or had a C-section. This is your body's reaction to the loss of blood and other physical and psychological stresses. You can't control it, but it will usually pass within an hour. Ask the nurse for a warm blanket. Although the shaking is not related to the room temperature, you may find this blanket comforting.

Breathe Easier

You may feel short of breath after delivering, especially if your baby is large and you've had to push for a long time. This may cause your chest muscles to spasm. If your hospital offers a postpartum massage, take advantage of the opportunity. A massage may also ease the cramps in your thighs and other aches and pains. If your hospital doesn't offer this service, you might consider hiring your own masseuse or ask your partner to give you a massage. Hot showers also help relax your muscles.

Exercise

After nine months of pregnancy, you probably don't want to hear this, but it is time to start Kegeling again—you can do it before you've even left the delivery bed. At first, you won't feel anything; it won't even feel like you have any muscles there, but keep trying every few hours, and eventually you'll get a response.

Kegeling increases the blood flow to the vaginal area, which will help healing and tone up the muscles that keep you from peeing when you laugh. (These muscles will also come into play when you eventually think about having sex again—see Chapter 19.)

QUESTION

How do I Kegel?
Tighten all the muscles around your urethra, vagina, and anus, hold tight for three seconds, and release. The best time to do this is when you are urinating because you'll know you are doing it correctly when you shut off the urine flow. Repeat twenty times, twice a day.

As soon as you can, get up and walk around. This stimulates your digestive and circulatory systems (which are probably sluggish after the birth), prevents blood clots, and starts the general recovery of your muscles. Be sure to have someone accompany you for that first walk, as you may feel shaky and like your legs are going to buckle.

Post-C-Section Pain

Moms recovering from a C-section often don't have perineal pain, although some may if they tried to push. The primary pain is at the incision site, and this can be exacerbated by the internal pressure of trapped gas created when the digestive system is slowed by anesthesia and other drugs.

You can reduce gas pains by getting up and moving as soon as possible (shuffling slowly down the hall counts, so don't try to do too much). Pressing a pillow against your incision as you climb out of bed can reduce the pain of getting up and moving.

There Is Always Paperwork

Fill out the birth certificate. If you don't do this before you leave the hospital, your baby may end up labeled "Baby Smith" on this critical document, with the first name merely recorded as an amendment.

Order photographs, even if it's against your better judgment. Your newborn may be a blotchy-faced conehead, but his first picture is one worth having—particularly since hospital photographers seem to be able to catch the babies with their eyes open and their mouths shut. Don't go for the supersized package, however. This will not be your child's best picture and you don't need a hundred copies of it.

You will also need to order your child's Social Security card from the hospital. Doing it at the hospital is much easier than figuring out where your local Social Security office is and trying to handle documents with a baby carrier and diaper bag in tow. Be forewarned: you'll need this number sooner than you'd think.

Going Home

You'll need a properly installed infant car seat in order to take your baby home from the hospital. Do not ride in the car while holding your baby, even for a short distance.

The American Academy of Pediatrics has a complete car seat guide at their website, *www.aap.org/family/carseatguide.htm*. No one seat is the best or safest. You want a seat that is installed correctly, fits well in your car, can be used properly each time you drive, and fits your child at each age and size. Although a higher price does not necessarily mean greater safety, don't skimp on the car seat. Buy a new one if possible. Avoid used seats unless you know the seat's history. Check the manufacturer's label on used seats and don't use one that is too old. Check with the manufacturer to see how long they recommend using the seat. Never use one that has any visible cracks, is missing parts, or does not come with instructions. You can check to see if a used seat has been recalled by calling the manufacturer or by contacting the Auto Safety Hotline at 888-327-4236 or the National Highway Traffic Safety Administration (NHTSA) at *www.odi.nhtsa.dot.gov/cars/problems/recalls/chiseat.cfm*.

Whichever style you choose, be sure to read the manufacturer's instructions carefully before installing and using the seat.

Here's what you need to know about car seats:

- Use a rear-facing car seat, installed in the backseat of the car.
- A five-point harness is preferred, keep chest clip at armpit level, not on the neck or tummy. Harness straps should be at or below the shoulders.
- Newborns should have a 45-degree maximum recline (built-in angle indicators and adjusters will help you get the right recline).
- If you have questions or need help installing your car seat, you can find a Child Safety Seat Inspection Station by state or zip code on the NHTSA website at *www.nhtsa.dot.gov/cps/cpsfitting/index.cfm*. This site will also tell you which nearby inspection stations have personnel who speak Spanish.

CHAPTER 2

Home Sweet Home: The First Days

It may feel weird—and even a little scary—when you finally walk back into your house. It's only been a couple of days, but so much has changed. You walked out as a couple, but you're walking back in as a family. Maybe your baby slept on the way home and is still asleep in the car seat as you walk in the door. Or maybe she's woken up, looking around, and beginning to demand, with an increasingly loud voice, some attention, food, or a diaper change. Take a deep breath—it's just beginning!

Help at Home

It's fine to say that you're putting on your nightgown and taking it easy for a week—but who's going to do the literal and figurative heavy lifting while you recuperate and bond with your baby? Family and friends may ask what they can do to help. Be honest and specific so that the help you get is the help you really need. Focus on the basics: meals, laundry, and short-term baby care while you grab a nap.

QUESTION

How can I politely discourage visitors?
Not answering the door is awkward and makes you feel like you're hiding in your own home. That feeling is compounded when that door is knocked on repeatedly or the doorbell is rung continuously. In order to politely preserve quiet and privacy, hang a simple note on your front door explaining that mom and her new baby are sleeping. Ask delivery people to not knock or ring, but let them know where they can leave packages.

If possible, have your partner take vacation days the week after you give birth. You both need time to spend with the baby so each of you can become comfortable with your new roles as parents. You may also feel most comfortable and least embarrassed asking your partner to help with your personal needs, like sitz baths and ice packs for your sore bottom.

Keep the cooking and cleaning to a minimum. You don't need fancy meals, but you do want more than fast food drive-through dinners. If friends ask, let them prepare or buy simple meals that can be easily reheated; let them throw in a load of laundry; let them run some errands or drive you to the pediatrician for your baby's first checkup.

Hired Help

Some families hire professional baby nurses or doulas for the first week(s) at home. It can be a welcome gift from grandparents, especially those who live at a distance. These professionals provide newborn care, meal preparation, light housekeeping (such as the baby's laundry), help with sibling care, and other tasks as negotiated. The cost for a baby nurse varies regionally, but expect to pay about $200 per day (may be significantly higher on the West Coast). A good baby nurse can teach you the basics of newborn care (how to give your infant a bath, for example) and can help you establish a routine to your day.

Most baby nurses are not registered nurses (RNs), but instead are newborn care specialists. A postpartum doula (from the Greek, meaning "a woman of service") can offer similar services, and generally charges $18–40 per hour. Make sure that anyone you hire has been trained in infant CPR.

The advantages of hiring professional help in the first week at home are:

- A professional is trained in newborn care and can give clear support to new parents. Grandparents may not have taken care of newborns in many years.
- You may be less embarrassed or hesitant to give clear directions to someone you've hired, instead of a relative or friend.
- You don't need to "entertain" or keep company with a hired nurse.

To find a baby nurse or doula, check with friends, your doctor, and the hospital for recommendations. There are also agencies that provide baby nurses. The Doulas of North America (DONA) website, *www.dona.org*, has a search feature to find a doula in your area. Ask for references and check them carefully.

Rules for Your First Week at Home

This is the time to concentrate on yourself and your new family. You need time to get cued in on the different cries and sounds your baby makes and what they tell you about his needs: the cry when he's hungry; the sound he makes when he needs a diaper change; the wail he bellows when he wants company.

Here are some tips to help you get the necessary privacy and rest:

- In case not everyone was on the phone chain, record a baby announcement on your answering machine or voicemail, and then unplug or turn off the phone.

- Don't sit down without something to drink in front of you—especially if you're breastfeeding. It's important to stay well-hydrated, for your sake and your baby's.
- You should try to take at least two naps a day, but keep in mind that sleep is also dehydrating.
- Try to limit your visiting hours. Friends and neighbors may come bearing gifts or food. Graciously thank them, explain that you're too tired for company, and say you look forward to seeing them over the next several weeks.

ALERT

Reasons to call your baby's doctor postpartum: rectal temperature above 99.6°F; failure to successfully get the infant to latch on to nipples; yellow eyes, and jaundice (yellow skin) down to the toes; inability to wake baby for a feeding after six hours of sleep; abnormal breathing; blue color around lips.

Feeling Better Every Day

If you're still having perineal pain, ask your partner to keep those ice packs coming. Or find a discreet patch of sun and expose your perineum for a few minutes a few times a day to help it heal more quickly. You can also run a shallow bath, or use your sitz bath or baby tub. If you have a rubber donut, use it as a cushion in the bath. Add one of several herbal infusions to the water. For example, witch hazel or cypress may stimulate the constriction of blood vessels; comfrey or golden seal are soothing; and lavender may encourage new skin growth. You can buy these as extracts or as dry herbs that you steep in hot water.

C-Section Postpartum Days

Rest is important for any new mom, but never more so than for those who have had a cesarean. Again, remember that you've had major abdominal surgery.

Your emotions may be running especially high as you process your birth experience. You may have had an image in your mind about how your labor and delivery would go. Having surgery was probably not part of your fantasy birth. Or this may be the first time you've had surgery and the recovery is more difficult than you expected. Talk over your feelings with your partner and your health care provider. Conversely, you may not feel negatively about your cesarean, and this is normal, too.

The incision itself is held together with staples or stitches. Talk to your health care provider about whether they need to be removed, as some stitches may be self-dissolving, and when. Usually they are removed within a week after surgery.

The area around your incision may look bruised, red, and irritated. It may itch or feel numb as it heals. This is normal and will go away within a few weeks. Talk to your health care provider if it continues to bother you.

Precious, Elusive Sleep

Your priority during these first days is getting enough rest. The only way you can recover physically, establish your milk supply, and bond with your baby is if you are well rested. This is a special time—preserve it.

It's also time for your body to adjust to its new role. Your hormone levels are shifting and adjusting again, you're healing, you're up at all hours, and you're excited and maybe nervous, too. Simply put—you're tired.

You need someone, be it your partner, a family member or friend, or your baby nurse, to keep guard over intrusions into this milky, sleepy baby space. This means limiting visiting hours, phone calls, and all the details of daily life (from paying bills to replacing the toilet paper) so you can focus just on the baby and your recovery. All too soon, reality will return.

Sometimes it's hard to dial it down enough to grab a quick nap when the baby is sleeping. You may be tempted to do a few chores, make a few calls, write a few notes, or check in at work. You may also be too keyed up or convinced that the baby will wake up if you actually fall asleep, and all you'll have accomplished is ten minutes of rest. Regardless, you should grab those ten minutes when you can. Short, deep-sleep naps can be very effective in re-energizing you.

Here are some other tips to help you catch forty winks when you can:

- Go to your bedroom.
- Darken the room and close the door.
- Get in your pajamas, if you're not already in them. At a minimum, loosen restrictive clothing.
- Turn off the phone in the room.
- Make your mind go blank and then picture a place or setting of comfort, for example, floating on a raft down a calm river.

The Birth Experience

Your hormones aren't the only things adjusting themselves. Perryn Rowland, a certified childbirth educator, said, "As a doula (a labor assistant), the most important thing I do for postpartum mothers is help them process the birth experience. This is a major event, and you need to talk about it. You need to reminisce about how you were feeling when this nurse walked in, laugh about how mad you got at your husband, and go over the birth in detail. And the dads need to talk about what they were experiencing. Because only after you talk about this tremendous thing that you both went through, only after you process the birth, can you move on and meet the next challenge."

ALERT

If you burst into tears, go to bed. If you're still crying after you wake up, call your health care provider. You may need medical help to cope with depression while your hormones slowly return to normal.

Buy a journal, or a notebook, or even record your impressions in your baby book. Listening to your partner and seeing your story in your own words will add a whole new dimension to your experience.

Postpartum Meals

You may or may not have lost much, if any, weight by the time you leave the hospital. Remember, your body is still eliminating a lot of extra fluid from the pregnancy. The important thing to remember is that this is not the time for dieting. You need to eat sensible, healthy meals to regain your strength.

How much you eat is even more important if you are nursing. You need 500 calories a day more than when you were pregnant just to maintain your weight. This adds up to 2,700 calories a day for an average woman. Include eight eight-ounce glasses of non-caffeinated fluid. If you drink when you're thirsty and your urine is light in color, you know your fluid intake is adequate.

Maintaining your calcium intake is important; you need a total of five glasses of milk or calcium equivalents a day. Insufficient calcium won't affect your milk supply, but your body will raid its own calcium stores to make up the difference, weakening your bones and teeth. (If you keep up your calcium intake after weaning, your bone mass will return.) Fortunately, it doesn't take milk to make breastmilk. If you are allergic to dairy products make sure to eat plenty of green, leafy vegetables and drink enough other fluids.

ESSENTIAL

After a week or two in your robe, take the baby for walks in the stroller or snuggly. The exercise will improve your mood, the motion will settle your baby down, and everyone you meet will coo at the baby and fuss over you, giving you an ego boost when you need it most.

You may want to avoid gassy foods, such as cabbage and broccoli, as these bother some babies, and stick to decaffeinated coffee or limited amounts of regular coffee. The amount of caffeine that gets into breastmilk is small, but do you really want to risk your baby waking up more often? Feel free to eat all the garlic you want—the flavor gets into your breastmilk and, much to the surprise of the researchers who studied this, most babies like the taste and nurse better.

Pamper Yourself

Here are the top twenty favorite new-mom pampers (no, not the diaper kind).

20. A haircut that camouflages shedding
19. Sleep late in the morning while Dad takes the kids
18. A girls' weekend away
17. Time in a hot tub
16. A spa day
15. An afternoon movie
14. Painting classes
13. A girls' night out
12. A silent pedicure with a book
11. Dancing
10. A new outfit that fits your body right now
 9. Doing yoga
 8. Coffee (or a decaffeinated beverage if breastfeeding) alone
 7. A date with your significant other
 6. Having someone else clean your house
 5. Being home alone in a clean house
 4. A massage
 3. A long shower
 2. A long, hot bath
 1. Sleep, sleep, sleep

CHAPTER 3

Let's Talk Sleep

After the euphoria of the first few weeks wears off, sleep is all you're going to want to talk about. Face it, when you meet other mothers on walks or at the supermarket and stop to exchange coos, you don't want to know what book she's read recently or if she's seen the latest James Bond movie. You want to know how much her baby sleeps.

Back to Sleep

You most likely already know this, but it's important to repeat that the American Academy of Pediatrics (AAP) recommends healthy infants be placed on their backs to sleep. Recent studies have shown that in the twenty years since back sleeping was first recommended, the incidence of Sudden Infant Death Syndrome (SIDS) has been reduced by 50 percent. Without question you should put your baby down to sleep on her back as tummy and side sleeping positions are not as safe.

ALERT

SIDS is responsible for more deaths than any other cause for babies one month to one year of age.

Here are the National Institute of Child Health and Development recommendations to keep your baby safe while she is sleeping and reduce the risk of SIDS:

- The back sleep position is the safest, and every sleep time counts.
- Place your baby on a firm sleep surface, such as on a safety-approved crib mattress covered by a fitted sheet. Never place your baby to sleep on pillows, quilts, sheepskins, or other soft surfaces.
- Keep soft objects, toys, and loose bedding out of your baby's sleep area. Don't use pillows, blankets, quilts, sheepskins, and pillow-like crib bumpers in your baby's sleep area, and keep any other items away from your baby's face.
- Do not allow smoking around your baby. Don't smoke before or after the birth of your baby, and don't let others smoke around your baby.
- Keep your young infant's sleep area close to, but separate from, where you and others sleep. Your baby should not sleep on a couch or armchair with adults or other children, but she can sleep in the same room as you. If you bring the baby into bed with you to breastfeed, put her back in a separate sleep area when finished.
- Think about using a clean, dry pacifier when placing the infant down to sleep, but don't force the baby to take it. If you are breastfeeding,

wait until your child is one month old or is used to breastfeeding before using a pacifier.

- Do not let your baby overheat during sleep. Dress your baby in light sleep clothing, and keep the room at a temperature that is comfortable for an adult.

In the Beginning

When you first bring your baby home from the hospital, he will sleep an average of fifteen hours a day, generally in random chunks throughout the day and night. (Note: Your baby may sleep almost all the time, or as little as eleven hours or less.) Your baby may be at her most alert at 2 A.M. and have no interest in going back to sleep until 4 A.M. This day/night reversal is not unusual. While you were pregnant, your baby probably slept a lot during the day while you were walking around and rocking her with your movements, and then got more active as soon as you lay down for the night.

FACT

Some babies sleep more; others sleep less. These are the average number of hours per day, including naps, that babies sleep: newborns: sixteen hours; one to three months: thirteen to fifteen hours; four to seven months: twelve to fourteen hours; eight to twelve months: twelve to fourteen hours.

Finding a Rhythm

You can begin to teach your baby that it's much more fun to be awake during the daytime than it is at night. If your baby was in the nursery at the hospital, day differed little from night. There were lights on, babies crying, and people moving about twenty-four hours a day. At home, though, you can make day and night distinct. Try waking your baby up every two hours in the afternoon, and make these fun times. Talk to him, get out those baby toys, take him outside to listen to the birds, and introduce him to visitors.

At night, don't talk to him much, don't turn on anything more than a nightlight, don't play with him—don't even change his diaper unless it's dirty or soaking through. In time, most babies will welcome nighttime with their longest chunk of sleep—as much as four or five hours. (Realistically, though, you probably won't go to bed the minute your baby does, so you still won't be getting nearly as much sleep as you need.)

Between six and twelve weeks, your baby should begin sleeping for five to six hours at night. (But still not, unfortunately, in long enough stretches to make you feel like you've really slept.) In addition, by three months your baby will probably be taking two one- to two-hour naps during the day. But like all other statistics, lots of babies sleep less; some sleep more. Talk to your health care provider about your baby's sleep patterns.

Sleep Deprivation

After three months (often sooner), the sleep deprivation will start to wear on you, and you will begin to wonder if your baby will ever sleep through the night. The effects of sleep deprivation are much more pronounced than being simply tired. While you'll notice delayed reaction times, clumsiness, and blurred vision, you might be too exhausted to notice impaired reasoning and judgment, apathy and agitation, and an increased sensitivity to pain.

In addition to being forgetful, confused, and increasingly irritable, you will seriously start to resent the mothers of babies who are sleeping 7 P.M. to 7 A.M. (you will meet these people) and wonder if you're doing something wrong. Rest assured that you're not. They simply drew good cards for this hand and have kids who like to sleep. If you're one of those, you can skip the rest of this chapter and save your energy for the next challenge your child throws at you. (But try to keep quiet about the amount of sleep you're getting; the rest of us really don't want to hear about it.)

The real issue isn't how much sleep your baby is getting—it's whether you are getting enough hours of sleep to cope as a parent, and how many of those hours are unbroken. Only you know how much is "enough" sleep and how you can best get it. If you are dangerously sleep deprived and your baby will drink from a bottle, ask your partner to handle the nighttime feeding duties from time to time.

Sleep Strategies

There are plenty of programs to help you get your baby to sleep just a little longer; some may work for your new baby but won't work for your next one. Some may seem remarkably sensible to you, but to someone else they may seem crazy.

Before exploring the different programs, let's look at the relative importance of sleep issues. You may read that it is important for your baby to learn to fall asleep by herself because learning this will make her self-reliant. You may also read that babies will sleep more soundly if alone in a crib.

Whatever the program or strategy, you've got to decide what works best for you and your baby. No one practice will work for every baby. Rather, it's what works best with this specific child. Don't be intimidated just because a program is very popular. If a program makes you uncomfortable, try something different.

Tried and True

In addition to structured sleep methods, there are some simple practices that, while they won't work for all babies, should prove helpful and work for yours. When your baby is a newborn, let her fall asleep in your arms, then gently put her down (on her back) in the crib, keeping one hand on her chest the whole time. Place both hands on her for a moment after she's down, and then lift them very slowly.

Keeping your baby awake when she's tired during the day will not make her sleep better at night—it will just make her crankier. Nap timing does have an effect, however, and you'll be much better off if your baby takes an afternoon nap than if she stays awake all afternoon and falls asleep at 5 P.M. Don't worry about building a bad habit in a baby who's less than three months old—if it works for tonight, it's good enough!

You don't have to turn your house into a library when your baby is sleeping—let the radio play, the dishes clatter, and the doorbell ring. She'll quickly learn to sleep through the noise, and you'll be able to relax instead of tiptoeing around.

The Real World

In the real world, mothers are reading stacks of books about sleep, talking about it with their friends, and doing whatever works for them. Sometimes, of course, they don't tell anybody about it, feeling guilty that they aren't following the rules. "Sure my baby is sleeping through the night," a mom you meet at the park will tell you, not bothering to mention that her definition of "through the night" is midnight to 4 A.M. Some mothers are better with hype than others.

FACT

A 2007 study from the Centers for Disease Control and Prevention found that parents were more likely to report insufficient sleep than adults without children. Mothers, particularly unmarried mothers, mentioned insufficient sleep more often than fathers. Insufficient sleep was reported by nearly 36 percent of unmarried mothers and almost 34 percent of married mothers.

Gearing Up

Sleep specialists may laugh at moms who fill shopping carts with sleep aids such as automatic crib vibrators and tapes of ocean sounds, but some moms have reported success with a number of products.

Motion is usually effective, so look for anything that keeps your baby rocking or gently bouncing. In addition to a glider or rocker, try holding the baby while bouncing on an exercise ball. Sitting and bouncing will also be more restful for you, and beats pacing the floor. But be sure and support your baby's head while gently bouncing on the ball.

QUESTION

What are the effects of sleep deprivation?
Research has shown that sleep deprivation can impair a person's motor skills; increase stress levels, anxiety, and depression; and may encourage the individual to take unnecessary risks.

If you need a hands-free device, a wind-up swing or vibrating bouncy seat will soothe him to sleep. The constant hum of you working in the kitchen might work on your baby. Get a CD player with a repeat function, and stock up on lullaby CDs or your own favorite soothing tunes. If all else fails, there's always driving. Rumbling bumps, a rocking motion, and the running engine combine the best of everything.

Sleep Programs

In the following pages you'll find summaries of a variety of techniques designed to help your child learn to sleep through the night. If one works for you, bravo! If it doesn't, use trial and error to develop a system that you and your baby can live with. Don't be afraid to modify the experts' suggestions. Don't worry that you must stay with whatever strategy you choose. You may find that the method you used for your first child is completely ineffective for your second.

There are a few rules that many—but not all—of these programs share. If you don't want to go all the way with any one approach, you might start with these elements as you work out a system of your own:

- Try to put your baby down to sleep when she is drowsy but awake. This may teach her to put herself back to sleep when she wakes up.
- Establish a pre-bed ritual and don't vary from it. For example, you might have bath time, then read a book(s), and sing a few songs or lullabies. Whatever the ritual, your child will associate these steps with bedtime.
- Get your baby attached to a "lovey," also known as a "transitional object." The idea here is that the baby will look for the lovey when she wants to calm down. Some people question whether you want your baby to bond with you, the mother, or with a stuffed yellow duck. The truth is that children understand the difference between their mom and a toy, and lovies are a reminder of the reassurance and love that you provide.
- Don't rush in at the first sound your baby makes. Often she will fall back asleep on her own.

And there is always one other option: don't do anything. Your baby will eventually sleep through the night—at least some time before she's a teenager, at which point your problem will be dragging her out of bed before noon.

ESSENTIAL

If you want to encourage your baby to become attached to a lovey (a blanket, stuffed animal, or comfort object other than your skin), nudge her toward something that can be purchased in bulk and then buy multiples. Inevitably, the lovey will get lost and having a backup may avert a crisis.

American Academy of Pediatrics (AAP)

All humans, adults and children, go through sleep cycles that include arousals and wakings. For that reason, the AAP's *Guide to Your Child's Sleep* encourages parents to help infants over three months old learn how to soothe themselves so that they can quickly fall back asleep between one of those cycles.

The key once again is to have a routine for naps and bedtimes. Starting when the baby is about six weeks old, you should go through your pre-bed routine of singing song(s), reading a book, rocking, etc., but keep the baby awake until he is in the crib. The nursery should be dim and quiet. Offer him a "lovey" if it helps.

If the baby wakes up in the middle of the night, don't rush into the room as soon as he cries, as he may fall back asleep on his own. If he doesn't, go in to comfort him, but don't pick him up. Pat him gently, speak in a low voice, and leave once he calms down.

Ferberizing

This program was proposed by Dr. Richard Ferber in his 1985 book *Solve Your Child's Sleep Problems*. Recently updated and expanded, it's intended for babies six months or older—not newborns. Dubbed "Ferberizing" by moms, the goal is for the baby to learn to put herself to sleep alone in a crib, and then to put herself back to sleep without a fuss when she wakes up during the night. This is meant to be a positive experience that gradually teaches the child to fall back on her own resources for comfort.

Ferber likens the process to what an adult would have to go through should she be forbidden to sleep with a pillow. At first she'd have trouble falling asleep and would wake repeatedly, but, after a few nights, she'd get used to it and sleep just fine.

Ferber's system, like many others, starts with a bedtime ritual (a bath perhaps, followed by a book or a song). You or your partner then put your baby to bed while she is still awake. The parent leaves the room, and the baby cries. On the first night, the parent returns in five, then ten, then fifteen minutes, and at subsequent fifteen-minute intervals to reassure the baby that she has not been abandoned. The parent does not stay in the room, rock the baby, or give her any "crutches" (like a bottle or a pacifier). Instead, you let the baby hear your voice, you rub her, and stay only two or three minutes each time you go in to offer comfort. No matter what, the parent does not take the baby out of the crib. This is repeated every time the baby wakes during the night. Starting on the second night, each interval is extended by five minutes.

While Ferber offers gradual alternatives (sitting next to the crib in a chair, for example, and moving the chair farther away every night), the approach of leaving for timed intervals is the one he most recommends.

Ferberizing may go on for hours a night, for days, or even weeks and eventually works. The big question is whether or not you are able to make it to the "eventually." (In most cases dads have an easier time sticking to this program; the hormones released in nursing mothers when listening to a screaming baby for an extended period of time do not make things any easier.)

ALERT

The Consumer Product Safety Commission, American Academy of Pediatrics, and the National Institute of Child Health and Human Development recommend that infants under twelve months be put to sleep in a crib with no soft bedding of any kind under or on top of the baby. They recommend using a sleeper or other sleep clothing as an alternative to blankets with no other covering.

Since Ferber's book came out, a number of similar but slightly modified plans have been published. Maybe the best news is that recent research has shown that you may not need to repeat the Ferber process each time the baby wakes up during the night. Do it once at the beginning of the night, and then go ahead and rock her to sleep when she wakes up. In most cases this won't delay the baby from consistently sleeping through the night.

Dr. Sears and the Family Bed

Parents, babies, and young siblings sleeping together in the family bed is the way babies have slept throughout most of history—and still do in much of the world. In the United States today, it has been repopularized by Dr. William Sears as one of the tenets of a childrearing philosophy called "attachment parenting." In his books, *Nighttime Parenting* and *The Baby Book*, Sears wrote that babies sleep differently than adults, with more waking periods and longer periods of light sleep, for a reason—they need to be able to wake easily when they are hungry, cold, or their breathing is compromised. He stresses that it's more important that a baby feels reassured and has a sense of intimacy than that he learns independent sleep habits.

The family bed has several benefits beyond the closeness and awareness it fosters between you and your baby. You may find it easier to get your baby to sleep, and your sleep cycles will become synchronized. When you do wake up, it will be out of a light sleep rather than a deep one, and soothing or feeding him will be that much easier.

Putting your baby in a crib has its own benefits. You may find that you sleep better with more room and without a squirming, kicking bundle beside you. If you can't sleep for fear of squashing the baby, or if you have a panic attack every time he makes a noise, you won't sleep at all or function well when you're supposed to be awake.

Sears suggests nursing or rocking the baby into a sound sleep before putting him down, either in a cradle or the parents' bed. You should get to the baby quickly whenever the baby wakes up, he says, since you'll probably have an easier time getting him back to sleep if he doesn't scream himself into hysteria first. Here's where having the baby in bed with you is an advantage—you can often soothe, or even breastfeed, your baby without fully coming awake yourself.

The family bed became controversial in 1999, when the Consumer Products Safety Commission (CPSC) issued a warning against adults sleeping with babies in adult beds. This warning was based on information obtained when the Commission used death certificate data in a study that attempted to identify products associated with infant suffocation. The study was criticized for its methodology, most significantly for not taking into account other risk factors such as parents under the influence of drugs and alcohol; the number of babies sleeping on sofas or waterbeds; and the number of mothers who smoked during pregnancy or at the time of the baby's death. Despite the criticism, there has been no better study since.

Dr. Sears supports the CPSC's continuing research on the safety of the family bed and suggests using an Arm's Reach Co-Sleeper Bassinet as an alternative. This crib-like bed fits safely and snuggly adjacent to the parent's bed. The co-sleeper arrangement gives parents and baby their own separate sleeping spaces, yet keeps baby within arm's reach for easy nighttime care.

Alternatively, you may get many of the same benefits of a family bed by room sharing, or putting your baby's crib in your bedroom. One British study found room sharing lowered a baby's risk of SIDS.

If you decide to have a family bed, follow these steps to help ensure your baby's safety:

- Keep the bed away from walls and other furniture (to eliminate the danger of the baby getting trapped on the side of the bed).
- Move pillows away from your baby.
- Don't use a waterbed.
- Never sleep with your baby if you have taken any sedative, such as alcohol, over-the-counter cold medications, or narcotics. If the label says that you shouldn't be driving or handling heavy machinery when taking the drug, you shouldn't be sleeping with your baby either.
- For comfort, get the biggest bed you can.
- Don't sleep with your baby if you are a smoker.

Dr. Weissbluth and Sleep Training

Dr. Marc Weissbluth, a sleep disorders specialist at Children's Memorial Hospital in Chicago and the author of *Healthy Sleep Habits, Happy Child*, believes that establishing healthy sleep habits in infants is critical to a child's long-term overall health. Dr. Weissbluth insists that parents need to establish consistent naps and early bedtimes to avoid the baby becoming overtired. In that state, he maintains, it's more difficult for the child to fall asleep. He warns against keeping a baby up late in order to accommodate a parent's schedule. The price, he cautions, is a sleep-deprived child.

When the baby is very young, Weissbluth advocates putting her to sleep after two hours of wakefulness, and doing whatever it takes to achieve this (rocking, singing, etc.). Your baby may cry in protest. Allow the crying to continue from five to twenty minutes, then pick her up and try again. From four to twelve months, Weissbluth recommends your baby take two naps a day (never in the car or stroller) and then enforcing an early bedtime. If the baby cries at bedtime, says Weissbluth, do not go in her nursery at all, because "down is down."

The No-Cry Sleep Solution

Elizabeth Pantley, author of nine parenting books, offers a series of steps to help parents tailor a sleep program for their child. Her book, *The No-Cry Sleep Solution*, is a thoughtful, practical guide that has become a bestseller by offering useful advice in a gentle, reassuring manner. She believes no baby should cry himself to sleep and urges parents to be realistic about what constitutes "sleeping through the night" (usually about five hours straight for a young baby). Her ten-step program will lead you through the process of helping your baby sleep. Pantley's plan involves discovering the stumbling blocks that are keeping your baby from sleeping; developing a sleep log so you can analyze your baby's sleep patterns; working with your baby's biological sleep rhythms; and offering a variety of sleep solutions that match your parenting style.

Focal Feedings

This modified "cry it out" approach is advocated by Joanne Cuthbertson and Susie Schevill, authors of *Helping Your Child Sleep Through the Night*. Their program varies slightly with the age of the child, but in essence includes waking up your baby at 11 or 11:30 P.M.—or just before you are ready to go to bed—and feeding her. This will theoretically prevent her from waking up an hour or two later and interrupting your deepest sleep.

If you are breastfeeding and the baby wakes up before the scheduled feeding, have your partner try to settle her in her crib without picking her up. If the baby doesn't fall asleep within ten to twenty minutes, your partner should pick her up, walk her around—anything to distract her for another hour or so before the next feeding. The idea is to get the baby adjusted to longer periods of sleep between awakenings. An alternative is to limit the amount of time the baby nurses in the middle of the night (which can be easier on both of you than not feeding her at all).

Scheduled Wakings

In this program, you try to take control of your baby's night wakings. Note which times your child typically wakes up, then set an alarm clock to wake you up before he does. Wake him up, feed him, and put him back to sleep. After he's used to this, start waking him up later and later, so he'll eventually forget to wake up on his own.

CHAPTER 4

Crybabies

When your child is born she typically greets the world with a wail. You will probably be thrilled to hear that first cry, as it's evidence that your baby is alive, though probably not pleased with the cool air and bright lights of the delivery room. This will probably be the last time you will be happy to hear your baby cry. For the next few years you'll be putting a lot of effort into getting your child to stop crying.

The First Cry

All babies cry. Infants cry an average of one to four hours a day. Some infants cry more—a lot more—and some cry less. Your baby may do nothing but sleep the first few days after birth and hardly cry at all. Don't congratulate yourself yet. Crying often doesn't really get going until babies are a few weeks old, and usually peaks at six weeks. A baby's cry makes both moms' and dads' heartbeats speed up, blood pressure increase, and palms sweat. It also heats up the breasts of nursing mothers, so hearing your baby cry may soak your shirt with milk.

A crying baby is trying to tell you something. She may be trying to communicate that she's hungry, or that she ate too much and her stomach hurts. She may be saying that her diaper is wet and it feels yucky, or that she liked that nice warm wet diaper on her and now that you took it off she's cold— and mad! She may be saying that she's tired and wants you to rock her to sleep, or that she's bored and wants you to samba dance for her entertainment. She may be saying that she's furious that she can't scoot across the carpet and grab the fireplace tools. When you first hold your baby in your arms, you won't understand any of this.

ALERT

Never shake your baby. It won't make the crying stop and can cause permanent paralysis, seizures, blindness, brain damage, or death. Because babies have large heads and weak neck muscles, shaking a baby causes the brain to bounce about in its skull, tearing blood vessels. If you feel overwhelmed, put the baby in a safe place and walk away.

Your job is to figure out how to understand your infant's language, because crying is a language. The sooner you figure it out, the sooner you'll spend more time listening to your baby coo and babble and less time listening to her shriek.

What you shouldn't be doing, at this point, is trying to teach your baby patience. In fact, the faster you respond to her cries, the better because it's easier to calm a baby that's just started crying, before it escalates into hysteria.

Translation, Please

While no one has created a baby-cry/English dictionary, the pitch and rhythm of your baby's cry can provide a clue as to where to begin to look for the problem.

- **Tired**—A whimper or somewhat musical cry, it can be irregular, sometimes accompanied by eye or cheek rubbing. You might think he fell asleep because he got so tired from crying. It's more likely that he was crying because he was tired.
- **Sharp pain**—A shriek, followed by a long silent pause and another shriek. (You'll definitely hear this one when your baby is vaccinated. It can also mean an air bubble is making his stomach hurt, his foot is caught in the bars of the crib, or he is being stabbed by a diaper pin.
- **Hunger**—Short, rhythmic cries that can sound desperate.
- **Pooping**—Starts out as more of a grunt than a cry, often while eating.
- **Too hot, sick, or feverish**—A whiny cry.
- **Anger or frustration**—Your baby may let out screams of outrage when you take a nipple from his mouth or unfasten his diaper, or for no apparent reason.
- **Boredom**—Progresses from gurgling and grumbling to wailing. The crying usually stops instantly when you pick up a bored baby.

Settling a Fussy Baby

Many of the same things that put your baby to sleep when she's tired will soothe her when she's fussy. To create homemade white noise, turn on the bathroom fan, tune in static on the radio, or run the vacuum cleaner or dishwasher.

Don't be afraid to hand him over to someone else. Your baby will know it if you're getting tired or frustrated, and a fresh pair of arms may solve the problem. If none are available and you're reaching your limit, put her down in a safe place and take a short break. Go into another room and calm down.

Even better, if possible, give both of you a breath of fresh air—literally. Put the baby in a front pack and go outside for some exercise. Going for a walk may soothe your baby, and do the same for you. If the weather isn't cooperating, stay inside and dance, holding your baby close, supporting her head (music is optional).

ESSENTIAL

When your baby won't stop crying, place her in a front carrier and vacuum. The combination of the warmth of your body, the sound of the vacuum, and the rhythmic motion as you move back and forth across the floor is almost guaranteed to settle her down. (The clean rug is a bonus.)

The Basics

Here are some the basics of soothing your crying baby:

- **Keep it moving**—Rock away in your glider or rocking chair, or just rock back and forth wherever you are, sitting or standing. Dance slowly around the room.
- **Go for a walk**—Walk her in the stroller inside, outside, wherever.
- **Sing or chant**—Soft, rhythmic coos may take your baby's mind off whatever is bothering her. You don't need to have a great voice or know the words, just hum something. If you really hate to sing, turn on the vacuum cleaner. It may not sound like much to you, but that annoying hum is music to some babies' ears.
- **Change the temperature**—If your house seems overly warm and you can't go outside because of the weather, stand in front of the open fridge for a minute or two.
- **Change the scenery**—Give your baby something interesting to look at. A plant, a mobile, or even a brightly patterned tablecloth will be interesting enough to distract her. Describe what you're looking at, and keep talking softly. She'll start to realize that she can't listen and scream at the same time.
- **Get naked**—Babies like skin-to-skin contact—and Dad's warm skin works just as well as Mom's. Kangaroo care, or skin-to-skin contact, is especially helpful for premature babies. It can help stabilize the preterm infant's heartbeat, temperature, and breathing. Lay the baby

down on your chest with your arms wrapped around her. Or, if she likes water, take a warm bath together.

- **Get quiet**—Some babies may just need peace and quiet, without toys or distractions. Leave her alone. Put her in a comfortable position in her crib or on a blanket on the floor, turn down the lights, and keep the noise down.

More Soothing Options

You've picked your baby up, offered to feed him, burped him, changed his diaper, wrapped him in a blanket, and taken the blanket off again—and he's still crying. You don't much care why anymore, and he may have forgotten why. When you just want him to stop, it's time to try these all-purpose soothers.

Rock-a-Bye Baby

As old-fashioned as it sounds, a rocker or glider can be your best friend when trying to soothe a crying baby. Add one to your list of must-have nursery furniture. The gentle rhythmic movement mimics the sensations your baby experienced in the womb. Your scent and warmth combined with the connection you share as you hold your baby and rock are calming and soothing. For moms it's simply a relief to get off your feet and sit down.

Rockers have been around for centuries and rock on curved runners. The more modern rocker-glider has wooden arms under the seat that pivot front-to-back on steel ball bearings (which makes for an effortless, smooth, noiseless, horizontal gliding motion.) Often you can purchase a matching ottoman.

Pacify Me

Babies like to suck and are calmed and comforted by sucking. You'll hear lots of pros and cons about pacifiers, called binkies by some parents. Almost every parent (and grandparent) has an opinion, but the American Academy of Pediatrics approves the use of pacifiers for baby's first year.

Here are some points to remember before introducing a binky.

- Avoid introducing a pacifier during the first month of breastfeeding as it can lead to nipple confusion.
- Use a one-piece, dishwasher-safe pacifier. Two-piece units pose a choking hazard.
- Buy extras of whatever kind your baby prefers, and replace a pacifier as soon as it begins to deteriorate.
- Don't overuse pacifiers. Try other means of soothing your baby (e.g., rocking or a new position).

Swaddling

In their first few weeks, some babies feel more secure, and are less likely to fuss, when wrapped snugly. Swaddling him will contain the flailing arms and legs, which may be startling the baby, and the heat from a slightly dryer-warmed blanket will calm him down. (Other babies hate this and will quickly let you know.) If your baby likes to be swaddled, see Figure 4-1 to learn how to do it.

1. Position a square blanket like a diamond, and fold the top corner down.
2. Lay your baby on his back on the blanket, the top corner just above his neck. Tuck one arm down and fold the blanket around his body and behind his back.
3. Fold up the bottom part of the blanket, folding down any excess that would be covering his face.
4. Tuck the other arm down and fold the remaining corner of the blanket around his body and behind his back.

You can also buy pre-made swaddling gear such as Miracle Blanket (*www.miracleblanket.com*) and Aden + Anais muslin swaddling cloths (*www.adenandanais.com*).

FIGURE 4-1(A):
Set up

FIGURE 4-1(B):
First wrap

FIGURE 4-1(C):
Second wrap

FIGURE 4-1(D):
Final Wrap

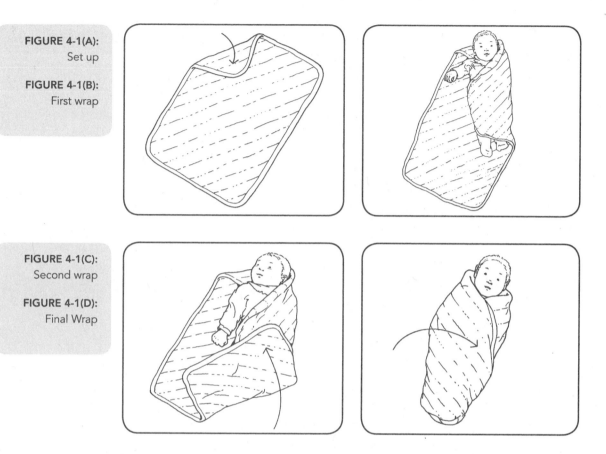

Gear for Soothing

Following are some soothing gadgets you may want to add to your baby's collection:

- **Sling**—Sizes vary, depending on your height. You'll carry your baby more comfortably if you have the right size. Consider two slings, sized for mom and dad.
- **Front pack**—a Snugli, Baby Bjorn, or Ergo will keep the baby close, and both your warmth and heartbeat may calm him.
- **Aquarium**—The sound of the filter is soothing, and the fish are distracting.
- **Swing**—The tick-tick of a wind-up swing can be soothing, but this type needs to be rewound fairly often, and rewinding is loud. A

battery-operated model may be a better choice. You won't use this for very many months, though, so borrow one if you can.

- **Sassy seat**—A cloth-covered baby lounge chair that you can gently bounce with your feet.
- **Music**—Try all kinds. If classical doesn't work, reggae might.

Minimize Crying

Babies are meant to be carried. In some cultures babies are carried as much as 90 percent of the time, and they don't cry as much as babies in industrialized countries (who spend more of their time alone). In fact, researchers have confirmed that extra carrying results in dramatic reductions in crying. If you don't want your baby to let out more than a whimper once in a while, don't put her down.

This isn't as onerous as it may seem. With such options as front packs and slings and backpacks for older babies, your child can be "worn" comfortably for hours, leaving your hands free to do other things.

The Secret of the Sling

Once you figure out how to use it, slings will be great for you and your baby. Your baby can hear your heartbeat, see your face, and catch a ride similar to what she felt in the womb. Her weight is evenly distributed on your back, so you're comfortable, and both your hands are free to do what you want. That she can sleep whenever she wants, you can nurse discreetly, and you're touching her constantly are benefits for you both.

ESSENTIAL

If you're going to use a sling, wash it many times before you first use it. The fabric will soften and it will be a lot more comfortable for you and your baby.

Unlike putting a baby in a front pack, which has a clear place for her head, arms, and legs to go, securing a baby in a sling is not intuitive. Your best bet is to get an experienced sling wearer to show you. If that's not possible, review the following and Figure 4-2 for one method. (Note: Slings come in different sizes. Make sure yours fits.)

1. In your left hand, hold the sling by the ring, so the padded area, if there is one, is facing you, and the unpadded area is away from you.
2. Put the sling down on a couch, and smooth it out so that the ring is on the left end and the widest area is on the right. Open up the section that's on the bottom.
3. Place your baby on her back on the opened fabric so her head comes within a hand's width of the ring and her feet are pointed toward the widest end.
4. Raise your right arm in the air, next to your ear, and dive into the sling with your arm and head. Adjust your position so the pad is on your left shoulder and the ring is near your left armpit.
5. Stand up, supporting your baby until you are sure she is secure.

FIGURE 4-2(A):
The sling

FIGURE 4-2(B):
Place the baby in the sling

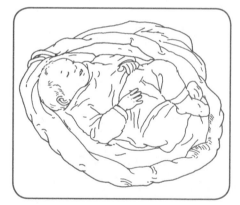

FIGURE 4-2(C):
"Dive" into the sling

FIGURE 4-2(D):
Final position

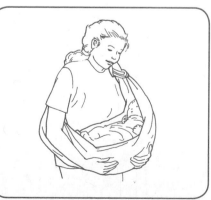

Carrying Power

Here are some suggestions for holds that might calm or soothe your baby. Don't forget to always support a newborn's head and bottom, and keep the baby as snuggled as possible—a baby that suddenly finds herself surrounded by not much but air may startle.

FIGURE 4-3:
Snuggle

FIGURE 4-4:
Football

Snuggle: Hold baby facing you, with her head resting on your chest, supporting her head and neck with one hand, and her bottom with the other.

Football: Hold baby on one side of your body, supporting the head and neck with your hand and forearm.

FIGURE 4-5:
Knee rest

FIGURE 4-6:
Shoulder

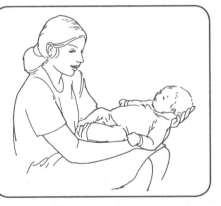

Knee rest: With your legs together, put baby face up on thighs, head toward knees, baby's legs bent, holding your hands on either side of her body.

Shoulder: Supporting baby's head and neck, place her so that her head is resting on your shoulder. Support her bottom with your other arm.

Could It Be Colic?

Then there are the cries that seem to have no rational cause and don't respond to soothing for very long. This may mean a baby is venting at the end of a long day, but if the crying goes on for hours every day, at roughly the same time, several days a week, then you can feel justified in calling it colic. Some pediatricians use the Rule of Three to diagnose colic: crying for no apparent physical reason for three hours a day, three days a week, for three weeks. By this definition, one out of five babies has colic.

ALERT

Get help if you have a colicky baby. Incessant screaming can be over-whelming; make sure you have some time for yourself—for everyone's sake.

In spite of trying for more than fifty years, doctors haven't pinpointed the cause of colic. Historically, it is believed to be some kind of abdominal pain (the word colic is derived from *kolon,* which is Greek for large intestine), but even that's not certain.

Colic may be caused by an immature digestive system that spasms rather than uses smooth muscle contractions. Or it may be that certain babies just notice the workings of their digestive system more. Some researchers have suggested that it may be an allergic reaction to something in the mother's diet—cow's milk in particular. This theory is controversial, as colicky babies don't have any symptoms of the stomach problems associated with such an allergy, like diarrhea or vomiting. Colic may be the reaction of a baby worn out by trying to make sense of a busy day. Or, colic may simply be the ordinary crying of a particularly strong-willed and persistent baby.

Colic Remedies

Since no one really knows what colic is, no one really knows how to fix it. You can try laying him face-down with his stomach over a small roll of towels or a slightly warm (comfortable to the touch) hot-water bottle. Here are some other suggestions.

- **Motion:** Rocking, riding in a stroller or a car, swinging in a baby swing (or even a car seat swung back and forth), dancing, bicycling his legs.

- **Medication:** Simethicone is an over-the-counter remedy that is given to the baby in the form of drops and breaks down gas bubbles (brand names include Mylicon and Mylanta). While commonly used, evidence does not support its efficacy in treating colic. Your doctor may prescribe the drug Levsin, or hyoscyamine sulfate. This smooth muscle relaxant is believed to help relieve intestinal spasms, but it may work by generally calming the central nervous system. Use caution, as the possible side effects include drowsiness, dizziness, urinary retention, and increased sensitivity to heat because of decreased sweating.

- **Dietary changes:** Try eliminating dairy products from your diet if you're nursing, or, after consulting your pediatrician, switch to a soy formula if you're bottle-feeding. The connection between cow's milk and colic is anecdotal at best, but some mothers have had success with this.

And If That Doesn't Work . . .

In spite of reports that all of these strategies work for some babies some of the time, odds are if your baby is truly colicky none of this will help much and you'll just have to wait it out.

Colic is tough. When your baby first starts crying, you may be calm, soothingly saying, "Oh my poor sweetie, let's change your diaper and see if that helps." By the third hour you'll feel like shouting, "WHAT? WHAT IS IT? TELL ME WHAT'S WRONG SO I CAN FIX IT!"

The point is to keep trying (and enlisting your partner, your relatives, and your friends to help.) Hold your baby, rock your baby, dance with your baby, or just sit and pat him—do anything that seems to help him calm down, even a little. It may seem pointless but you will know you're trying, and maybe your baby will know, too.

You may be surprised what works. One mother discovered it was the sound of the hairdryer that was the answer (sound, not heat). What works for one baby may not work for the next, but take the peace and quiet where you can get it.

Teething Blues

The good news is that parents of colicky babies should see the colic episodes begin to wind down significantly by the beginning of the fourth month (the Chinese consider a hundred days of crying to be normal). The bad news is that older babies can find new reasons for crying.

One significant reason for older babies to cry is teething, which typically starts at six or seven months (although a few babies don't get their first tooth until twelve or even eighteen months old). The gums swell just before a tooth appears, and this can hurt your baby for days. You can help soothe her with things to chew on—teething toys, a leather band, a cold washcloth, a frozen bagel (take it away when it starts to soften). You can offer her a bottle of ice water to suck (although sometimes sucking makes the pain worse), or try rubbing her gums. There are mixed reports on topical anesthetics, like Baby Anbesol or Orajel. It can be hard to apply, they tend to work only for a limited time, and they taste terrible. Ask your health care provider before using.

FACT

Separation anxiety is another reason for tears in an older baby. By about eight months your baby is aware enough to notice when you leave but doesn't understand that you will come back. So she cries—even when you just step out of sight for a moment. When all you want to do is duck into the kitchen to get a glass of water, this response can be challenging.

Teething babies fuss, cry, and wake up more often. While most experts do not believe that teething causes loose stools, runny noses, or fevers, many parents are convinced that there is a correlation between these symptoms and teething. To be safe, check with your doctor if your child has a temperature of 101°F or higher (100.4°F or higher for a baby younger than three months). Do not give any medication for teething, including acetaminophen and ibuprofen, without checking with your health care provider.

CHAPTER 5

Breast Is Best

More than 95 percent of mothers are physically capable of breastfeeding, so if you can breastfeed, you should. The research overwhelmingly proves that breastfeeding is good for both the baby and the mother. The next two chapters will give you the information you need to successfully nurse your baby. But this is not intended to make you feel guilty if you can't or if you choose not to breastfeed. Parenting is much more than any one decision, and bottle-fed babies thrive like their breastfed counterparts. You'll find information on how to bottle-feed your baby in Chapter 7. But first read ahead to learn more about nursing your baby.

Benefits for Baby and Mom

Human milk is designed as the perfect food for infants. It contains elements that researchers are only beginning to discover. Over time, breastmilk changes from the colostrum produced in the first few days—which provides babies with antibodies to protect them from the germs they are encountering—to a blend of colostrum and milk, and eventually to pure milk. Milk then adjusts in subtle ways as the baby matures, even changing during the course of a feeding. A nursing baby first receives milk with a lower fat content; as she continues to feed, the fat content of the milk that follows increases.

ESSENTIAL

If breastfeeding doesn't work for you, you can phase in bottles at any time. However, if a week goes by without breastfeeding, it is very hard (though not impossible) to resume. Recent research indicates that women must breastfeed exclusively during the first three weeks in order for their milk supply to develop fully; otherwise, their supply will always be a step behind their baby's needs.

The American Academy of Pediatrics recommends that:

- Mothers breastfeed for at least the first twelve months of life and as long after as is mutually desired.
- Babies breastfeed exclusively for the first four to six months of life.
- Newborns nurse whenever they show signs of hunger.
- No supplements—including water or formula—should be given to breastfeeding newborns unless there is a medical indication.

Breastmilk is powerful stuff. It can kill bacteria, viruses, intestinal parasites, and even stop the growth of cancer cells. Breastfed babies develop fewer allergies and have a lower risk of developing diabetes. Statistically speaking, breastfed babies are smarter and have enhanced cognitive development.

For the mom, breastfeeding releases oxytocin from your pituitary gland. This produces uterine contractions, which help your uterus return to its nonpregnant size (thereby reducing the risk of postpartum hemorrhage). Nursing also burns calories, which will help you lose those pregnancy pounds.

Prolactin, the hormone that produces milk, induces calm, so nursing may help you cope through the crazy first months of parenting. Finally, breast-feeding reduces your risk of developing breast, ovarian, cervical, and endometrial cancers.

FACT

Breastfed infants are less likely to be overweight first graders. According to a British study, children who were breastfed for more than a year were four times less likely to be overweight at school age than children who were breastfed two months or less.

You can probably still breastfeed even if you require certain prescription medications for your own health. Most medications enter breast milk in small amounts that won't affect a nursing baby. But it is vitally important that you discuss with your doctor all drugs you currently take (including over-the-counter medications and herbal supplements) before you begin breastfeeding, as well as check on the safety of any new drug prescribed for you.

There are other good reasons to breastfeed your baby:

- **Breastfeeding is relatively easy.** Most of you will discover this after the initial awkwardness, while others may find the first few weeks of figuring out how to breastfeed correctly are a struggle. But, hey, it took you at least that long to learn to ride a bicycle, and aren't you glad you did? In the long run, breastfeeding will make your life much easier, just like that bicycle. When your breastfed baby is hungry, you pick her up, unsnap your nursing bra, and dinner is served. Once you get the hang of it, you'll probably manage to have a free hand—until it's time to unsnap the other side of your bra. You can read, dial a telephone, or even shop online while your baby nurses in a sling.
- **Breastfeeding keeps you free during feeding times.** When your bottle-fed baby is hungry, you have to check the refrigerator or the diaper bag and hope you find a prepared bottle, then warm it up while trying to distract your hungry and increasingly agitated baby. And bottle-feeding is a two-handed operation; you can't do much else while you're holding both the baby and the bottle.

- **Breastmilk is easier to digest than formula,** so breastfed babies rarely get diarrhea or constipation and their dirty diapers don't stink. There is an odor, but not a particularly bad one. In fact, the stuff looks and kind of smells like Dijon mustard.
- **Breastfeeding is significantly cheaper than formula.** In addition to the health and nutrition benefits of breastfeeding, there are also the perks of simplicity and cost savings. Breastfeeding babies are portable; you can take them anywhere for any amount of time without worrying about how long you can keep a bag of bottles cold or where you can find clean water to mix with powdered formula.
- **Breastfeeding is environmentally responsible**—you don't have packaging, cans, or containers to throw out. You also don't have to worry about packing and lugging bottles, nipples, and paraphernalia with you, or trying to find what you need if you're away from home.
- **If you're small-breasted, you may only need one hand free.** Women with small breasts can easily breastfeed with one hand (or no hands, after a little practice), since they don't have to support the breast, just the baby.

ALERT

The first two weeks of breastfeeding are the hardest, and they don't give you a true picture of what breastfeeding is like. Stick with it through these challenging times before you consider giving up.

You May Need to Feed Your Baby Formula

Here are some situations and physical conditions that may require you to bottle-feed your baby part- or full-time. Talk to your doctor and to a lactation consultant before you make a final decision.

- You need to take a medication that would pass into your breastmilk and harm your baby (be sure to get clear information from your doctor).
- You return to work and either do not have the opportunity to pump or are unable to pump enough milk.
- You have had significant breast surgery. Often women with minor breast surgery, like the removal of benign lumps, have no problem

breastfeeding. (Breasts that were augmented also function fine, as long as the milk ducts were not cut. Breast reduction surgery typically causes most breastfeeding problems.)

- You have a highly contagious disease, like HIV or tuberculosis.

The First Feeding

Your baby has just made his entrance into the world and, if he's doing fine and you had a vaginal delivery, your partner or a nurse has placed him on your stomach. You can try to nurse him right away if you're up for it, but don't feel like you have to. Waiting until you both get your bearings is fine. Don't sweat it if you're ready and your baby isn't. There really is no rush. You'll both probably need a nap in the hours following the birth, after which you'll both wake up and be ready to tackle this new experience.

You should attempt that first feeding whenever your baby is ready. According to midwife Jean Rasch: "The baby is born, the baby is hungry, the baby wants to eat, you put the baby on your breast, and the baby sucks. It's going to work—why wouldn't it work?"

Get Organized

You'll probably want to start with the football hold or cradle hold (diagrammed on page 60). Sit up in bed, pull up your hospital gown, and settle a pillow on your lap. Make sure your back and elbows are supported; you may need more pillows. Get comfortable. If you have large breasts, tuck a rolled-up washcloth or towel under the breast you intend to nurse with to help support it. Then ask the nurse to hand you the baby.

Step-by-Step

Unwrap your baby and pull up his T-shirt, if he's wearing one. You want skin to touch skin. Rotate your baby to face your breast, supporting his head. Then, with the opposite hand, form a C with your thumb and forefinger and cup beneath your breast. Bring the baby close to your breast (don't lean down to the baby, that's a sure path to back pain), and lift up your nipple making sure that your hand doesn't cover the areola (the darker skin around the nipple). Tickle the baby's lips with the tip of your nipple. Wait until he opens really wide and then, bringing his head to your breast, shove your breast in as far as it will go. If you weren't quick enough, your baby may have only the nipple in his mouth. Use your finger to break the suction, take him off the breast, and try again.

Once he's on, check his position. His mouth should be covering at least a third of the areola and you should hear sucks and swallows. Don't fuss about whether or not his nose seems to be covered by the breast—he'll move if he can't breathe. Switch sides when you think your baby has drained the first breast; you won't hear swallowing anymore or see his jaws or cheeks working. This may take as few as five minutes or more than twenty. Take a burp break when you switch breasts.

Breastfeeding Positions

FIGURE 5-1:
Cradle hold

FIGURE 5-2:
Cross-cradle hold
(opposite arm)

FIGURE 5-3:
Football hold

FIGURE 5-4:
Side-lying hold

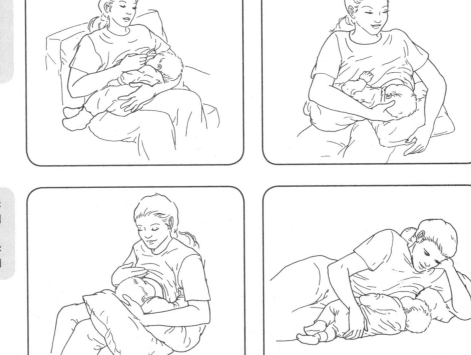

Burping Positions

FIGURE 5-5:
Double Football
(for twins)

FIGURE 5-6:
Shoulder (high
over the shoulder)

FIGURE 5-7:
Lap (sitting
upright)

FIGURE 5-8:
Knees (tummy
down)

Establishing a Good Milk Supply

Nurse your baby on both breasts, and do a minimum of eight times a day for at least the first week. It will take a few days for your milk to come in, so don't worry if you don't seem to have any milk yet. Frequent nursing at this point is intended to establish a good milk supply.

At the first feeding, and over the next few days, your baby will be receiving colostrum, a yellowish fluid. Colostrum is full of antibodies and will protect your baby from a host of viruses and infections. It also acts as a laxative that flushes out the meconium—the black, tar-like waste accumulated before birth.

Your baby's feeding during these early nursing sessions will trigger the release of prolactin, which relaxes you and stimulates milk production. It will also release oxytocin, a hormone that causes muscle contractions in the milk lobes (which will force the milk down into the milk ducts), and contractions in the uterus, which will speed your postpartum recovery.

Keep It Simple

Breastfeeding is natural, rewarding, and good for both you and your baby. However, it is not always easy. While you're both still learning, there are several things you can do to keep things going smoothly:

- Get comfortable.
- Bring the baby to your breast, instead of moving yourself to the baby.
- Make sure the baby is latched on correctly. She should have the areola in her mouth, not just the nipple. If it hurts, it's wrong.
- Make sure your baby's head is tipped slightly back and her chin is pressed into your breast. It is the movements of her chin and tongue that draw out the milk.
- Keep your wrist straight. Flexing the wrist supporting your baby's head may tip her down into a less efficient nursing position, and the strain on your wrist may cause inflammation and pain.
- Nurse at least ten to twelve times a day for the first few weeks—that's an average of once every two hours.
- Don't watch the clock; let your baby tell you when she's done.
- Vary your nursing position. The baby will press on your breasts differently depending on how she is positioned.
- Use your finger to break the suction before taking your baby off your nipple. Pulling her off will hurt.
- Have a drink of milk, water, or juice. When your baby is drinking, you should be, too.
- Don't forget to burp your baby. Most babies swallow a little air along with the milk, and this trapped air can cause stomach pains. Try burping when you switch sides and after breastfeeding, but don't worry if your baby doesn't burp, some just don't.

Ask for Help

If you're feeling insecure, aren't sure if the baby is sucking correctly, or feel uncomfortable in any way, get some expert advice. The maternity nurses, as well as your child's pediatrician, may be able to help you. You might also want to talk to a lactation consultant, who is trained to help you learn how to breastfeed. Many hospitals have lactation consultants on staff (often ob-gyn nurses will also get this specialized training). If your hospital doesn't have a lactation consultant available, contact the La Leche League (*www.lalecheleague.org* or 1-800-laleche) for help or for a referral to a consultant in your area.

Breastfeeding Post-Cesarean

Breastfeeding after a cesarean is more difficult, but well worth the effort. The postpartum benefits are the same as for the mother who delivered vaginally: early bonding with your baby and the release of oxytocin to help the uterus contract for the mother, and the immunological benefits of colostrum for the baby.

Depending upon what kind of anesthesia you had for your C-section, you may need a little extra time before you physically feel able to hold and nurse your baby. If you had an epidural you'll be awake and alert sooner than if you've had general anesthesia. Once you are fully conscious and feel physically able to hold your baby, you can begin nursing. Ask your partner or a nurse to stay with you when you first start breastfeeding, in case you need help or get tired and need to hand the baby to someone else.

Your baby may be a little drowsy and lethargic, especially if you have had anesthetics for a prolonged period (e.g., you labored with an epidural for hours before the cesarean). You will need to encourage and stimulate him so he stays alert during breastfeeding (rub his back, change his diaper, talk to him, and try to make eye contact). The anesthesia will be out of his system within a day or two.

Don't be a martyr about pain relief. You have had major surgery and will need some pain medication in the first few days. You will also probably be taking some antibiotics to avoid infection, so take only those medications prescribed by your doctor. While these drugs do pass in very small amounts into your milk, they will not harm your baby.

Finding a comfortable breastfeeding position after surgery is a little more difficult, but through trial and error you will find what works for you and your baby. The side-lying position is often preferred in the first few days after surgery. Turn slowly on your side and put a rolled-up towel next to your incision (in case the baby kicks). A nurse or your partner should place the baby on his side next to you, chest-to-chest, directly facing your breast. You will need help to roll over when you want the baby to nurse on the other breast. The football hold is less comfortable immediately after surgery, but is often preferred a few days later. Rest the baby on a pillow, over your incision, and hold him along the side. Whatever position you use, remember: always be sure that the baby opens wide and latches on correctly to avoid sore nipples and ineffective milk transfer.

ESSENTIAL

Before breastfeeding, you should find a comfy spot, get lots of pillows, a big drink of water, milk, or watered down juice, and a book or the TV remote. Put the portable phone within reach or turn the answering machine on.

Some hospitals require, as a precaution, that all C-section babies be transferred for observation to the NICU immediately after birth. Healthy babies are usually reunited with their mothers within a few hours, if not sooner, and you can initiate breastfeeding then. Should your baby need to stay in the NICU longer for observation or treatment, ask about the availability of electric breast pumps and start pumping as soon as possible. This, along with pumping every couple of hours, will help stimulate your milk supply, prevent engorgement, and provide the valuable colostrum for your baby which can be fed to him in the nursery until he is able to breastfeed.

Breastfeeding Styles

As with sleeping and crying habits, feeding styles vary from baby to baby depending on what the baby needs at the time. You may notice your baby prefers one of the following styles. (The first five names were coined by researchers at Yale University.)

- **Barracuda:** Immediately latches on and feeds vigorously for ten to twenty minutes.
- **Excited Ineffective**: Goes wild at the sight of the breast, grabs it, loses it, and then screams. Try to feed this baby before she's too hungry, and consider getting help with your latch-on technique.
- **Procrastinator:** This baby will wait for the real milk, thank you very much, and she'll pass on the colostrum. Don't let this initial lack of interest trick you into giving her a bottle of water or formula; just keep trying to latch her on at regular intervals. Pump between feedings to ensure a sufficient milk supply.
- **Gourmet:** This baby will take a delicate taste of the milk, roll it around in her mouth, and perhaps play with the nipple a little before getting down to business. She doesn't like to be rushed.
- **Rester:** This baby likes to nurse a few minutes, rest a few minutes, nurse a few minutes more, take a nap, and then come back for more. Make sure you find a comfortable seat and surround yourself with books, snacks, or whatever you need to keep you happy for what can be a long feeding session.
- **Billy Goat:** This baby butts, tugs, and pummels you while she feeds. She may be frustrated with your milk flow, which may be too slow or too fast for her taste.
- **Regurgitator:** This baby nurses contently for about twenty minutes, then throws half of it back up on your shirt. Then, of course, she's hungry again.
- **Barnacle:** This baby latches on tightly and nurses constantly, almost around the clock.
- **Sightseer:** This baby doesn't want to miss the passing scene, so her eyes and head wander about while she's nursing. If you have a sightseer, you'll be surprised by just how far your nipples can stretch. Sightseeing tends to emerge in the fourth or fifth month.
- **Desserter:** About twenty minutes after a full nursing session, this baby comes back for a couple more sips—for dessert.

Milk's Here

When your milk comes in—two to four days after birth—and replaces the colostrum, you will know it. Your normally squishy breasts will get bigger than you ever imagined possible and may seem as hard as rocks. For some women, this transition from colostrum to milk can be rough, but at least it doesn't last long (typically just a day). You may feel like you are going from a size C to a size ZZ.

QUESTION

How do I know if my baby is eating enough?
Rest assured, he's fine if: he nurses eight to ten times a day; he has six to eight wet diapers a day after the first week; your baby's poop resembles Dijon mustard mixed with cottage cheese by the fifth day; he seems healthy and alert; he gains weight after the first week; and your breasts feel full before each feeding and softer afterward.

Fetch your baby and start nursing because the longer you wait, the more your breasts will hurt. If your breasts are too hard for your baby to latch on to, put a warm washcloth on them for a few minutes or take a shower. You can also massage your milk glands toward your nipple and squeeze out a little milk. If you are still uncomfortable after your baby nurses, put ice on your breasts for a few minutes, or tuck a cold cabbage leaf into your bra. While this may seem like odd advice, cabbage, possibly because of its sulfur content, draws out the excess fluid to reduce swelling and the cold feels good.

FACT

Think about what you are going to name the act of breastfeeding because, sooner than you think, your baby will be using that word. (It may sound cute to ask your infant if he wants "tittie," but having a toddler scream "tittie" in a crowded grocery store is not that cute.) Some options other parents have used include: num-nums, boobie, the boob, ba, snack, lunch, nurse, nurch, drink, dahda, mimi, mother's milk, or bup.

Now when your baby begins to feed, you may feel a tingling or burning sensation a moment before milk begins to leak from your breasts. This is the let-down reflex, caused by the release of oxytocin, the hormone that triggers contractions in the muscles surrounding the milk-producing cells to squeeze the milk into the milk ducts. (You don't need to be feeding a baby to trigger this reflex. It can happen during sex, when you see a picture of a baby, if you hear a baby cry, and sometimes for no apparent reason.) If you don't feel it, you'll still know milk is flowing because your baby will start gulping. (He may also pull away for a moment if the milk is spraying too fast.)

Gearing Up

The nice thing about breastfeeding is you really don't need anything but your baby and your body. But it can be nice to have:

- Lots of pillows to tuck around you.
- A nursing pillow. There are several types: a wedge that sits on your lap; a wide, partial ring for your waist (great for football holds or nursing twins); and the Brest Friend, which is a smaller ring with a back support.
- A nursing stool. This low stool lifts your legs just enough to ease the strain on your lower back.
- Cloth diapers, and lots of them, to catch messy burps and drool.
- An electric pump. The popular Medela Pump In Style is usually powerful enough, but rent a hospital-grade pump if you need more suction.
- A sling. Great for nursing while on the run.
- Paperback books. Nursing is a great time to catch up on your reading, but magazines or hardcover books are hard to manage.

Breastfeeding Fashions

Just because you are nursing doesn't mean that you can't look good. Breastfeeding fashions have moved into the twenty-first century. You can find sleek, comfortable clothes, including professional outfits for when you return to work but want to continue pumping. In the haze of those early weeks, look for comfort and easy access in whatever you wear.

- **Bras:** You will probably have more cleavage than usual, so you'll need comfortable nursing bras that offer good support. You may find the snap-front styles easier to manage than those with hooks. Avoid tight or underwire bras.
- **Casual wear:** Look for washable button-front shirts and T-shirts for easy nursing access. You can always drape a baby blanket for discreet breastfeeding in public.
- **A nursing dress:** You may eventually get sick of untucked shirts, so one official nursing dress, with its discreetly hidden slits, is nice to have.
- **Breast pads and shells:** To absorb milk leakage, tuck some cotton or flannel breast pads into your bra. Especially in the early weeks, when your milk lets down as your baby sucks on your breast, you'll want something to absorb the leaking from the other breast. Breast shells are made from silicon and tuck into your bra and are especially helpful in the first weeks. They keep your nipples protruding, which relieves engorgement and makes it easier for your baby to latch on. Any dripping milk collects in the shell, and you can freeze it for future use.

Maintaining Your Milk Supply

You will have more success breastfeeding—barring a medical situation—if you get plenty of rest, surrender to your baby, and surround yourself with people who support you. Don't be discouraged by friends or relatives who are uncomfortable at the sight of you breastfeeding, or keep questioning your ability to feed your baby. If your baby wants to nurse every hour or two, let her. Her stomach will eventually get bigger, she'll become strong enough to feed more efficiently, and the time between feedings will increase.

If you are concerned about your milk supply, take more naps and make sure you are eating and drinking enough. Let your baby feed more frequently (if she's using a pacifier, you might want to take it away for a while) and consult your doctor or a lactation specialist.

What about Bottles?

You'll find a full discussion about bottle-feeding formula to your baby in Chapter 7, but most breastfed babies do have an occasional (or more) bottle of expressed breast milk. If you think you'll want your baby to take a bottle, get her used to it after the third week and before the eighth week. Too soon could affect your milk supply unless you pump regularly, and she might not cooperate if you try too much later.

CHAPTER 6

Breastfeeding Hills and Valleys

Think back to when you first learned to ride a bike. You might have been riding along just fine for weeks, but then you varied your route and encountered your first hill. For breastfeeding moms, there are a few hills in the early weeks. Some, like the growth spurt and occasional leaking, will be faced by most. Others, like a breast infection, are rarer. Whatever the challenge, most can be mastered with determination and perseverance.

The Growth Spurt

It's almost noon. You've been up with your baby since 5 A.M., and you haven't yet taken a shower or gotten dressed because twenty minutes after he finished nursing, he wanted to nurse again. Clearly, you think, your baby is starving. You wonder if you should start supplemental bottles of formula. The answer is no, because this is a growth spurt.

FACT

Growth spurts are typical at two weeks, six weeks, three months, and six months, but they can sneak up at any time. Your baby's seemingly endless appetite will let you know when another one has arrived.

Your baby has suddenly jumped up to a higher nutritional requirement level, and will nurse to increase your milk supply—which is exactly as nature intended. You may have a rough day or so, but very quickly your baby's hunger and your milk supply will be back in synch and feeding times will be back to normal.

Expect days when you do nothing but nurse. Console yourself with the fact that you are actually accomplishing a lot—building up your milk supply—and don't go running for a bottle.

Stumbling Blocks

Leaking and sore nipples are two of the most frequent problems you'll face when you first start breastfeeding. Here are some solutions.

Leaking

Leaking is most common in the early weeks of nursing, but can happen at any time, particularly when you're accustomed to nursing your baby at fairly regular intervals but get delayed. Leaking can also be triggered by the sound or sight of a baby—any baby—or by sex. While leaking itself isn't a problem, the round wet spot on your shirt can be. To avoid or minimize this, wear print shirts, use breast pads or a thick cotton bra, and press against your breasts with your forearm when you begin to feel the tingle that signals a let-down.

Ouch! (Sore Nipples)

Sore nipples are typically caused by incorrect positioning or improper latch-on. To get over a case of sore nipples, first solve the positioning problem (see Chapter 5). Then you can:

- **Air-dry your nipples after each time you nurse.** You can also make sure your nipples get air by using a breast shield (see Chapter 5). For a homemade solution, cut off the handles of two tea strainers (preferably plastic) and place them over your nipples, inside your bra.
- **Catch some rays.** Find a private sunny spot, or carefully use a sun lamp, and expose your nipples for three minutes several times a day.
- **Express a little breastmilk and dab it on your nipples.** Breastmilk has a number of healing properties—take advantage of them.
- **Make a cup of tea, then save the tea bag.** Place the tea bag (at room temperature) on your sore nipple for a few minutes.
- **Soothe them with lotion.** Rub on lanolin (check that it has been treated to remove any pesticide residues), olive oil, or aloe vera gel. Wash your nipples and pat dry before breastfeeding.
- **Apply ice before nursing.** Ice acts as a painkiller and helps bring out your nipples for a better latch-on.
- **Take a break.** Spend a day nursing on only one side to give the other nipple a chance to recover. Either hand express or pump the resting breast as often as you would nurse.

Quirks

Your baby will develop his own breastfeeding habits that may create problems for you. Here's how to handle these issues.

Breast Favoritism

Most babies will prefer one breast to the other. It may be because of the way you support the baby with your stronger arm, the fact that one breast produces more milk, or that the baby simply prefers to lie on one side instead of the other. To avoid having the less-desired breast go completely into retirement (and make you look lopsided for the duration of breastfeeding), start each feeding with the breast that is out of favor. Your baby may be less likely to be picky when he's really hungry.

Rejection

You can feel pretty insulted when your baby pulls off and cries after nursing for a few minutes and refuses to latch on again. The key to ending rejection is finding the cause. The most common source of rejection is a flood of milk—too much for your baby to handle. If you suspect this is the problem, express or pump a little milk before you nurse. If that doesn't fix it, your baby may be teething, have a cold or earache, hate your new deodorant, or have found that something you ate changed the taste of the milk. It may be as simple as the weather—on a hot day your baby may not want to snuggle against your warm body—or a developmental spurt—your baby suddenly has noticed the world around him. If you can't figure out the cause, hang in there; hunger will eventually prevail. In the meantime, pump so that you maintain your milk supply.

Biting

Most breastfeeding moms get bitten at least once when the first teeth come in. They typically let out a yell, startle their baby into tears, and then feel horrible about scaring their child. The baby, however, doesn't try that again for quite a while. If you have a biter, use your finger to take the baby off of your breast, say "No" distinctly and calmly, and hold him off for a few seconds before letting him suck again. This usually works after a few bites.

Speed Bumps

These are more serious problems you may encounter while breastfeeding. Most can be easily resolved and should not stop you from continuing to nurse your baby.

Clogged Milk Duct

A clogged milk duct is fairly obvious—you feel a small lump in your breast, and it can be painful. (The lump can be anywhere in the ducts, which run all over.) To treat it, put a warm washcloth over it for five minutes, then massage the lump gently, pushing the milk down toward your nipple. Then start nursing your baby, making sure the baby is positioned so she faces the clogged duct, and continue massaging. The more you nurse, the faster the clogged duct will drain.

Breast Infections (Mastitis)

Breast infections are serious. If you have flu-like symptoms, a low fever, red streaks or patches on the breast skin, pain in your breast, or a hard lump in your breast, you may have one. Check with your health care provider. She may prescribe antibiotics (which won't hurt your baby). She will also tell you to go to bed, drink lots of fluid, apply warm compresses on the infected side, and continue to nurse on the infected side.

Absolutely do not stop nursing, as that will only make the infection worse. Do not delay treatment of a breast infection, since untreated infections can abscess and require surgery.

Thrush

Also called a yeast infection, thrush may present with cracked nipples that burn the entire time your baby nurses. Your baby may also develop thrush in her mouth (white patches) and diaper area (rash). Talk to your health care provider for a definite diagnosis. To control thrush, make sure your nipples and everything that touches them are clean, use a nipple wash (one teaspoon of vinegar in one cup of water), or nystatin cream (a prescription drug) that stops yeast from reproducing.

Common Drugs: Are They Safe for the Baby?

Be sure and tell your doctor that you are breastfeeding before he prescribes any medication. Most are safe for your baby, but here is a list of common drugs and whether they are considered safe for nursing infants.

Safe	Not Safe
Acetaminophen	Tetracycline
Antihistamines	Cyclosporine (maybe, check with your doctor)
Ibuprofen	
Robitussin (guaifenesin)	Amphetamines
Antidepressants	Nicotine
Decongestants	Anticancer drugs
Most antibiotics	
Antacids	
Thyroid medications	
Insulin	
Kaopectate	
Vitamins	
Vaccines	

No Let-Down Reflex

Some women have trouble breastfeeding at first because they aren't experiencing a let-down. In fact, some women who give up breastfeeding because they think they don't have enough milk actually have plenty of milk; they just don't have a let-down reflex. Without the let-down reflex the baby gets a trickle of milk, enough to sip but not gulp. Stress is the biggest inhibitor of the let-down reflex, so anything that can reduce stress helps, such as a warm bath or listening to music. There are also prescription medications that can jump-start a let-down, including Reglan, a prescription antinausea drug that can increase milk supply. It's vital that you discuss the issue with your doctor, as Reglan should not be taken by anyone with a history of depression.

Milk Flow That Is Too Fast

Milk coming too fast may make your baby gulp, choke, or pull away. You may want to express a little milk first. Try nursing from just one breast at each feeding (you may have to pump the other one in between feedings if you're uncomfortable). Try leaning back in a recliner or on pillows while nursing, positioning your baby so the top of her head is above the top of your breast, so she can sip at the milk without it pouring down her throat.

Flat or Inverted Nipples

If your nipples don't protrude when you're aroused—or in a cold breeze—you may have what the breastfeeding books define as inverted nipples. To check, squeeze the areola at the bottom of the nipple and press it toward your chest. If your nipple doesn't protrude, it is flat. Truly inverted nipples can prevent successful breastfeeding, but most will respond to treatment—manually rolling your nipples several times a day, wearing a breast shield inside your bra that presses the areola and encourages the nipple to protrude, or pumping with a heavy-duty pump.

Call a Doctor If . . .

Below are signs that you should check with your doctor about your baby or yourself. Remember: check with your health care provider if you have a question, whether it's a sign on this list or not. Odds are that everything is fine, but trust your instincts and don't hesitate to ask.

- Your baby hasn't had a wet diaper in twenty-four hours.
- It is the fourth day after the birth and you see no evidence of white-colored milk (in leakage from your breast or spit from the baby).
- Your baby has no bowel movements on the fourth day after the birth.
- Your baby cannot latch on to a breast.
- Your baby is lethargic and is difficult to wake for feedings.
- Your baby latches on readily but feeds for only a minute or two and then appears to doze off.
- Your baby feeds endlessly, for an hour at a time, and doesn't seem satisfied, then sleeps for less than an hour before crying for another feeding.
- Your breasts are painfully hard and swollen (full and firm is fine, hard and painful is not).
- Your nipples hurt during the entire feeding, not just for a moment at latch-on, and you find yourself dreading feedings or shortening them because of the pain.

Out to Lunch

People eat in public all the time. They eat in restaurants, they eat in parks, and they eat walking down the street.

Breastfeeding babies are people, and therefore they should be able to eat in public too. There is absolutely no reason why they shouldn't. People won't stare—if they do, they, not you, need an attitude adjustment. You'll probably get more compliments than criticisms.

FACT

Mothers have a right to breastfeed wherever they have the right to be with their baby, whether or not there is specific legislation in a state. However, many states have passed legislation explicitly clarifying this right, and, in some cases, have set fines for people who try to interfere.

Think about it. Which would you prefer to sit next to at a restaurant: a quietly breastfeeding baby or a screaming, hysterical baby?

When nursing in public, you will set the tone for the reaction of others. If you fumble with your clothes and worry more about flashing a bit of skin than about getting your baby fed, the people around you will feel as awkward as you do. But if you matter-of-factly help your baby latch on, adjust your shirt, then continue your conversation, you shouldn't receive any negative attention.

You can also reduce the amount of attention you attract by being proactive. Don't wait until your baby is crying with hunger. Rather, pick your place and time before your baby is starving. If you are shy, drape a lightweight baby blanket over your infant so you can have privacy while you get him latched on to your breast.

Slings are great for public breastfeeding. Hitch the sling a little shorter so your baby's head is at your breast, turn the baby toward you, supporting him with one arm, and, after he has latched on, adjust the extra fabric to hide him from view. You can even breastfeed with many styles of frontpacks. Simply lower the frontpack to get the baby's head in the right place, and then keep walking.

Dress for Success

While special nursing clothes are available, you don't really need them. You can't wear regular dresses and breastfeed easily, but any untucked shirt is fine for nursing. A nursing bra is good for easy access. Avoid tight bras or underwire bras; they can cause clogged milk ducts.

You'll probably want at least a small supply of breast pads to catch leaks in the early weeks, and then for any time you think you'll be away from your baby for longer than usual. Change the pads regularly to keep your breasts dry. Disposable pads lined with plastic block air, washable cotton breast pads are better because they allow your skin to breathe. You can also make your own pads by folding up a cloth handkerchief or cutting circles from cotton diapers or old T-shirts (you'll need several layers).

The Commitment

During the first few weeks, you're struggling to figure out how to breastfeed and feeling like all you do all day is feed your baby. This is not the time to decide how long you'll breastfeed. Just get going without a stop date in mind. You may add bottles—of breastmilk or formula—into the routine when you go back to work or need some time to yourself. By the age of six months, your baby will probably start eating cereal and other mushy foods, and you'll be nursing even less.

The current recommendation of the AAP is to breastfeed throughout the first year of your baby's life and then as long as is mutually desirable. Your baby may even wean herself before then. You may find that you want to continue breastfeeding into the second year. You may wean to a bottle or find that your baby does just fine with a cup. You may decide to wean because you are pregnant with another child, or choose to continue breastfeeding through your next pregnancy. Once you've made a successful start at breastfeeding, the options for continuing are all yours.

Back to Work

You don't have to stop breastfeeding your baby when you return to work. You can continue to provide him with your milk by pumping and freezing it, so it can be defrosted and fed to him during your work hours.

FACT

Unfortunately, there is no national legislation that requires employers to support your efforts to continue breastfeeding. Minnesota is the only state that mandates employers to reasonably accommodate nursing mothers. Talk to your employer about your intention to continue breast-feeding and take the initiative to develop a plan for how often you will need breaks and where in your workplace, if not your own office, you plan to pump.

Organization Is Key

Start to build up a supply of breastmilk in your freezer a month before you return to work. Pump just after you have fed your baby or in between feedings. Don't be discouraged if you don't get much milk at first. Your milk supply will increase after a few days of pumping.

Store milk in breastmilk storage bags (available online and at major retailers) in two-ounce and four-ounce portions (single feeding amounts). The smaller portions are easier to defrost and less milk will be wasted if your baby doesn't finish the bottle (or cup). Label the bags with the date and amount.

Breastmilk can be stored in the refrigerator for up to seventy-two hours. You can freeze breastmilk, but safe storage depends on the temperature of your freezer and where you store the milk. According to the La Leche League you can store breastmilk in:

- Freezers located inside a refrigerator—two weeks.
- Separate door refrigerator/freezer—three or four months (temperature varies because you open the door frequently).
- Separate deep freeze at constant -19°C (0°F)—six months or longer.

Defrosted milk can be kept for up to twenty-four hours in the refrigerator and can be safely kept at room temperature for several hours.

Workplace Logistics

Before you return to work (perhaps before you go on maternity leave), talk to your employer and your coworkers about your intention to breastfeed. If you have on-site day care or your caregiver can bring the baby to you, try to schedule at least one nursing session. If that's not possible you'll want to pump when you would normally feed your baby. You need to know when, where, and how often you can pump. You may need to adapt your schedule so that you can include pumping sessions. With a good pump and practice, you will only need about fifteen minutes to pump both breasts.

Ideally, the room you use for pumping will have privacy, a chair, and electrical outlets. You'll also need a refrigerator for storing your milk (a small, bar-sized one will do). If there is no refrigerator available, many breast pump carrying cases also come with built-in, cooler-type compartments that stay cold enough to store your pumped milk until you can get home.

FACT

The U.S. Department of Health and Human Services has a helpful website on breastfeeding and tips for continuing to nurse when you return to work at *www.4woman.gov/breastfeeding/index.cfm?page=230.*

If you don't have a private office, ask if there is a conference room or another space you can use. Sitting on a toilet seat in the restroom is not a reasonable option. Point out to your employer that you will be able to pump more efficiently if you are in a space that is comfortable and private. Some mothers, when faced with no better option than a restroom, have chosen to pump in their cars during their breaks.

Pump It Up

To effectively return to work and pump several times a day, you'll need to invest in or rent an electric breast pump that expresses breast milk from both breasts at once. These cost between $200 and 300, or can be rented for between $30 and $60 a month. You can also purchase car AC adapters, built-in milk coolers, travel cases, and hands-free kits. It may be worth the investment, especially if you plan to have more than one child. A more detailed description of breast pumps can be found in Chapter 7.

Weaning Your Baby

Hopefully, your baby will wean herself, gradually showing less interest in nursing as you begin to introduce solids. Take your cue from your baby. When she refuses the breast or nurses less frequently and for shorter intervals, it may be a sign that she's ready to wean.

If at all possible, you want to avoid an abrupt end to nursing. Going cold turkey can be hard on both your child, who can't understand why she's no longer nursing, and on you. Your breasts will become engorged, and you risk clogged ducts or even mastitis. In addition, your hormones will plummet and you increase your risk of depression.

When it's time to wean your baby, taper off gradually. Eliminate one feeding per day, stretching out the process over several days so that your milk supply diminishes slowly. Usually the first feeding in the morning and the last one at night are the hardest to remove. You may decide to leave it at that level for a time.

Continue to cuddle your baby, even if you avoid the cradle hold. You want to maintain the wonderful physical closeness, even when you are no longer nursing.

CHAPTER 7

Bring Out the Bottle

Unlike breasts (you've got one pair, and your baby is pretty sure to accept their shape and what comes out of them), when you begin bottle-feeding you have a number of somewhat confusing options. Whether it's equipment or formulas, prepare yourself for a trial (and error) period as you figure out what you and your baby like best. If you have decided to bottle-feed your baby, ignore the comments and guilt that breastfeeding proponents will try to heap upon you. You've got enough on your plate that you don't need to waste time worrying about the breastfeeding police. Refuse to second-guess yourself. Your child will give you plenty of other things to stew about, so save your energy.

Choosing Your Equipment

You'll probably want to "test drive" some bottles and nipples to find the right ones for your baby. Here are some options.

Bottles

The three types of bottles (glass, plain plastic, and plastic with disposable liners) come in two sizes: small (four ounces) and large (eight or nine ounces). That's where the simplicity ends. Since each manufacturer tries to distinguish itself from the others, and there are hordes of variations within each category. You will find short, fat bottles and long, thin ones. There are ones with a bend in the middle and ones with handles.

The general idea behind all these bottle designs is to make it harder for air to get into the baby. Bottles with liners collapse as the baby sucks. The bottles with the bend are intended to be easier to hold at just the right air-bubble-preventing angle, but they're harder to clean. Except for your convenience and your baby's preference, the bottle you choose doesn't matter all that much.

ESSENTIAL

Buy more bottles and nipples than you think you need. You'll end up scrubbing bottles all day if you don't have enough.

Of greater concern is whether your bottle is manufactured with Bisphenol-a (BPA), a chemical used to create the plastic called polycarbonate. BPA is an artificial estrogen and has been previously used by most major U.S. baby bottle manufacturers in their production. It's also found in many food storage containers and toys. There has been a growing dispute over the safety of BPA, with some studies showing that even low levels of BPA are harmful to animals and people and may increase your risk of cancer, diabetes, obesity, and early puberty.

To be safe, don't use bottles manufactured with BPA. There are plenty of BPA-free bottles on the market you can use. For an excellent overview of the issue, check out the Smart Plastics Guide at *www.healthobservatory.org/library.cfm?refid=77083*. For an update on which bottles (and sippy cups) are BPA-free, check *www.safemama.com*.

Nipples

Nipples differ in size, shape, and flexibility, but look for a nipple that most resembles the human breast. If you're bottle-feeding from the beginning, your options are open—a generic "breast" nipple is fine. If you are transitioning to bottle-feeding from breastfeeding, however, you need to be more selective. The nipple's shape should resemble yours. For example, if you have large breasts with fairly flat nipples, your baby may not be comfortable drinking from a long nipple on a small base. You may need to let your baby test a couple of shapes before you discover what works best. If your local supermarket doesn't have a wide variety, check the web.

QUESTION

How do you increase a bottle's milk flow?
For a faster flow, loosen the neck ring. If that doesn't help, you can enlarge the hole in latex nipples with a needle heated over a flame or boil the nipple for a few minutes with a small toothpick stuck through the hole.

When you're shopping for a nipple, you'll notice brownish nipples and clear nipples. The brown nipples are typically made of latex; the clear ones are silicon. If you can find a silicon nipple in the size and shape you need, choose it over the rubber one, which has a more noticeable flavor and gets sticky when it gets old. Because the rubber ones are opaque, it's also harder to be sure they're clean.

FIGURE 7-1:
Standard nipple

FIGURE 7-2:
Orthodontic
nipple

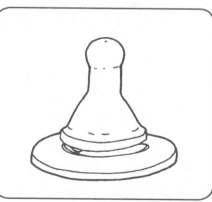

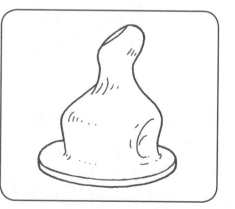

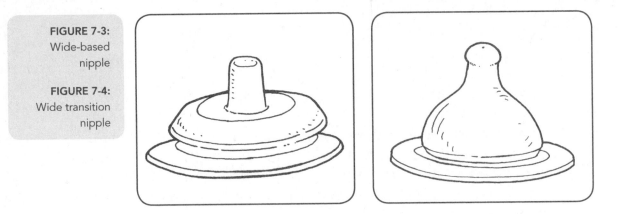

FIGURE 7-3:
Wide-based nipple

FIGURE 7-4:
Wide transition nipple

The other key variable is the hole in the nipple. Some nipples have multiple holes, while others have one. Some holes are small, some large. Some have round openings and some are cut in an X shape. According to the manufacturers' labels, the small, slow-flow holes are for newborns while larger, faster-flow nipples are intended for older babies. The manufacturer doesn't always know best—your baby may have a different idea. If you're transitioning from breastfeeding and have a strong let-down, your baby may be used to gulping milk. A slow-flowing infant nipple might frustrate him. Try opening up the hole to permit a faster flow, or replace newborn nipples with faster-flowing ones.

Even with the right nipple, you may not always get the right flow of milk, or even the same flow you got the last time. Turn the bottle upside down and shake it a few times. You should see a spritz of milk followed by slow, steady drops. You can adjust the flow by loosening or tightening the bottle's ring. You also may find that some supposedly "fast-flowing" nipples are slower than those advertised as "slow-flowing"—check the flow rates for yourself. Be aware that nipple flow may change (typically, but not always, slowing down) with repeated washings.

Additional Paraphernalia

After you choose your bottles and nipples, you'll find that you need a few more gadgets to simplify preparing, cleaning, and traveling. The good news is that you won't need everything on this list. The better news is that most of the items will be useful long after your baby is beyond bottles.

- Bottles (If you're bottle-feeding exclusively, you'll need eight four-ounce bottles for a newborn and eight eight-ounce bottles for an older baby).
- A bottle brush.
- A graduated pitcher for mixing batches of formula.
- A basket designed to hold rings and nipples for the dishwasher (you'll use it later for all sorts of things).
- Bottle warmers (these pads heat up when activated by pinching, and can be recharged by boiling).
- Formula dispenser for traveling (a plastic case with several compartments for premeasured powdered formula; a two-chambered bottle—one chamber holds powdered formula, one holds water; or premeasure formula into bottle liners, twist-tie shut, and mix with premeasured water kept in a separate bottle).

On the Menu

Next is the question of what goes in the bottle. If you're pumping and have a supply of breastmilk, you're all set. If not, you need to select a formula, one that is fortified with iron. There are milk-based and soy-based formulas. According to recent research, soy-based formulas do not lower the risk of allergies or colic, and may have problems of their own. According to the AAP, there are only three circumstances where a soy formula is preferred:

- The parents are strict vegans (who don't eat red meat, poultry, fish, or any products that come from animals like eggs or dairy products).
- The baby is diagnosed with lactose intolerance, which is rare among infants and more commonly found in older children and adults. This isn't just an allergy to cow's milk. Lactose intolerance is the inability to digest sugar lactose found in cow's milk and cow milk formula. Soy formula is lactose-free.
- The baby has congenital galactosemia, a rare disease in which the baby doesn't have the enzyme that converts galactose, one of the two sugars found in lactose, into glucose, a sugar the body can use. For these children, consuming breastmilk, cow's milk, or other dairy

products can result in a galactose buildup and eventual blindness, severe mental retardation, growth deficiency, and death.

ESSENTIAL

Take an educated guess at how many bottles your baby will need during a day and make them in one batch, preferably in the morning when your baby is not screaming with hunger.

Should your baby be unable to tolerate cow's milk formulas, your doctor may recommend a hypoallergenic formula over a soy-based formula. Hypoallergenic formulas, however, can cost up to three times more than standard cow's milk or soy formulas.

The bottom line is to always talk to your pediatrician about which formula to use at first and before you switch types. There may be other reasons why your baby is showing signs of discomfort.

You may have to try various formulas if your baby seems to reject one, vomits after most feedings, has constant diarrhea, or gets a rough red rash on her face or bottom. Any standard formula is fine as long as your baby likes it and seems to digest it well.

Formulas come packaged as a powder, concentrated liquid, or ready-to-serve liquid. Powder is the cheapest, most compact, and most portable, but it is slightly more difficult to blend than the concentrated liquid. Some researchers have expressed concern about liquid formula in cans, since most are lined with BPA. While formula manufacturers concede the presence of BPA in the cans, they insist that it is a trace amount that presents no danger to infants. To be safe, you may prefer to use powdered formula, prepared and served in BPA-free bottles.

There has been concern about trace amounts of melamine, an industrial chemical, that have been found in U. S. manufactured infant formula. The Food and Drug Administration (*www.fda.gov*) has issued a report that insists the formula sold in the United States is safe. According to Dr. Stephen Sundlof, director of the FDA's Center for Food Safety and Applied Nutrition, "The levels that we are detecting are extremely low," and do not pose a health risk to infants (even those who are fed formula exclusively for a year). Parents "should not be changing [their infant's] diet. If they've been feeding a particular product, they should continue to feed that product. That's in the best interest of the baby."

QUESTION

Is your local water fluoridated?
If you're not sure, check with your water department. At the age of six months, your child will begin needing fluoride in her diet to ensure the healthy development of her teeth. If your tap water doesn't contain fluoride, you can purchase fluoridated bottled water marketed for infants, have fluoridated spring water delivered, or ask your pediatrician to prescribe fluoride drops.

Fill 'er Up

Here are step-by-step instructions on how to prepare bottles of formula.

1. Boil the nipples and other bottle parts before the first use (this both sterilizes them and gets rid of the plastic flavor). You don't really have to sterilize them again after that if you had a healthy, full-term infant, as long as you have a chlorinated water supply. (Well water can be a concern. Have your water tested for safety or boil the bottles in a pot for five minutes prior to each use.) For all subsequent washings, a run through the dishwasher or hand washing in hot, soapy water will get them sufficiently clean. You'll find it's best to wash or soak bottles soon after using, as curdled milk can be difficult to scrub out.

2. Wash your hands, wipe off the top of the formula can, and mix the formula exactly according to the directions (unless you're using a ready-to-use formula). Too little water can cause dehydration while too much means your baby won't be getting enough calories. If you are concerned about the amount of chlorine in your tap water, use bottled water. It isn't necessary to boil the water unless the available water supply has known problems.

3. Pour the formula into the bottle. You probably think the next thing you need to do is to warm the bottle and then shake a few drops on your wrist to check the temperature, just like you've seen on TV. Wrong. In fact, unless your baby is used to a warm bottle, he probably won't care

if you serve it to him at room temperature or straight out of the refrigerator, although he may get used to (and come to prefer) the bottle temperature he gets most often. Think of the advantages of a baby who will drink a cold bottle. There's no struggling to warm a bottle while holding a hungry, crying, and increasingly agitated baby and no looking for hot water while on a trip. You can put a bottle in a cooler of ice right next to your bed for nighttime feedings.

If your gourmet child insists on warm bottles, go ahead and do that little wrist ritual—if the milk feels at all hot, it is too hot. If you've microwaved the bottle to heat it, shake it well so there are no hot spots. Most experts recommend against microwaving because of the danger of hot spots, but most formula-feeding mothers end up using the microwave. If you do microwave, however, stick to plain plastic bottles; bottle liners can explode and glass bottles can crack. Never microwave breastmilk because it contains too many fragile antibodies. Put a bottle of breastmilk in a cup of warm water if you want to warm it.

Top Ten Bottle-Feeding Mistakes

Following are some things you should avoid while bottle-feeding:

10. Boiling bottles to sterilize them is not really necessary. A trip through the dishwasher or a soap-and-hot-water wash is sufficient.
9. Don't change the proportion of water to formula (either because you think it's a hot day and your baby needs more water, or that extra formula will make him sleep better). You risk dehydrating or starving your baby.
8. Don't boil water to mix with powdered formula. Unless your water supply has known problems (in which case you may wish to use bottled water), water straight from the tap or filter is fine.
7. Don't leave the top on the bottle while heating in the microwave.
6. Don't microwave breastmilk (it kills the antibodies).
5. Don't forget to shake microwaved bottles well to eliminate hot spots.
4. Don't give your baby a bottle to hold in the crib. This can cause tooth decay and ear infections.

3. Be careful not to screw the nipple ring down too tightly. This cuts off the flow of milk and makes bottle-feeding frustrating for the baby.

2. Never prop up a bottle to feed your baby. If she is too young to hold a bottle, someone should be holding her. Propping a bottle to let a baby feed herself can cause choking.

1. Don't urge your baby to finish a bottle. Breastfed babies eat until they are full; bottle-fed babies should be allowed the same privilege.

Dinner Is Served

Feeding your baby, whether it's from your breast or a bottle, is an opportunity to bond with your baby. Enjoy those close moments. All too soon, your baby will be grown up, and grabbing a meal with mom may not be as high on his list of priorities.

Settle into a comfortable chair with a nearby table on which to rest the bottle when you stop to reposition the baby. Turn off the phone and try to minimize other distractions. Hold your baby snuggled close, positioning his head in line with the rest of his body. He should be at about a 45-degree angle, so that his ears are higher than his mouth and his head tips back slightly. (Adjust the angle if your baby spits up during the feeding, but don't hold your baby completely flat. The milk can back up into the Eustachian tube and cause an ear infection.) Pick up the bottle and then, with one finger on the hand holding the bottle, stroke the baby's cheek that is closest to your body. When he turns toward you, brush his lips with the nipple, and let him latch on himself; don't stuff it in. Make sure the tip of the nipple is in the back of his mouth. Hold the bottle firmly so it resists his suction; otherwise, he'll just be moving the bottle around instead of getting the milk out.

As he drinks, keep adjusting the angle of the bottle so that the nipple is always full of milk and not air. Don't tip the bottle up any more than you have to; the more you tip it up, the faster the flow, and a gulping baby is likely to swallow air. If the flow is too slow, however, your baby may get frustrated and fuss, or lose interest and doze off.

When your baby seems to fuss or pull away, stop for a burp, and then offer him the bottle again. If he's not interested, don't push him to finish the bottle. And don't obsess about how much your baby eats. Nursing mothers don't know how much their babies get, and breastfed babies do just fine.

The amounts will vary from day to day, so just make sure that your baby is steadily gaining weight.

If your baby doesn't finish a bottle of pumped breastmilk, you don't have to throw out the leftovers. Put it back in the refrigerator and bring it out for the next feeding, but don't do this more than twice. Leftover formula breeds bacteria more easily than breastmilk, so unfinished amounts should be thrown away.

Timing the Introduction

If you're breastfeeding and intend to occasionally use a bottle or eventually switch to a bottle full-time, timing is everything: after the third week and before the eighth week. If you start too early, you may permanently reduce your milk supply. If you start too late, your baby may not want to have anything to do with a bottle. After the third week, conduct bottle practice every day. You don't have to continue with daily bottles once your baby has demonstrated that she is willing and able to suck from a bottle's nipple, but do remind her at least several times a week that milk does, indeed, come in bottles. (Be prepared, though: At six or eight months, she may pull a fast one on you and begin refusing bottles no matter how successful she's been with them until that point.)

Another Chance

If you miss this introduction window, your baby may want nothing to do with a bottle and it may not be worth forcing the issue. You can just wait another month or two and then begin teaching your baby to drink from a cup. But if you must wean an unwilling baby to a bottle (because you have to be away from your baby or must take medication that would be dangerous for your baby, for example), it can be done.

First, make sure that you are holding the baby in a different position than the one in which you breastfeed—facing out, for example—or feed while walking around the room. Act thrilled and excited when you are getting ready to give your baby the bottle, as if you are just about to give her the most delightful treat. Don't act apologetic or worried. Expect your baby to reject your first attempts. Give up for a few moments and then try again, still acting as enthusiastic as you possibly can. Remember that even a few swallows taken from a bottle count as a win.

You can start by offering the bottle a few times a day when the baby is hungry, but take it away if she refuses. You might try offering a cup, or waiting a little while and then nursing her. The opposite method may work for some babies. That is, introduce the bottle when the baby is not frantically hungry, in the hopes that it will be perceived as something fun to play with, and then—what a bonus—the baby gets some milk, too. If this doesn't work, temporarily switch to a dropper or syringe; try anything that will get the milk into the baby's mouth from a source other than the breast.

If you're the nursing mother and are having no success with bottle-feeding, get yourself out of the picture. Let someone else struggle with this early introduction. Typically, most moms turn to the dads, but even better is an experienced bottle-feeder—her confidence will communicate to the baby.

The Joy of Pumping

Did you ever see a milking machine demonstration at a county fair? Now try to picture yourself in the cow's place.

Having a supply of pumped breastmilk on hand may be a good idea. Even if you rarely give your baby a bottle, at least he will recognize what's inside of it. However, if you don't have a reason to pump—for instance, no plan to go back to work or to attend an event to which you can't bring your baby—and you don't want to, then don't force it on yourself. You should, however, plan on bringing your baby with you whenever you go out for more than a few hours until he's eating solids, about six months old.

If you do decide to pump, get the most powerful pump you can. Some women with hair-trigger let-downs can use a hand pump or even express milk without a pump, but you'll have a better chance of success with a hospital-grade pump. Portable briefcase-style electric pumps aren't bad but are not quite as strong as the less stylish ones. You may want to rent a pump before investing in one.

Getting Started

Wait until your baby is at least four weeks old and, hopefully, settled into a regular nursing schedule. Pick a time at least an hour after he's nursed and an hour before you expect him to nurse again (or a time when there is something on TV that you like, since it's hard to pump and do much else but sit) and try to pump at the same time every day. If your baby for some reason cuts a feeding short, pump out the remainder. If you experience a let-down during a free moment, grab the pump and take advantage of it.

Use clean pump equipment and bottles (wash with hot soapy water and air-dry on a clean towel or run through the dishwasher). Wash your hands, get comfortable, and then do whatever best produces a let-down. This may be music, silence, or looking at a picture of your baby.

When you start to pump, unless your baby has just nursed, you'll probably get very little milk until your milk lets down. You should then pump until the milk flow stops. (For the first week don't expect to get much milk; your body has to adjust to producing extra for your pumping sessions.) Start on the minimum setting, and dial the pressure up until you're getting milk. If you're using a single pump, pump for five minutes on each side, alternating for as long as you are producing milk. Or you use an adapter that lets you pump both breasts at once—after all, you really don't want a pumping session to last longer than it has to.

Storing Breastmilk

Breastmilk will keep at room temperature for six to ten hours, depending on how cool your room is. You can leave it out if you're planning on using it that day (to eliminate having to heat it). It will keep in the refrigerator for as long as eight days, and you can add to it during that period. It will keep in the freezer for up to four months if your freezer has a separate door, and in a deep freezer for more than six months. Once thawed, it can be refrigerated for twenty-four hours, but not refrozen.

When you're ready to use the frozen milk, defrost it in warm running water. Don't use hot water, or you'll compromise the milk's immune-boosting effect. Shake it up, as the fat will have risen to the top. If you feed the baby unshaken milk, he'll get all cream, will get full, and may not get enough overall fluid.

CHAPTER 8

Real Food Comes Next

By the time you're finally feeling comfortable about breast- or bottle-feeding, or whatever combination of the two you have worked out, people will start asking you whether or not your baby has started eating solids. Odds are people will ask you sooner than they should. Until recently, moms began mixing up bowls of baby cereal when their infants were around four months old. Some started sooner in hopes that solid food would help their babies sleep longer. It didn't.

Time for Mush

Currently, the AAP advises parents to wait until their infants are six months old before giving them any food except formula or breastmilk. Complementary feedings do not increase total caloric intake or growth rate, and lack the protective components of human milk.

QUESTION

How much is enough?
During the first year, solid food is only a supplement—the baby's primary nutrition source remains breastmilk or formula. Don't panic if it doesn't seem like your baby is eating all that much.

Reasons for Waiting

By about six months most babies are physically ready to swallow solid foods. The tongue extrusion reflex, in which most things that go into a baby's mouth are quickly pushed out by her tongue, fades away. An older baby's digestive enzymes have matured to the point where she can fairly efficiently break down solid foods. Her intestines have started secreting a protein called immunoglobulin A (IgA), which prevents allergens from passing into the bloodstream. It's important to wait for these capacities to develop, because a breastfed baby may lose some of her protection against infections and allergies once she starts solids.

Be Patient

Besides the health reasons for holding off on solids, there are a few practical ones. Solids will quickly transform the reasonably tolerable smell of a breastfed baby's poop into foul sludge. Cleaning up spit-up stains will become challenging. If you've got a trip planned, take it before you enter the solid food stage; a couple of days' worth of baby food can really weigh down your suitcase. (You'll also be happier if you can postpone the challenge of feeding a baby squirming on your lap in an airplane seat.)

The only reason for jumping the gun on solids is if your baby is at least four months old and is acting like she's going to go ahead and start solids without you. Talk to your pediatrician before you do. She may be ready if she stares at you when you eat and grabs at your food, mouths all of her toys, can sit up (with support) fairly well, or nurses frequently or drinks huge amounts of formula but still seems hungry. Most importantly, she's ready if she doesn't immediately use her tongue to push out anything you put into her mouth.

But wait the six months—or a little longer—if you can. The window for the introduction of solid food is a lot wider than the window for the introduction of the bottle.

ESSENTIAL

Try not to pass your food hang-ups on to your children. You many think tofu is gross and avocados are slimy, but your child may love them if you feed them to her without comment.

Babies can do without solids for as long as eight months without ill effect. Soon after eight months, however, your baby will begin to require the extra nutrients that come with solids. She ought to have a little experience with this new way of eating before that time comes, so starting daily eating practice sometime before eight or nine months is a good idea.

Your Baby Is Ready for Solids When . . .

- She's at least four to six months old.
- She's like a vulture when you're eating, ready to pounce on your food.
- She stops sticking her tongue out when her mouth is touched.
- She sits with support and controls her head well enough to lean forward when she wants more food.
- She's almost ready to sit up on her own.
- She indicates she's full when you are feeding her.
- She drinks more than thirty-two ounces of formula, or breastfeeds six or seven times a day and wants more.
- She's at least twice her birth weight or at least thirteen to fifteen pounds.

First "Real" Food

Rice cereal is easy to digest and unlikely to cause an allergic reaction. Alternatives, particularly if your baby has a tendency to be constipated, are barley and oat cereal. (Avoid wheat at first, as wheat allergies are fairly common.)

Instant, ready-to-mix rice cereal is widely available, and the standard brands are basically alike. To prepare instant rice cereal, mix about two teaspoons of the cereal with breastmilk or formula (if you're using a cereal that already includes powdered formula, all you need to add is water). Experiment with the texture to see what your baby prefers, but start out with the mixture a bit soupy (but not so thin it runs off of the spoon).

You can also make rice cereal from scratch, but the downside is that homemade cereals are not iron fortified, and at six months your baby is ready for a boost of iron. The cereal-making process can be as simple (rice plus water cooked into a mush) or as elaborate as you choose. Talk to your doctor about whether your baby needs the extra iron fortification, especially if he's being fed with iron-fortified formula.

Suppertime

For your baby's first supper, pick a time when she's starting to seem hungry, but not frantically so. Forget about assembling the highchair; she won't be ready for that for a few weeks. Instead, put your baby in an infant seat or on the lap of an available adult, making sure she is basically upright with her head tipped slightly back.

Do not put solid foods in a bottle or an infant feeder unless your doctor has told you to do so (which she will suggest only if your child has one of a very small list of medical conditions). It is easy to overfeed using a feeder, unlike a spoon that your baby can easily push away.

Scoop a tiny bit of cereal on an infant or demitasse spoon—or even your own finger—and put it just into the front of your baby's mouth. Don't shove it in; she needs to learn for herself how to get the food off of the spoon and far enough back into her mouth to swallow. Since you're introducing this at a stage when she is mouthing everything in sight, she'll probably open her mouth as soon as the spoon gets close.

Then let your baby do whatever she wants with the cereal. She may try to suck the spoon. She may push the cereal out with her tongue. Matter-of-factly scoop it off of her chin and back into her mouth. Eventually she may swallow and then open her mouth for another bite. Once she turns away she's had enough, even if it's only been a few spoonfuls. Respect her appetite and stop when she's full; don't try to coax in one last bite. Let your baby decide how much she wants to eat. The average baby eats the equivalent of one jar of baby food at each meal once she is eating confidently and has moved to three meals a day.

If she starts to get bored with this new game, wipe her off and put away the spoon and bowl, but bring it out again at around the same time the next day. If she balks completely—closes her mouth from the beginning, turns away from the spoon, or just starts screaming—try again tomorrow. If she balks several days in a row, give it up for a few weeks and try again; some babies just aren't ready when you think they should be.

Tricks of the Trade

Be prepared: Most feedings don't go all that smoothly. It may seem like it takes you an hour for your baby to eat a meal—and then an hour for you to clean up!

Your baby may grab at the spoon—so give him one of his own to hold. He may want to smoosh the cereal with his fingers. Let him—he'll probably suck some off of his fingers as well. He may refuse to open his mouth. Try opening yours wide and take a bite yourself. It will be pretty bland, but make smacking noises like it's the best chocolate you've ever tasted (or whatever is your favorite food).

Gearing Up

Following is a list of handy things to have when your baby is ready to try solid food:

- Infant feeding spoon or demitasse spoon
- Big bibs for baby; an apron for you

- Sturdy highchair with a safety strap (although you won't be using that for a few weeks) or infant seat
- Topless plastic cups, preferably with handles; no-spill cups
- Food processor or blender; food grinder
- Washcloths
- Disposable self-stick placemats for restaurant tables or highchair trays
- A plastic mat, towel, or a dog to catch spills
- Portable clip-on highchair for restaurants or visits

Don't Stress over the Mess

This eating thing is supposed to be fun. If the messiness is making you crazy, turn up the heat, strip her down to her diaper, and put a towel or shower curtain (for wider coverage) under her chair.

ESSENTIAL

Wash and save your glass baby food jars. You can use them to store homemade baby food, a meal-sized portion of food for travel, or a serving's worth of dry baby cereal—simply add liquid when you're ready. (Later on, they make great bug keepers for older kids.)

Moms who have the easiest time with the mess that comes with feeding a baby are the ones who own a dog, preferably a big one, with an omnivorous palate. Such dogs position themselves strategically under the highchair and lap up any spills as soon as they hit the ground. These moms say they wouldn't feed a baby without one. If you don't have a pooch, there are always newspapers, towels, a plastic mat, or just a mop to clean up the remains on the floor. If you're really lucky and the weather's cooperative, feed your baby outside. Hose down the highchair and area under it afterward. (Remember to remove your baby first.)

Life after Rice

Stick to rice cereal, once or twice a day, for two weeks or so—or even as long as a month. This food is easy to digest, unlikely to cause allergies, and can be prepared with a thicker consistency as your baby gets more proficient at eating.

Slowly introduce other foods to your baby's diet. "Slowly" is the key word here. Feed your baby a single new food, in tiny portions, for at least three days straight before moving on to another food, and watch for signs of allergic reaction. (Don't serve a mixed food until you've allergy-tested the ingredients first.) It is much easier to allergy-test at the food introduction stage than figure out what caused an allergy later. It's a good idea to keep a chart of what foods you've introduced, and what reaction, if any, you noticed.

While there is wide agreement that rice cereal is the perfect first food, there is less agreement on what the second food should be. One theory is that the next few foods should be vegetables, not fruits, so your baby doesn't get the idea that all food is sweet. The other theory holds the opposite: that fruits, because of their sweetness, are more likely to interest your baby and therefore should be introduced before vegetables.

Both theories make sense, so go with what seems to work for you and your baby. Every few weeks introduce a new type of cereal into the mix as well. In general, the order doesn't matter that much.

▼ **TOP TEN FIRST FOODS**

10.	Peas
9.	Sweet potatoes
8.	Squash
7.	Pears
6.	Avocado
5.	Bananas
4.	Applesauce
3.	Barley cereal
2.	Oat cereal
1.	Rice cereal

Homemade Baby Food

Commercial baby food is easy and convenient, if relatively expensive. While it's easy enough to make your own, don't be guilted into preparing homemade baby foods if you have no time or interest. Buy the jarred food for the few months until your baby is eating table food.

Simple Food Made Simply

There's nothing complicated about making baby food. In fact, simplicity is the key. You can make a batch and freeze it to be defrosted as needed. Here are some simple steps to making baby meals:

- Buy the freshest vegetables and fruits and use them within a day or two.
- Peel, remove any seeds and cores, and then steam or boil until soft. Bananas don't need to be cooked—just mash with a fork.
- Puree the mixture well (in a blender, baby food grinder, or food processor).
- Freeze individual portions in ice-cube trays. Once frozen, you can take the cubes out of the trays and store them in bags in the freezer. Be sure to label and date the bags. Frozen fruit and vegetable purees are good for three months; pureed meat, fish, and chicken will last up to eight weeks.

Don't mix ingredients while you are still introducing them to your baby. You can mix two together—like carrots and sweet potatoes—once you know that your baby is not allergic to a particular fruit or vegetable.

Defrost in the microwave, but just until barely warm and stir thoroughly to get rid of any hot spots. If necessary, add breastmilk, water, or formula to smooth or thin the puree. Avoid butter, oil, sugar, and salt.

Organic for Baby?

You may see some food labeled "natural," "free-range," and "hormone-free," but that doesn't guarantee that the food is organic. Only baby food labeled "USDA organic" has met standards set by the United States Department of Agriculture, and only those foods that have been certified to meet USDA standards can be legally labeled "organic."

In order to qualify as "USDA organic," the food must be at least 95 percent organic, meaning that all but 5 percent was produced without conventional fertilizers and pesticides. Organic food can't be irradiated, genetically modified, or produced with antibiotics or hormones. Any meat products must come from animals that have been fed organically grown feed.

While organic jarred baby food may be slightly more expensive, you can save if you shop at sales and buy in bulk.

If you are going to make your own baby food, look for fruits and vegetables that have been certified as USDA organic on their labels.

ALERT

Constipation is common in the early weeks of introducing solid food. You're giving your baby something a lot harder to digest than breastmilk or formula, and the most typical first foods—rice cereal, banana, and applesauce—are binding. Sometimes adding fluids (a bottle or cup of water a day) is enough to solve the problem. You can also feed your baby a little prune juice, or switch from rice cereal and applesauce to oat cereal and pureed pears.

Nitrate Alert

Fresh beets, turnips, carrots, collard greens, and spinach may contain nitrates, chemicals found in abundance in the soil from certain parts of the country. Nitrates can cause a type of anemia in infants up to six months of age. It's not a question of whether or not the vegetables are organic. To avoid this problem, the AAP recommends you buy commercially prepared forms of these vegetables. Baby food manufacturers screen the produce for nitrates.

Baby Food Safety Tips

Take care to make sure that the food you feed your baby is safe and fresh.

- Don't feed your baby directly from the jar. Once saliva enzymes from the spoon touch the food, they break down nutrients and speed up spoilage. To avoid waste, spoon a meal's worth of food into a bowl. If you must feed from the jar, throw what's left away.
- Refrigerate unused food immediately.

- Don't keep an open, refrigerated jar of baby food longer than two days—even if it tastes fine to you, bacteria can make your baby sick.
- If you're giving your baby food from a can, either run the can opener through the dishwasher or use one reserved for this purpose (not the one you use to open the dog food).
- Give your baby only pasteurized juices.

Meat and Dairy

At around eight months you can, if you'd like, give your baby his first taste of meat. Don't panic if those little jarred meats never make it into your baby's mouth. Many babies never take to the taste of canned meats. You can try mixing meats with pureed vegetables or grind up meat from your family's dinner, which at least smells better than the jarred meats. Or you can just wait until your baby is old enough to pick up a bit of chicken and chew it for himself. Meat is not necessary in the first year; your baby is getting all the protein he needs from formula or breastmilk.

Wait until your baby is at least twelve months old before feeding him dairy products. The protein in cow's milk can be difficult to break down.

Vegetarian Baby

A healthy vegetarian diet that also includes milk and eggs can easily meet all your baby's nutritional needs. Discuss your baby's proposed vegetarian diet in detail with your pediatrician. A vegetarian diet should include lots of iron-rich foods (stewed dried fruits, beans, and fortified cereal), and a daily multivitamin with iron (make sure this is stored out of reach of your baby as iron poisoning can be fatal).

Fat is important in brain development, and babies under age two need more calories and fat than at any other time in their lives. Some foods used to increase calories and fat in the diet are mashed avocado, vegetable oil, and nut and seed butters.

Vegan Diet

Meeting all of your baby's nutritional needs is less easily accomplished on a vegan (vegetable foods only) diet. Vitamin B12 can only be supplied by animal products, and it is also difficult to provide sufficient calcium, vitamin D, and riboflavin, which originate largely, but not exclusively, in dairy products. It can be especially difficult for infants on a vegan diet to consume the quantity of food required to provide the necessary amounts of these essential nutrients. As previously stated, infants need much higher levels of fat in their diet than adults, and a vegan diet is typically a low-fat one. Discuss your concerns with your health care provider to see what adjustments you must make to your baby's diet so she gets the nutrients, calories, and fat she needs.

Allergic Reactions

Any of these symptoms indicate that your baby has reacted unfavorably to the new food you just tried:

- Skin reactions: Rashes on the face or trunk, severe diaper rash, hives, eczema
- Digestive problems: Vomiting, diarrhea, gas
- Swollen lips or eyelids
- Crankiness
- Stuffed nose
- Wheezing

Wheezing, though rare, is a reason to call your doctor immediately. Discuss with your doctor whether the wheezing was caused by the food and whether the food should be eliminated. Milder symptoms mean you should just put the food away for a while. Try it again in a couple of months, and odds are it'll be just fine.

Peanuts

Although high in protein, calories, and fat, neither peanuts nor peanut butter should be given to babies. About 1.5 million Americans have a severe allergy to peanuts. The symptoms can range from the mild, an itchy throat, to the serious, anaphylactic shock, which can result in death. The AAP recommends that children at higher risk of developing a food allergy should not be given peanut butter until they are three years old. Your child is at higher risk if you or a family member has a food allergy, asthma, eczema, or hay fever.

If you do serve your child peanut butter, remember that young children often swallow without chewing. Sticky foods like peanut butter can increase their risk of choking. To avoid this problem:

- Always spread peanut butter thinly on a cracker or bread.
- Do not serve dollops of peanut butter.
- Always make sure your child is seated when eating.
- Make sure an adult is with your child when he is eating.

Label Literacy

You would think a jar of pureed plums would contain, simply, plums. But you can't assume that, so check the label. In the past, baby food companies would regularly add sugar and thickeners (like tapioca starch) to their products, reasoning that babies preferred sweeter, smoother foods. (This may be true, but may not be the preference to reinforce.) After a fuss in the press a few years ago, jarred baby foods, at least those designed as first foods, became purer. You should still check the label, however, in particular for foods labeled "fruit desserts" or "stage-three" foods. Don't be fooled if the label says that the product includes fructose, dextrose, or maltodextrins— these are all different forms of sugars. Be on the lookout, too, for corn products, including corn syrup as a sweetener and cornstarch as a thickener. These can trigger allergies in a sensitive baby.

Also watch out for and avoid artificial flavors and colors (red #40, yellow #5, etc.). These can cause unpredictable allergic reactions, and there is some unconfirmed evidence implicating them in neurological disorders.

All about the Cup

You can begin teaching your baby to drink from a cup at about the same time you start solids, or even a little sooner.

Offer sips of breastmilk, formula, or water from a cup beginning at about five months—not for nutrition, but for practice. You can also let her have a drink from your glass of water by putting the cup to her lips and tipping it until a tiny sip pours out. Since most of it will trickle down her chin at first, try it when you're getting ready to change her clothes anyway. It's also a good idea to hold cup practice at bath time.

When your baby starts eating solids, she can also have small amounts of juice, preferably mixed with water. Keep the amount of juice small (less than four ounces a day), or she may fill up on juice and not get the other nutrients that she needs.

There are three basic kind of infant cups, and you'll eventually want to get your baby used to all three of them. She should learn to drink from a cup without a top, controlling the flow with her lips. Like eating, this is a skill that has to be practiced. You will also want her to drink occasionally from a cup with a spouted lid. These cups allow the liquid to flow out in a small stream, and are perfect for when she's eating finger foods in her highchair and you want her to have a drink available, but don't want her to soak herself if you step away. The baby still has to control the flow herself, but the liquid pours out fairly slowly when the cup is tipped over.

You'll also want your baby to drink from a no-spill cup. These cups have valves inside their spouts and don't spill even if shaken. They're great for the stroller, the car, or even wandering around the house. The experience of drinking from them is closer to that of sucking from a bottle than it is drinking from a cup, so they shouldn't be your baby's only cups.

Buy BPA-free sippy cups. Check *www.safemama.com* for a list of manufacturers who produce BPA-free cups.

Finger Foods

At eight or nine or ten months, most babies will be pretty proficient at slurping and swallowing, and you'll be used to the feeding routine. You've allergy-tested a number of foods and have a fairly long list of things your baby can and will eat. He's opening his mouth like a little bird whenever he sees the spoon, and you're getting a lot more of his food in his mouth than on his clothes. Daily menus are easy: a few bowls of cereal, a few servings of pureed fruits and vegetables, and you're set.

Then your baby pulls a fast one. "No more mush!" his pursed lips seem to say as he knocks the spoon out of your hand and pureed carrots spatter across the floor. Your baby is sick of goop. However, he has only a few teeth and is not nearly ready to handle a knife and fork.

QUESTION

How will I know my baby is ready for finger foods?
Signs your baby is ready for finger foods include: sitting up well in a highchair by himself, eating a number of different pureed foods, including thicker ones, and picking up things with his thumb and forefinger, a sign that his motor skills are advancing.

One Lump or Two?

One option is moving to lumpier baby foods. The prepared versions are marked "stage three" or designated for older babies. If you are making them yourself, don't puree them as long and leave in some chunks. The change in texture and the more complex tastes of these foods may get your little bird opening his mouth again. Just in case, here are some other menus to try if your child starts to gag at the lumpier foods.

Cereal Strategies

Grab the Cheerios, or, to be brand neutral, oat cereal rings. Scatter a few on your baby's tray, and he'll try to pick them up and put them in his mouth. These may entertain him enough for you to slip in a few spoonfuls of mush in between bites.

Finger food can be a fun distraction. While your baby's busy getting the Cheerios near his mouth, you can be ready with the spoonful of squash or pears, waiting for that split second when he opens his mouth and doesn't yet have the Cheerio in place.

Cheerios are a popular food for nascent self-feeders for a number of reasons. First, they are made of oats rather than wheat, so allergies are unlikely to be an issue. Second, they are spit soluble and quickly soften into easy-to-swallow mush. They are also difficult to choke on and more likely to stick to your baby's mouth than to be inhaled. Third, they give your baby great practice at picking things up with his thumb and forefinger. This pincer grasp is a developmental milestone (see Chapter 16) that he is likely to be working on around the same time he becomes interested in self-feeding.

Another option is a teething biscuit. There are a number of varieties available, or you can make your own. Read the labels carefully, because some have a lot more sugar than others. Teething biscuits dissolve into mush as your baby gums them. (But don't leave your baby alone with one since large pieces can break off and pose a choking danger.)

Finger Food Buffet

There is no reason your self-feeder should have a boring diet. Provide him with a variety of foods to enhance nutrition and give him important experience with different tastes and textures. In addition to Cheerios, try (in baby-sized pieces): rice crackers; boiled, sliced carrots; cooked sweet potato sticks; thin slices of cheddar cheese sticks; plain yogurt; unsweetened applesauce.

ALERT

If your baby is under twelve months, do not feed him: whole hot dogs, whole grapes, raisins, nuts or seeds (including sunflower and other seeds sold as snack food), olives, popcorn or potato chips, ice cubes or hard candy, or uncooked carrots or apples.

Finger foods must be soft, break down into small pieces, and be easy to swallow. There are a host of fruits that meet those criteria, including cantaloupe, peaches, pears, plums, kiwis, avocados, and even apples, if they are first steamed or poached (slice them, add a spoonful of water, and cook them in the microwave). Just remove any peels and pits and cut into baby-bite-sized pieces. For vegetables like broccoli, squash, and carrots, steam or boil them until reasonably soft.

Pasta makes a great early finger food as long as you pick small shapes and cook them soft. Serve it plain, with tomato sauce, or even with pesto.

Breakfast foods are also good finger foods for any time of the day. Whole-grain waffles (purchased frozen and heated in the toaster), pancakes (use a whole-grain mix, make a batch, and freeze them; they are easily reheated in the microwave), and French toast (for babies under twelve months, make it with separated egg yolks mixed with formula or breastmilk). You can spread any of these with a fruit or vegetable puree to bump up the nutrition.

Whatever you're serving, give your baby only a few pieces at a time, and consider mealtime finished as soon as throwing the food on the floor becomes more interesting than putting it in his mouth.

The finger food stage can start as early as six months or not until several months later. It depends on your child's personality, for one. Babies with strong individual preferences and a lust for independence will move into this stage earlier than more easy-going babies. It also depends on the environment. If you don't mind a mess, your baby probably gets his hands into his cereal regularly, and that has already become his first finger food experience. If neatness is important to you and you are quick to wipe up spills, your baby may have gotten the message that he should keep his hands out of the way at mealtime.

Either way, by twelve months your baby will probably do most of his feeding himself. Most of that will be with his fingers—although he may begin to experiment with using a spoon, he probably won't be very successful yet.

ALERT

These foods are the most likely to trigger allergic reactions in some babies. Be alert if you try any of them: citrus fruit, tomatoes, strawberries, wheat, corn, soy products, egg whites, cow's milk, shellfish, and peanuts.

Eggs

Doctors recommend that you wait until your baby is ten months old before introducing egg yolks into his diet. You should wait until your baby is at least a year old before offering him egg whites, as they often cause allergic reactions if introduced too early.

Honey

Honey is not recommended for infants under the age of twelve months, as it may carry botulism spores that can be deadly for babies. Even baking may not destroy these spores. While not all honey contains botulism spores, there's no reason to take the risk since babies don't need honey.

Finger Food Options

Since a baby's airway is the size of the tip of his pinky, you should always serve finger foods under constant adult supervision. Only give finger foods to a child who is sitting up—not lying down or walking around. Be sure that all finger foods are soft and cut into small pieces.

▼ **TOP TEN FINGER FOODS: SIX TO EIGHT MONTHS**

10.	Graham crackers
9.	Mashed potatoes
8.	Peeled carrots (to gum on, before teeth emerge)
7.	Arrowroot cookies
6.	Teething biscuits
5.	Bagels
4.	Soft-cooked vegetables
3.	Bananas
2.	Zwieback
1.	Cheerios

▼ **TOP TEN FINGER FOODS: NINE TO TWELVE MONTHS**

10.	Ripe peaches
9.	Avocado slices
8.	Small meatballs
7.	Rice
6.	Scrambled egg yolks
5.	Tofu
4.	Toast
3.	Rice cakes
2.	Egg noodles
1.	Cheerios

Setting the Pace

Meals at the finger-feeding stage will be messy and may take a long time. Resist the temptation to step in and neatly tuck each bite of food into your baby's mouth. Eating isn't just about nutrition at this point—it's about learning. This is your baby's time to learn to like different tastes and textures; to learn to skillfully get food from the bowl to the mouth, gums, or throat; and to learn about when to eat and when to stop.

CHAPTER 9

Diaper Diaries

As a new parent, you are expected to instinctively be an expert on taking care of a baby—from washing her hair to cutting her toenails. If you had your baby in a hospital, you might come away thinking the most important thing to know is how to give your baby a bath, but the numbers tell a different story. The bath-to-diaper-changing ratio suggests that you'll need to know a lot more about the care of a baby's body than how to bathe her.

Wet Diapers

When you first start breastfeeding, it's important to count how many wet diapers your baby has (six to eight in a twenty-four-hour period is good) as a judge of whether she is getting enough milk. Once your milk has come in, some babies urinate every one to three hours, while others only four to six times a day. If she's sick or if it's very hot outside, she may urinate less and it would still be normal.

Urination should never be painful. If you think your baby is in distress while urinating, call your doctor as this could be a sign of a urinary tract infection.

If you see actual blood in your baby's urine or bowel movements, talk to your health care provider. It could be simply a result of diaper rash, but it could also be a sign of something more serious.

The Scoop on Poop

In your baby's first few days, his poop will look like tar—black, sticky, and hard to remove. This is meconium, a thick, dark green or black paste that fills a baby's intestines in utero and must be eliminated before he can digest normally. If you're lucky, he'll have eliminated most of the meconium in the hospital. If not, you'll be wiping it off at home. (It's sticky stuff, and may not come off with plain water. Try a little baby oil on a cotton ball.) Following the meconium, your baby's bowel movements will turn yellow-green.

If you're breastfeeding, your baby's poop will resemble seeded, slightly runny Dijon mustard once your milk comes in. It will be more tan if you're formula-feeding, and thicker than peanut butter.

The most amazing thing about this bodily function is how much noise can be generated from such a small person. There you are, holding your precious, dozing baby as relatives coo over how sweet he is, when you hear the sound of a volcano erupting. It's definitely a conversation stopper, and a clue to run, not walk, to the changing table.

Your baby will typically dirty several diapers a day, but he may have bowel movements as often as ten times a day or as infrequently as once a week. Both are normal. The ten-times-a-day baby does not have diarrhea, and the once-a-week-baby is not constipated (unless the poop, when it comes, arrives in pellets). If your baby is eating well, growing nicely, and seems comfortable, don't be concerned about how often he poops.

Diaper Wars

Be forewarned: You will need lots of diapers. First, you have to choose sides—are you going to be on Team Cloth, or Team Disposable?

There are women who can argue about their diaper choices for hours. One concern is the impact on the environment (disposables become solid waste that must be disposed of in landfills; cloth diapers use energy and water for laundering and, if you're using a diaper service, transporting). The other concern is the health of the baby (cloth diapers are more natural and you're likely to change them more often; disposables keep baby drier, but leak synthetic pellets when they get overloaded). Luckily, there is a middle road—disposable diapers called Tushies that don't contain chemically synthesized absorbents.

Team Cloth

The main complaint about cloth diapers is that too often "poop happens." In other words, the poop leaks out of the diaper and stains the baby's clothing, especially in the first couple of weeks when explosive bowel movements are common. More changes and more laundry ensue. Plus, unless you use disposables when you're out of the house, you're left carrying around dirty diapers. Environmentally speaking, cloth diapers are the best choice and, with good planning and organization, may work for your family.

Reasons to Use Cloth Diapers

There are many good reasons to use cloth diapers:

- Cloth diapers have a hundred other uses (including a peek-a-boo toy, burping rag, and, sooner than you might think, dust rag, and silver-polisher).
- You'll be more attentive to your baby's needs since you'll have to change her diaper more quickly when she wets.

- Kids may potty train earlier because they can feel the wetness when they urinate, unlike in disposable diapers, which wick the moisture away from the skin.
- They are less expensive than disposables.
- Fewer chemicals are touching your baby's skin.
- They're environmentally correct.
- Even taking into account the cost of doing laundry or using a diaper service, cloth diapers are generally cheaper to use than disposables.

Applied Skills

Unlike disposable diapers, you may need to prepare cloth diapers for use. Below are the different styles of cloth diapers. Whichever kind you choose, you can fasten it with diaper pins, clips, special tape, or a wrap that fastens with snaps or Velcro. If you're using pins, open them up and stick them in a bar of soap before you start the diaper change. Make sure they are out of baby's reach.

Prefold Diapers

Prefolds, common in the United States but less so in other countries, have a thick center and thinner edge sections and are rectangular in shape; nonprefolds are squarer and of uniform thickness.

FIGURE 9-1(A):
Set up

FIGURE 9-1(B):
Fasten

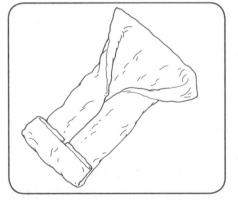

Square Diapers

Fold a standard square diaper into a triangle. Put one point between the legs, and pull the other two points around the side to meet it near the middle of the belly.

FIGURE 9-2(A):
Set up

FIGURE 9-2(B):
Fasten

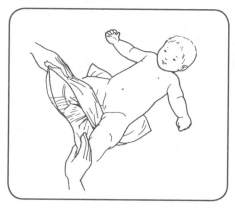

Diapering with a Twist

Or fold the diaper in thirds but then twist the part that goes between your baby's legs to make it extra thick where it counts. You can fold the diaper down in the front before wrapping it around your baby to give a boy extra thickness where he'll need it most.

FIGURE 9-3(A):
Set up

FIGURE 9-3(B):
Fasten

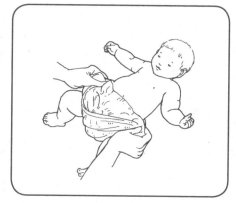

You can also use two diapers. Place one, folded in half or in thirds, between the baby's legs. Wrap the second diaper on top (using whichever method), and pin only the outside diaper to hold everything in place.

Contoured Diapers

Contoured diapers that resemble a fitted sheet are considered better than the prefolded or unfolded square diapers. These don't need to be folded— they are designed to fit easily around your baby's butt. Unfortunately, these aren't commonly offered by diaper services.

QUESTION

What's the best way to wash cloth diapers?
First, after removing from baby, rinse messy diapers in the toilet. Keep wet diapers in a diaper pail that's about half full of water; add one-half cup of vinegar to the water. Keep a secure lid on the pail. Put diapers in the washing machine and run it on the spin cycle to remove excess water. Reset the machine to the full wash cycle in hot water, using mild detergent and bleach. Add one-half cup vinegar to the final rinse and either machine dry at highest heat or line dry in the sun.

Team Disposable

One possible reason disposables are more popular is that putting them on is more intuitive. Open one up with the tapes or Velcro tags underneath your baby, put her bottom in the middle of the diaper, bring the front of the diaper up between her legs, and fasten the tabs at her waist. Some disposables contain substances similar to barrier creams (e.g., Desitin or Balmex). If your baby develops a diaper rash, it may be a reaction to the built-in protective cream. Change to a different brand (or try cloth diapers).

FACT

According to the California Integrated Waste Management Board, disposable diapers represent about 50 percent of the personal garbage produced by parents of a single child.

Reasons to Use Disposable Diapers
- Disposables are required by most day care centers and preferred by babysitters.
- They're less bulky so your baby's clothes will fit better.

- You have less financial commitment up front, and you don't need pins or wraps.
- Used diapers go right out to the trash.
- You'll have fewer changes and less laundry to do.
- Fewer changes also mean there is a better chance your baby will sleep all night.

Tricks of the Trade

There are a few tricks to diapering with disposables.

- While your baby still has her umbilical cord, fold the top of the diaper down to turn it into a bikini before fastening.
- Make sure the leg edges are turned out, not folded back under the elastic. This creates a better seal.
- If your disposables fasten with adhesive tapes, make sure not to get anything on the adhesive—lotions, water, or powder will ruin their stickiness. If your disposables fasten with Velcro tabs, don't pull the tabs too hard or they might rip off.
- When you're diapering a boy, make sure his penis is pointed down in the center of the diaper. If you accidentally diaper his penis up, or tucked out a leg edge, you will end up with a wet lap.
- Even though today's disposables are unlikely to leak until they weigh more than your baby, change them once they get a little squishy. Otherwise, the little pellets of super absorbent gel burst out of the diaper and are pretty much impossible to get off of your baby's skin unless you give her a full bath.

Eco-Friendly Disposables

Although more expensive, biodegradable disposable diapers like Nature Boy and Girl are made of cornstarch instead of plastics. Critics, however, maintain that these diapers aren't better for the environment or the health of babies. The real issue is that regardless of whether or not the diaper is biodegradable, no diaper can break down in an airtight landfill. Furthermore, those who argue the environmental benefits of using cloth diapers can be confronted with the idea that cloth diapers excessively use a precious resource, as well—water, especially important in drought-stricken areas. Consider: you need water for the growing cotton plants, you need water to wash the diapers, and you need water for the extra loads of laundry necessary when cloth diapers leak.

Base your decision about which kind of diaper to use on what works best for your family.

Generics

The amount of advertising dollars spent on promoting brand-name disposable diapers is staggering. Do brand names make a difference? One advertising exec commented that parents buy brand name diapers for their first-born and then happily buy the generics or store brands for subsequent children. Do the math: is it still a bargain if you have to double the cheaper diapers to get the same leak-proofing? You might use generic during the day when you can change the baby more often, and a more absorbent brand at night when your baby's sleeping. You may need to try different brands to find the one that works for your baby.

Universal Diapering Strategies

Make sure you have everything you need within reach before you put your baby on the changing table, countertop, bed, or floor to change him. Use the dirty diaper to do as much preliminary wiping as you can before you bring out the clean cloths or wipes.

Try not to look disgusted; you want your baby to think getting his diaper changed is fun. Sing, spin a mobile, or hold a toy in your mouth—anything to keep your baby entertained and on his back. Clean the baby's bottom with plain water (using an infant washcloth, cut-up towel, soft paper towel, or cotton balls) for the first month. Save commercial diaper wipes for later, as they may irritate your baby's skin.

For a girl, make sure you wipe front to back, using a clean section of washcloth or piece of cotton each time, to prevent spreading poop to the vagina. Although you don't typically need to clean the inside of the lips of the vulva, it sometimes seems as if poop is in every fold, back and front.

For a boy, toss an extra diaper over his penis while you're cleaning him. This reduces the chance of getting a fountain in the face. This isn't a bad precaution when changing a girl, either.

When you're done diapering, put your baby down in a safe place (never leave your baby alone on the changing table, even if he is belted in). You want to dump whatever is loose from the dirty diaper into the toilet. (This goes for disposable diapers, too. Their biggest environmental hazard may not be the amount of paper in the diapers, but rather the problems caused by leaching bacteria.) When you're done, wash your hands thoroughly.

Diapering gets more challenging as your baby gets more control over his body and can kick away your hands, flip over, and, eventually, try to stand up. If he's persistent in wriggling, move the scene of operation to a washable rug on the floor. You may have to swing a leg over his torso to gently hold him on the floor during some of the wrigglier stages. And once your baby learns to stand up, you may have to learn to change his diaper while he's vertical.

Gearing Up for Diapering

Whether you go cloth or disposable, you will spend a lot of time with diapers over the next couple of years. Over time, you'll discover what brands and methods work best for you and your baby. If you have a two-floor home, set up a changing station on both floors to save time and energy from constantly running up and down the stairs. While you're perfecting your technique, there are a few things all changing stations need.

- Make sure your changing surface (changing table or empty counter) is tall enough so you don't hurt your back when bending over it.
- If you plan on using disposables, keep one bag in the current size, and one bag of the next size up waiting in the wings.
- If you're using cloth, you'll need three to four dozen in each size.
- You'll need three to six diaper wraps to go over the cloth diapers.
- Use washcloths for the first month before switching to diaper wipes.
- Get a diaper pail designed for whichever type of diapers you're using.
- Get a variety of changing pads—one for the changing table, one for traveling, and a larger, waterproof pad for naked time.

- Keep two pad covers in rotation (one on the pad, one in the wash).
- Have cream or ointment for diaper rash. Odds are you'll need it eventually.
- Invest in a waterproof flannel crib pad or disposable bed pads to put underneath the sheet. You'll need them now, and they're a good idea to keep for the crib-to-bed transition.
- Above all, keep your sense of humor.

Diapering Tips

Here are some strategies to improve the quality of time spent diapering:

- First and foremost, get all your gear together BEFORE you open a dirty diaper. You'll be glad you did.
- If your changing table has a strap, slip your hand between your baby's belly and the clip before you try to fasten it to avoid pinching your baby's delicate skin.
- Speed counts—the faster you can get your baby diapered and dressed the happier you're both likely to be.
- Accuracy counts—if the diaper isn't lined up correctly on your baby before you fasten it, it will probably leak.
- Treat diaper rash at the first signs—don't let it get out of hand.
- Put a towel or extra cloth diaper under your boy or girl baby and another one over your boy baby while you're changing. Babies do pee when their diapers are off.
- If you have an active child, give up your changing table and get good at diapering your child on the run.
- Stash several special toys in a box near your diaper table, and let your child see these toys only at changing time.
- Always have some diapers on hand that are one size bigger than the diapers that your baby is currently wearing. Babies can grow out of diapers seemingly overnight and too-small diapers contribute to diaper blow-outs.
- Use a cloth diaper or a waterproof flannel mattress pad as a changing pad when you're away from home. The cute little changing pads

that come with diaper bags are so waterproof that any accidents run right off the pad onto the couch/chair/lap you're changing her on.

- Good-quality paper towels moistened with water can substitute for diaper wipes.
- Cut up a cloth diaper into four squares and use the squares as an extra liner (for either cloth or disposable diapers) at night.

Diaper Rash

Diaper rash can be as mild as a little redness or as severe as bleeding sores. Some babies seem to get it all the time; others hardly ever. Peak diaper rash times are when babies start to eat solid foods, when they sleep through the night in a dirty diaper, and when they are taking antibiotics. The best way to treat it is to prevent it.

Change diapers frequently (immediately if they're messy). Expose your baby's bottom to air as often as you can and light (even a light bulb helps). This is pretty easy when your baby's an infant. In a warm room, put him belly down on a disposable absorbent pad (the kind you sat on in the hospital) or use a waterproof crib pad with a cloth diaper on top of it. Do not leave him alone.

ESSENTIAL

Once your baby is mobile, it is less likely he'll stay put. If it's summer, let him run around bare-bottomed outside. If it's winter, you might consider heating up your bathroom and giving him a little extra naked time after his bath.

It's not necessary to slather on ointment with every diaper change to prevent diaper rash. If you notice a little redness—the first symptoms of diaper rash—begin treating it immediately. Don't just hope it will go away on its own, as it's likely to get worse and become a lot more uncomfortable for your baby and a lot harder for you to treat. Also understand that, left untreated, a simple case of diaper rash can become a yeast infection, which is a lot harder to get rid of than ordinary diaper rash. (A yeast infection typically comes on quickly and intensely, characterized by a bright red rash around the diaper area with small red pimples here and there in the surrounding areas.)

You can let him go au naturel in the house, but be prepared for him peeing on the floor. If that sounds too messy for you and it's warm outside, let him roll around on a towel on the grass. You can also put a cloth diaper down in your stroller, sit your baby on top of it, and go for a long walk.

FACT

The AAP recommends that you don't use any baby powders. The concern is that, if inhaled, powder can cause breathing problems and lung damage. If you do use a powder, use the cornstarch-based product sparingly, shake it into your hand (away from the baby), and don't allow it to build up in the neck or groin folds.

Rash Remedies

Ointments come into play when your baby has diaper rash and can't be naked. These are typically oil-based (Vaseline, A&D ointment, or plain olive oil) or zinc-oxide-based (Desitin, Balmex, or Johnson & Johnson). Ointments create a barrier, protecting your baby's skin, and have to be spread on thickly to work. If standard ointments are ineffective, you might ask your drugstore to order a thick cream called Triple Paste or Aquafor. Both are hard to find and expensive, but some moms swear by them. Others reach for Bag Balm, an ointment intended for use on cows with chapped udders. Bag Balm, used to treat a variety of skin problems, soothes soreness and inhibits bacteria growth, but it is only FDA-approved for use on animals. Check with your health care provider before using.

Don't apply over-the-counter hydrocortisone cream unless you've discussed it with your doctor. Extended use of hydrocortisone cream can thin a baby's skin.

If you suspect a yeast infection, ask your pediatrician to prescribe an antifungal ointment or use an over-the-counter antifungal cream like Lotrimin. However, if your doctor prescribes a combination steroid-antifungal cream like Lotrisone, only use it as long as recommended. Do not use it as a regular diaper cream, because the steroid can lead to serious side effects in children, including thinning of the skin.

In Hawaii, where the humid climate makes diaper rash a real problem, moms use pure cocoa butter to prevent diaper rash. Cocoa butter is available at most drugstores and comes in solid bars or sticks that must be warmed. (Put it in a jar, then sit the jar on a sunny windowsill or in a bowl of warm water. Test it on your own skin to make sure it's not too hot before applying to your baby.) If you live near a grocer that caters to a Latino community, you have access to another remedy—plantain leaves. Crush fresh leaves, and use them to line your baby's diaper.

If you're battling diaper rash and using home-washed cloth diapers, add vinegar to the rinse water. Urine is irritating because it is alkaline, and the acid in vinegar can make it less so. (Diaper services often treat their diapers in this way as a standard practice, or will upon request.) You can also add vinegar to your baby's bath water. Use about one cup of white vinegar in about six inches of water in a normal tub, or less than one-third cup in a sink or baby tub.

If you're using disposable diapers, consider peeling off the outside plastic cover and fastening a cloth diaper around it. That combination will prevent leaks while allowing air to get through.

If your baby has graduated to wipes, you should go back to using plain water to clean your baby's bottom while she's rashy. Diaper wipes may make the rash worse.

Intimate Care

Keeping your baby's private parts clean will reduce the risk of infection. Don't panic if you see a spot of blood the first time you change your baby's diaper. In the early days red spots are not a concern. They can come from urates, which are normal crystals in a baby's urine that turn to a salmon color on the diaper. Talk to your health care provider if you see any blood after the first couple of days.

Just for Girls

In girls, spots within the first week home may also be a small amount of bloody vaginal discharge caused by the mother's hormones. Talk to your doctor if you see blood in your baby's diaper after the first couple of days.

Penis Care

You will be asked in the hospital if you want your son circumcised. If there are no religious or cultural reasons to circumcise your son, you need to decide if this is the right decision for your family. The benefits of circumcision include:

- Reduced risk of urinary tract infections during the first year.
- Possibly reduced risk of cancer of the penis.
- Possibly reduced risk of sexually transmitted diseases.
- Decreased association with AIDS.
- Easier genital hygiene.
- If father is circumcised, he may want his son to look the same.

Critics argue that circumcision:

- Can be painful.
- May reduce sexual pleasure and performance (proponents disagree).
- Is a violation of human rights when performed on an infant since he can't make an informed decision about this permanent medical procedure.

If your son is circumcised, don't clean his penis at all for the first four days. After that, wipe it gently with a wet cotton ball, then pat it dry with a clean cloth diaper. You'll probably be given a tube of sterile petroleum jelly from the hospital. For the first four days or so after the circumcision, squeeze some onto a gauze pad and cap the pad over the tip of the penis every time you change him. This keeps it from sticking to the diaper. After a few days, you may see a yellowish discharge that forms a crust. This is normal, as are a few spots of blood. If the penis oozes blood, call the doctor.

If your son is not circumcised, don't retract his foreskin for cleaning; if you force it, you could cause bleeding and scarring. Normal bathing will keep him clean.

Bellybutton Care

Your baby's bellybutton needs special attention until the cord dries up and falls off (usually two but perhaps as long as five weeks), because this area can get infected. To prevent infection, keep his bellybutton dry and clean, and expose it to air as much as possible.

That doesn't necessarily mean you shouldn't immerse your baby in water until the cord is gone, only that you shouldn't cover the cord area until it is completely dry. (Pediatricians have different opinions about this; check with yours.) If you see any signs of redness or pus, however, don't immerse him and call your pediatrician.

You'll probably be told to wipe around the base of the cord with a cotton swab dipped in rubbing alcohol several times a day. This has a dual purpose—alcohol both kills bacteria and dries out the cord. (Although recent studies have shown that water may work just as well, your doctor will probably recommend alcohol.) You may see a few drops of blood as the cord detaches. This is normal, as is a small amount of yellow discharge. Redness on the skin around the bellybutton or oozing pus is not normal. If you see either, call your doctor immediately.

CHAPTER 10

Baths and Beyond

There's no big rush to give your baby her first bath—the nurses bathed her at the hospital. Infants don't get all that dirty, so one bath a week is plenty until she's eating solid foods (and smearing them all over herself) and crawling in the dirt. Just be sure to wash her face, hands, neck, and diaper area daily. If your baby likes her bath, feel free to bathe her every day. It won't bother her skin as long as you limit her bath to no more than ten minutes, use water and a mild soap only, and, if she has unusually dry skin, use a lotion afterward.

Bath Time

The first bath is a major photo opportunity. There are a couple of approaches, and with practice you'll discover which method works best for you and your baby. But we'll say here, and several times throughout the chapter, that you never leave your baby alone in the tub, even for an instant.

ALERT

The U.S. Centers for Disease Control and Prevention warn that children under age one most often drown in bathtubs, buckets, or toilets; among children ages one to four years old most drownings occur in residential swimming pools.

Gearing Up

The first few baths are relatively simple—you're just concentrating on keeping your baby warm, making him feel secure, and getting him clean. As he grows, of course, toys and boats and ducks will take up more room in the tub than he does. In the meantime, stock up on some simple, yet highly recommended, bath aids:

- Cotton balls (for cleaning eyes and ears).
- Plastic cup or spray bottle.
- Soft brush.
- Baby washcloths (lots, for washing, warmth, and play).
- Several towels.
- Giant bath sponge (for baby to lie on, or use another towel).
- Baby soap or no-tears shampoo (the two are pretty much interchangeable), or mild glycerin bar soap.
- Baby bathtub, dishpan, or clean sink.
- Foam pad to kneel on when you're bathing your baby in an adult tub (special pads are available for this purpose, or you can use kneelers designed for gardening).
- Non-skid mat (for use in the adult tub).
- Foam faucet cover (for adult tub).

The Sponge Bath

If you decide that your baby's first bath should be a sponge bath, give yourself plenty of time to figure out exactly where you're going to conduct this operation. You don't want to be running around the house with a naked baby trying to decide where to bathe him. Your best choice is a counter next to the sink if your counter is big enough. This has several advantages. Cleanup will be easy since it's waterproof, it's high enough to keep you from wrecking your back, it provides a ready source of warm water, and it makes it easier to rinse your baby's hair.

You'll need something soft to lay your baby on. A thick, folded bath towel is fine. If you have a baby bathtub that came with a thick contoured sponge, save the tub for later but place the sponge on the counter.

Make sure you have everything that you need within reach. You'll need several towels. In addition to the one on which your baby's lying, you'll need one to keep parts of him warm while you're bathing other parts, and another one to dry him. You'll also need:

- At least two washcloths (you don't want to wipe a spot of milk from his face with the same washcloth you just used to wipe his backside).
- Cotton balls or another clean washcloth for his eyes.
- Baby soap or mild bar soap (like Dove).
- A clean diaper.
- Clean clothes.
- Diaper rash ointment, if you're using it.
- A plastic cup.

Strip the baby down to his diaper and lay him on the towel. Cover him with the other towel; you'll uncover only the piece of baby you're washing at the moment.

Wipe inside the corners of his eyes, from inside out, using a clean cotton ball or different corner of the washcloth for each eye. You can use cotton balls to wipe his ear folds as well, but don't try to wash inside the ear canal, even if you see wax. The wax protects the inner ear. Then move on to washing his limbs and the front of his torso.

To wash his hair, wet it with the washcloth, add a dab of soap, and gently massage the entire scalp, including the soft spots. (You don't really need a special baby shampoo; liquid baby soap is an all-purpose cleaner at this stage.) Hold your baby so his head is being supported by one hand, and tip it slightly back over the sink. Using the plastic cup, pour warm water back over his head, avoiding his eyes. If some soap does get into his eyes, wipe them with plain, warm water; he'll open his eyes once the soap is gone.

ESSENTIAL

When bathing your baby, pay special attention to all the creases around his neck, which may be filled with gunk. With a newborn, this gunk is likely to be skin cells sloughing off; with an older baby, the gunk is likely to be dried food.

Next, take off his diaper and wash his bottom and genitals. (If you're bathing a girl, remember to always wash from front to back.) Finish by sitting him up, leaning him forward on your hand as if you're going to burp him, and wash his back. Check to make sure all the soap is rinsed off, and dry him with a clean towel, again paying particular attention to the creases in his neck.

Into the Tiny Tub

When you're ready to get your baby off the counter and into the tub, you don't need an official baby bathtub. You can bathe your baby in a clean dishpan, the tiny plastic basin the hospital gives you to hold your supplies, or even the sink itself.

Whatever type of tub you choose, think of your back when you're positioning it. Having the tub in the sink or up on the counter will be easier to manage than crouching over it on the floor. When you are trying to bathe two kids at once, put the baby tub with its stopper unplugged right inside the big tub—there should be room left for your older child.

Gather up all your supplies while your baby is still dressed. Line the baby tub with something soft (a special-purpose bath sponge or a towel), fill it with only two or three inches of lukewarm water, and test the temperature on the inside of your wrist or elbow. The idea here is that most of your baby's body and all of her face should be well above the water line. You'll keep her warm by layering extra washcloths over her stomach and pouring warm water on them regularly. (This is a great job to give a sibling.)

ALERT

Babies lose heat especially quickly when they are naked, so get your bathroom nice and toasty, around 75°F, before bath time starts. You can either turn up your thermostat or let the shower run and steam up the bathroom before tub time begins.

Bath-Time Tips

Try these strategies for improving bath-time efficiency, safety, and fun:

- Turn your hot water heater to a low setting (about 120°F) to avoid dangerous burns.
- Don't answer the phone, even a cell phone, while bathing your baby. Let the calls go to voicemail. It's too distracting to be talking on the phone while bathing a slippery baby.
- Remove shaving razors from the sink and edge of the tub
- Put liquid baby soap into a clean pump dispenser for one-handed use.
- Save the spray bottle the hospital gave you for cleaning your perineum and use it to rinse your baby's hair.
- Bring on the washcloths—the more the merrier. Besides the one you're using for washing, spread a few others across your baby to keep him warm. If you have another child, give him a washcloth to soak with water and drip onto the baby's tummy. You may be rewarded with tandem giggles.
- Pat your baby dry. Don't rub, as this can irritate delicate baby skin.
- Heat the towels in the dryer, and let them cool slightly—your baby will love the snuggly warmth.
- The kitchen sink makes a great place for a baby bath if you have a spray hose and faucet that turns out of the way and all the dishes are done.
- Save your back. Put the baby bathtub on a counter.

- Make your baby comfortable in the baby bath or sink and reduce the chance he'll slide around. Put a folded towel or special-purpose bath sponge on the bottom before you put your baby in the water.
- When your baby is ready to graduate from the infant tub to the big tub, start out by placing the infant tub inside the big tub for a few baths to get him used to the transition.
- Bathe with your baby. It's a lot easier on your back than leaning over the tub, and you're bound to get wet anyway. (If you have a hard time finding enough time for your own bath in a normal day, this idea is for you.). Have another adult nearby to pass the baby to you when you get in the tub and so you can hand off the slippery baby when it's time to get out of the tub.
- Get a spray hose that attaches to the tub faucet; you can use it to rinse your baby with clean water, and it makes hair washing much easier.

Graduating to the Big Tub

Your baby is ready to graduate to a regular bathtub once he can sit steadily without support (usually some time after six months).

You'll find that baby stores sell bath seats or rings for this stage. These will give your baby extra support, but probably aren't worth a trip to buy them. Your baby won't use a bath ring for long; as soon as he starts crawling, he'll want to explore the tub. A bath ring or seat may give you a false sense of confidence. Even when your baby is in a bath ring or seat, you need to stay within grabbing distance—these devices don't keep a baby from tipping over and slipping under the water.

FACT

Your best bet may be to get in the tub with him and support him between your legs. This is a two-person job. One person gets in the tub first, then the other one hands off the baby. (Reverse the procedure on the way out.)

Since a towel or sponge on the bottom of a regular tub will slide all over, get a non-skid mat if your baby seems not to like sitting on the bathtub's hard surface. This will be softer to sit on, as well as safer.

Bath Toys

Your baby will be interested in bath toys at this point, but keep them simple—a few things that float and a cup that pours water are plenty.

- Nylon bath puff, washcloth (use the cloth to wrap up tub toys for baby to unwrap)
- Plastic cups
- Floating plastic book, dolls, boats
- Sponges, cut into cute shapes
- Spray bottle
- Rubber ducky, boats, bath puppet
- Siblings

Hair Today, Gone Tomorrow—and other Scalp Issues

Some babies are born as bald as a cue stick; while others sport a full head of hair at birth. Even those who appear to be bald at birth, upon close examination, you'll find fine, downy, very light-colored hair. Your baby may lose her hair in the first six months. It can also come in a different color than what you saw in the delivery room.

Hair Facts

Telogen effluvium is the technical term for your baby losing his first hairs. All hair has two stages: growth and resting. When it's in the resting stage, the hair remains in the follicle. When new hair comes in, the old hair falls out. Stress, fever, and hormonal change can make hair stop growing and go into the resting stage . . . and then fall out. Your baby's hormone levels plummet after birth, which is why his newborn hair falls out.

You may be surprised to find that the new hair is a different color and texture.

Cradle Cap

When you're washing your baby's head, you may see thick, yellow scales. This is cradle cap, and, although it looks pretty yucky, it's benign. You could let it go away on its own, or try this instead. Rub baby or olive oil onto the scalp, let it soak for a few hours, then scrub the cradle cap away with a baby hair brush, baby toothbrush, or nail brush, followed by a dandruff shampoo to get the oil out.

Bald Spots

Your baby may develop a bald spot or two. Study how he sits and sleeps. If he sleeps with his head on the same side or rubs the same spot of his head against his mattress, he may develop a bald spot in that place.

To remedy the problem, alternate where you put him down for his nap and at night. For his nap, put him down with his head going toward one end of the crib; at night, put him down with his head at the opposite end of the crib. He will turn his head to look out the crib which will relieve the pressure on the bald side.

Trimming Nails

Of all the baby-care tasks, nothing seems to panic parents more than the idea of cutting their baby's nails.

Clippers or Scissors?

Parents are evenly divided between clippers and scissors. Clippers seem safer than scissors, but can actually cause more damage. The best guide is probably what you're more comfortable using on your own nails—experience counts. And you may discover, that your own manicure scissors are actually less likely to draw blood than blunt-tipped infant nail scissors. The blunt tip does keep you from stabbing your baby, but that isn't so much of a risk. The bigger problem is that the blades of baby scissors tend to be a little thicker and difficult to slip easily under your baby's nails, making it more likely that you'll pinch skin.

Trim Time

Wait until your baby is in a deep sleep when you're learning to trim nails. This means her arms and legs flop when lifted, and her hand is resting open, not in a fist. Hold the scissors or clippers in one hand; with the other, pull the tip of her finger down away from the nail. You should now have better access to the nail, so go ahead and cut. Cut straight across. If you're worried about sharp corners, you can gently file them later. If you do cut your baby, press on the cut and the bleeding will quickly stop. You can also dab on antibiotic first-aid cream.

You will get better with practice—and you will get plenty of practice. Your infant's fingernails may need to be trimmed several times a week. (The good news is you don't need to worry about cutting your baby's toenails. Don't worry if they look weird; they'll grow out slowly.)

Beginning Tooth Care

Do you really need to start thinking about tooth brushing when your baby won't have any teeth for ages? Well, yes, actually, you should start thinking about tooth brushing now. You need to get your baby used to having her gums cleaned before her teeth come in. The first few times you try it, she's likely to bite you, and you're much better off getting those bites over with before they can draw blood. Still, it's not likely to be fun.

The best toothbrush for an infant is a gauze square (sold in the first-aid section of a drugstore) wetted with plain water. It's amazing how much gunk this can remove.

An alternative is a fingertip brush—a brush with rubber bristles that sits like a cap over your finger. You can also go straight to a toothbrush; infant toothbrushes are very soft. (The downside is that they are quickly chewed into oblivion.) Hold your baby against you when you brush, facing into a mirror so you can see what you're doing—and your baby always enjoys mirror time. Your baby is less likely to clench his mouth shut or wriggle away than when you come at him from the front.

What you don't want to introduce at this point is toothpaste. Babies will swallow it, and swallowing excess fluoride can damage the enamel of the teeth yet to come in. That said, babies over six months of age do need a certain amount of fluoride in their diet to prevent future cavities. If the water in your community is not fluoridated, you can purchase bottled water that is or ask your pediatrician to prescribe fluoride drops for your baby.

QUESTION

What can I do now to make tooth brushing fun for my baby?
The following tips will make tooth brushing fun for both of you: babies love to imitate, so brush your teeth in front of your baby before you try to brush his teeth, name your baby's teeth and sing to them while you brush, look for something silly hiding behind your baby's teeth.

Sunshine and Naked Time

A number of infant care problems can be avoided by letting your baby lie around naked. If he can spend some of his "naked time" in the sun—outside, or in a patch of sun from a window—so much the better. Sunbaths help prevent diaper rash, heal the umbilical cord, and head off newborn jaundice by breaking down the bilirubin in the blood. We're not talking about going for the George Hamilton look, of course. Just five minutes of sun a day, in the early morning or late afternoon, are plenty. And make sure your baby is facing away from the sun or that his eyes are covered.

CHAPTER 11

Well-Baby Care

Hopefully your baby's first year will be smooth sailing, with nary a cold or ear infection in sight. But the truth is, this scenario is unlikely. While you can't protect your baby from all bacteria and viruses, you can take steps to keep her as healthy as possible. Make sure that you take your child to the doctor on a regular basis for well-baby visits; follow the recommended immunization schedule; develop a strong, comfortable relationship with your baby's health care professional so that you never hesitate to ask questions or voice concerns; and stock your medicine cabinet with the over-the-counter drugs and supplies you'll need when your baby does get sick. Here are some tips to help keep your baby healthy and happy.

Parent-Doctor Partnership

One of the most important steps to keeping your baby healthy is to find a good health practitioner whom you trust. Preferably, you interviewed several doctors while you were pregnant and settled on one before you delivered. You want someone who is well-qualified, listens to you and your child, and is covered by your health insurance. Make sure to check that the hospital where your doctor has privileges is also covered by your insurance. Using an out-of-network hospital can saddle you with thousands of dollars in out-of-pocket expenses.

Infant Alert: The First Month

You're more likely to need to call the doctor while your baby is a newborn. Symptoms that are not worrisome in an older baby can indicate real trouble during a baby's first month.

Jaundice

Many babies develop a yellow tinge to their skin color after birth. This is caused by increased amounts of a pigment called bilirubin, which is produced by the normal breakdown of red blood cells. Normal jaundice occurs in more than 50 percent of babies, appearing on day two or three and disappearing in a week or two. It's usually harmless, but talk to your doctor as she may want to evaluate your baby's jaundice. Usually it goes away on its own as the baby excretes the extra bilirubin in her feces.

So-called breastmilk jaundice occurs less frequently. It looks the same, but usually appears between days four and seven and can last three to ten weeks. You may find it helpful to nurse more frequently, every one and a half to two and a half hours during the day and at least every four hours at night. Frequent feeding may seem counterintuitive, but it will result in frequent pooping that helps cleanse bilirubin from the body. Your doctor will want to monitor your baby's condition, but usually it resolves itself.

- Call your doctor immediately if your jaundiced baby becomes dehydrated or feverish.

- Call your doctor during her regular office hours if your baby looks deep yellow or orange, has fewer than three movements a day, or still looks yellow after she is fourteen days old.
- Call your doctor if you have any concerns whether or not your baby's symptoms meet any of the above criteria.

If the bilirubin levels rise too high, your doctor may want to have your baby "go under the lights." Your baby may be readmitted to the hospital, although phototherapy can sometimes be done at home. Your baby's eyes are covered and she rests under the bili lights (either nude or with a small diaper). The lights break down the bilirubin, and it is then excreted in your baby's bowel movements. Once the bilirubin levels start to go down, they rarely rise again.

Fever

Call the doctor if your zero to three-month-old baby's temperature is above 100.4°F rectally. A fever in the first two months may be a sign of a serious infection, and an infection at this age can quickly overwhelm the developing immune system. Your baby may be hospitalized and treated with antibiotics.

Before you call the doctor, make sure you have the following information on hand:

- Your doctor's name.
- Your baby's temperature (even if it's normal).
- A list of his symptoms, starting with the ones that concern you most, and an estimate of their duration.
- Information about what you've done to address her symptoms.
- The phone number of a pharmacy that is open, convenient, and accepts your insurance.
- Your child's weight at her last checkup (in case your doctor wants to check on the dosage of a medication).

Diarrhea

Diarrhea in newborns can quickly lead to dehydration. Babies normally have several bowel movements a day, and these are typically runny. If the stool looks more like water than like mustard, however, it could be diarrhea. If you suspect diarrhea, and your baby is pooping more often than she is eating, call the doctor.

Vomiting

Projectile vomiting (vomit that shoots out of the mouth instead of dribbling down the chin) may mean your baby has an obstruction in the valve between the stomach and small intestine. Call your doctor immediately.

Vomiting after more than three feedings in a row may cause dehydration. Call your doctor if your baby doesn't pee in eight hours. You should also call if any blood appears in the vomit; if vomiting continues for more than twenty-four hours; or if your baby appears listless or just not right.

FACT

If your solids-eating baby gets diarrhea, avoid apple and grape juice, as they'll make the diarrhea worse.

Floppiness

While a newborn doesn't have a lot of muscle control, she typically kicks and squirms and waves her arms around. If she feels floppy all over or seems to lose muscle tone, she may have an infection, and you'll need to call the doctor.

Shakes

A quivery chin is cute, but if your baby seems to quiver all over, your doctor needs to find out why.

Older Baby Symptoms

If your baby is more than a month old, you don't need to be quite so quick to dial the doctor. But you should call if your baby:

- Is three to six months old and has an axillary (under the arm) fever higher than 101°F.
- Is over six months old has an axillary fever higher than 103°F.
- Has a fever for more than two days.
- Has a fever and a stiff neck, symptoms of meningitis (Check for this by holding a toy level with her face and then moving it toward the ground. If she can't follow its path by bringing her chin down to her chest, she may have a stiff neck).
- Is too sleepy (You may be relieved if your baby suddenly starts to sleep all day and night, but a big jump in sleepiness is not normal and may indicate an infection).
- Cries excessively.
- Vomits persistently (after every feeding within twelve hours), or if the vomit contains blood.
- Seems dehydrated (If your baby seems to be peeing a lot less than usual—i.e., you're changing fewer diapers—there is a problem.)
- Has trouble breathing (the skin between her ribs may suck in with each breath), or breathes extremely rapidly (more than forty breaths a minute).
- Has persistent bluish lips or fingernails (babies can briefly turn blue from the cold, or from crying).
- Has a cough that lasts longer than two weeks (although check with your doctor when your baby first develops a cough), or has a whooping or barking cough.
- Has eye inflammation or discharge.
- Has a rash that covers much of her body.

In the Medicine Cabinet

You'll be treating a lot of minor illnesses, so have the following on hand. For nonprescription medicines, check the label for the correct dosage. If no information is given for your baby's age or weight, call your pediatrician's office for the correct dosage.

- Thermometers—at least one oral and one rectal
- Infant acetaminophen drops or suspension
- Infant ibuprofen drops
- Topical anesthetic (useless for teething, but may help with splinter removal)
- Vaseline
- Pedialyte (oral electrolyte solution designed to replace fluids and minerals lost when child has diarrhea or vomiting)
- Benadryl (an antihistamine for allergic reactions)
- Calibrated syringes or droppers for giving medicine
- Nasal aspirator
- Saline nose drops
- Diaper rash cream
- Hydrocortisone cream
- Aveeno (an oatmeal bath, soothing for many skin problems)

ALERT

The America Academy of Pediatrics recommends that children do not take aspirin—even children's aspirin. There is a linkage between aspirin and Reye's syndrome, a serious neurological disease. As a result, most pediatricians do not recommend the use of aspirin for fevers from any illness. (Note: Pepto-Bismol contains aspirin, and its use should be restricted as well.)

Well-Baby Checkups

You'll see your baby's doctor a few days after you come home from the hospital (where she will check for jaundice, and any feeding problems). After that, the AAP recommends a checkup at two weeks and then at two, four, six, nine, and twelve months. Your baby is growing and developing at an exponential rate in that first year. Your doctor will be able to check for any deviations from the norm, advise and guide you through this tumultuous year, and give your baby the recommended vaccinations.

Most well-baby visits start with measurements—how much has your baby grown. It may not matter whether your baby is in the ninety-ninth percentile or the fifth—what matters is that there is steady growth from visit to visit. Any significant change from what your baby has previously shown would be something to discuss. Here's what your doctor will be checking at a well-baby visit.

- **Head:** Your doctor will measure your baby's head circumference. She will check the fontanels (soft spots) on your baby's head. These gaps between the skull bones give your baby's brain room to grow. The skull bones will fuse naturally between nine to eighteen months.
- **Ears:** Your doctor will check for any fluid or infection in the ears.
- **Eyes:** Your doctor will check for any eye discharge and blocked tear ducts. Later, she may use a bright light to track your baby's eye movements.
- **Mouth:** Your doctor will check inside your baby's mouth for thrush, and later for teeth.
- **Heart and Lungs:** Your doctor will check for normal heart sounds and rhythms and any abnormal breathing.
- **Skin:** Your doctor will check for various skin conditions—diaper rash, baby acne, birthmarks, jaundice, and others.
- **Abdomen:** Your doctor will palpate your baby's stomach, checking for any tenderness and enlarged organs. She'll also check for an umbilical hernia, which is a bit of intestine or fatty tissue that has broken through the muscular wall of the abdomen. Most umbilical hernias resolve themselves.
- **Hips and Legs:** Your doctor will check that the hips are not dislocated.
- **Genitalia:** For a boy, your doctor will check that both testes have descended into the scrotum. For a girl, your doctor will ask about any vaginal discharge. Your doctor will also check for any tenderness in the area, lumps, or signs of infection.
- Your baby may receive one of his immunizations.

After the physical exam, your doctor will ask you to talk about your baby: his activities, his diet, his sleep, and so on. Before you go to the doctor, make a list of any questions you may have. If you feel you need more time to talk and your baby is crying or needs your attention, ask the doctor for a phone appointment to review your concerns.

Fever Basics

"Does she have a fever?" That is one of the first questions you'll be asked whenever you call your doctor with a question about a sick baby—and it will soon be one of the first questions you'll ask yourself.

FACT

> *Do not* try to lower a fever by rubbing your baby with rubbing alcohol. Isopropyl alcohol is quickly absorbed through the skin, and large amounts applied topically can be inhaled, which can lead to alcohol poisoning and other problems.

Fevers do have a purpose, although their exact role is unclear. They may increase the number of white blood cells (which kill viruses and destroy bacteria) or raise the amount of interferon, an antiviral substance, in the blood and thus hinder bacteria and viruses from multiplying. Fevers aren't dangerous in themselves (although they serve as a warning of other problems), except when they rise very quickly or reach extremely high levels— above 106°F.

You will notice that your baby's fever will climb in the afternoon from a morning low. This is normal, and doesn't mean your baby is getting sicker.

Thermometers

Thermometers come in different styles: glass; digital; and tympanic. Avoid using a mercury-filled glass thermometer because of concerns about mercury. The American Medical Association issued a statement that non-mercury fever thermometers are just as effective, as well as safer than mercury-filled ones. Disposable strips aren't accurate enough for a baby under a year, and definitely not for newborns. You can take a baby's temperature rectally, under her arm (axillary), or by reading the heat off of her eardrum (tympanic). You can't, however, take his temperature orally; holding the thermometer under his tongue would be uncomfortable and he might gag or choke. Also, your baby might bite off the end.

Taking Your Baby's Temperature

For babies under three months, most doctors want you take a rectal temperature. It's the most accurate and, at this age, every degree is significant because treatment of a fever will be based on temperature.

If you are using a non-mercury glass thermometer to take your baby's temperature rectally, make sure you have one intended for rectal use. If you are using a digital thermometer, designate one for that purpose by marking it with an indelible "R." First clean the thermometer by wiping it with rubbing alcohol or washing it with soapy water. Then make sure it is reset by shaking the thermometer until the temperature gauge reads below 98.6°F. To reset a digital thermometer, turn it off and then on again.

Put a dab of petroleum jelly on the tip of the thermometer. Lay your baby stomach down on the changing table and hold her with one hand placed firmly on her back; add another dab of petroleum jelly at the opening of her anus. Insert the thermometer tip a half inch into her rectum (never forcing it), and hold it there between your second and third fingers, with your hand cupped over her buttocks. Wait two minutes for a glass thermometer, or until a digital thermometer beeps. A rectal temperature of 100.4°F and up in a baby under three months is considered a fever.

For older babies, open up or remove her clothing to take a temperature under her arm. Put her in a comfortable position, lying in your arm or against your chest. Put the glass or digital thermometer in her dry armpit and tuck her elbow against her body. Cuddle her, making sure she doesn't move her arm. (You can pace the floor with her, just keep her arm firmly over the thermometer.) Wait four minutes, or until the digital thermometer beeps its all-done signal. An axillary temperature of over 102.2°F is considered a fever.

How to Treat a Fever

If your baby has a fever, make sure she isn't dressed too warmly and that her room isn't hot. You can strip her down to her T-shirt, but keep a light blanket handy for when her temperature begins to drop.

With your doctor's permission and confirmation of the dosage, give her a fever-reducing medicine, like acetaminophen (Tylenol) or ibuprofen (Motrin). You should see the fever start to come down thirty minutes later, sometimes sooner. If it doesn't, or spikes back up again quickly, these medicines can be alternated. While doses of Tylenol are meant to be given four hours apart and Motrin six hours apart, pediatricians sometimes recommend giving a dose of Motrin only two hours after giving Tylenol. Just don't give a second dose of the same medicine any sooner than prescribed. Talk to your doctor about what she thinks is most effective in treating fevers.

You can also try to bring your baby's fever down by giving her a bath in a few inches of lukewarm water, using a washcloth to spread water over her, and letting her air-dry. Give your feverish baby lots to drink—she's sweating out fluids, and dehydration can make her feel worse.

Febrile Convulsions

You should, however, be aggressive in fighting fevers in children who are susceptible to febrile convulsions. Two to four percent of children, most between six months and six years old, are susceptible to these kinds of seizures, characterized by symmetrical rhythmic convulsions, eyes rolling back in the head, and a loss of consciousness. Convulsions can last as long as ten minutes, but usually disappear in less than two minutes. Although it's less common, some susceptible children experience them every time they get a fever. The seizures usually have no permanent effects and are not a form of epilepsy. A seizure is likely related to fever if:

- The seizure occurs within twenty-four hours of starting a fever
- The seizure lasts less than five minutes
- The seizure affects the whole body and is not confined to one side

While your child is having a seizure, you want to focus on her care—you can call the doctor once the seizure is over. If your child has a seizure:

- Turn her on her side
- Remove any hard objects she might slam into
- Look at your watch

You need to time the seizure—your doctor will want to know its duration. If the seizure lasts longer than five minutes, call your physician or local paramedics. After five minutes the child should get emergency care and be evaluated; but seizures of that duration are rare. If your child is prone to these seizures, you will probably want to administer fever-reducing medicine sooner, rather than later. Call your doctor after the seizure is over and review the incident.

Giving Medicines

"Give him one dropperful of Tylenol," or, "Give him one teaspoon of antibiotic," your doctor says. You dutifully fill the dropper or syringe up to the correct line, put it in your baby's mouth, and squirt it in. It immediately comes dribbling back out, at which point you madly try to shovel it back in with your finger. Giving a baby medicine is not intuitive. If you're lucky, your baby will like the taste and lap it up—but don't count on it.

Here are some strategies that may work:

- This method requires two adults. One adult sits on the floor, leaning against a wall, with her legs straight out in front of her. Another adult lays the baby on the first adult's legs, so his head is slightly higher than his body (which happens naturally since your thighs are fatter than your ankles), and the baby's feet point toward the adult's feet. The first adult then lifts the baby's arms above the baby's head; this keeps his hands from knocking the medicine away and opens up his throat. The second adult slips the dropper or syringe into the side of the baby's mouth, between his cheek and where his molars will eventually appear, squirts in just a few drops of medicine, then a few more, and then a few more until the dropper is empty. It doesn't matter if the baby's mouth is shut or if he's crying; the medicine will dribble down his throat.
- Another method is the cheek pocket. Use a finger to pull out a corner of your baby's mouth to make a pocket in his cheek, and drop the medicine into the pocket a little at a time. Keep the pocket open until all the medicine has been swallowed.

Distractions can help make the medicine go down. If you can call on another adult or sibling to wave a toy or make faces at your baby, do so. Otherwise, dangle a toy from your mouth as you use both of your hands to give the medicine.

ALERT

What you don't want to do is try to hide your baby's medicine in a bottle or in food. It still won't taste great, and if your baby doesn't finish the juice or food you'll have no idea how much medicine he consumed.

If giving your baby medicine orally is always a struggle, ask your drugstore for acetaminophen suppositories. The dosage, in milligrams, is the same as that for oral medication, but is less preferable than the oral form because the amount that is absorbed can vary.

Eye Treatments

You may also someday find yourself having to give your baby eye medication, in the form of drops or ointment. You'll need to have someone hold your baby's hands so she doesn't rub away the drops immediately, or you can wrap her in a blanket. Balancing your hand on her cheek, but being careful not to touch the dropper to the eye, aim the drops for the inside corner of her eye. (Her eye does not need to be open; when she blinks, the drops will get in.)

If you're administering ointment, you do not need to force her eye open. Instead, squeeze out a line of ointment along the roots of her upper eyelashes (kind of like eyeliner). Keep her hands away from her eyes until the ointment melts into them. You can also pull down her lower eyelid to make a pouch and put the drops or ointment inside that. If your baby really fights the eye medication, try applying it when she is asleep.

Healthy Baby Care Tips

The most important thing to remember about your baby's health is to trust your instincts. Don't back down if your baby's doctor dismisses your concerns but you feel something is wrong. Insist that your baby be examined until your baby is better or the cause of her symptoms is found.

Here are some other strategies for keeping your baby healthy:

- When taking your baby's temperature rectally, keep a cloth diaper or a diaper wipe nearby while you're waiting for the reading, just in case he poops.
- Bubble baths can be fun for older babies, but if your baby is a girl you might want to make them a rare treat. Bubble baths can irritate the sensitive labial and vaginal tissues, causing itchy or painful rashes.
- If giving medicine is a major struggle, ask your pharmacist if the drug comes in any other flavors. Parents report that some of the cherry-flavored medicines taste disgusting and the same medicine in an orange or another flavor is sometimes accepted more willingly.
- Try refrigerating your baby's liquid medicines—they may taste better cold. But check with the pharmacist to make sure refrigeration won't alter the medicine's effectiveness.
- If he really hates the taste of a medicine, have your baby suck on a popsicle first to partially numb his mouth.
- If your feverish baby is too fussy to nurse or drink from a bottle, wet a clean washcloth, freeze it, and then give it to him to gnaw on.
- Go for a drive. A sick baby may sleep better in the car than the crib.

Your baby will get sick and you will get through it. Rely on your good sense, and know that your baby will probably be better in the morning.

CHAPTER 12

When Baby Is Sick

The cry wakes you in the middle of the night. It's not the normal middle of the night cry, the "eh-eh-eh-eh" that let's you know that she's hungry—again. It's a cry that you've never heard before. You rush into her room, scoop her up from the crib, and cuddle her, your cheek against her head. And then you pull back, startled. She's hot. She's really hot. She's sick! Do you call the doctor? Run to the emergency room? Give her medicine? Just put her back to sleep? You're the triage nurse and you have to figure it out—which isn't easy, particularly because she's still screaming. The most important thing is don't panic.

Cold Strategies

Keep in mind that there are over 200 rhinoviruses that cause respiratory disorders like the common cold. Sometimes it seems like your baby is intent upon catching every single one of those viruses in the first year. Remember, your baby's immune system is still developing. While you will pass on some antibodies to protect him, especially if you breastfeed, your baby will still catch his share of colds and other common childhood diseases, although thankfully, probably not all in the first year! Here are practical suggestions to help you both survive those sick days.

Babies catch colds—a lot of colds—particularly if they have older siblings bringing cold viruses home from school. Until your infant is about two months old, you should try to protect him from exposure to non-family members who have colds. Babies this young really need their noses to breathe because they don't easily switch to mouth breathing when their noses are stuffy.

ESSENTIAL

While a cold itself will clear up on its own, colds can lead to secondary conditions such as ear infections, pneumonia, or bronchitis. If your baby doesn't seem to be getting better, or spikes a fever after recovering from his initial bout with fever, suspect a secondary infection and call your doctor.

Most colds are mild. A cold typically lasts a week to ten days. It may start out with a fever, followed by stuffiness, sneezing, and sometimes a cough. Don't try to guard your baby against catching colds forever or try to protect him from his siblings' colds. The former will make you crazy and the latter is impossible. Unpleasant as they can be, your baby needs to have a few colds in his first year. Exposure means that he will be less susceptible to cold viruses later on when missing a few weeks of school may set him back. It turns out that exposure to germs during the first year of life helps make a child's immune system function correctly. A recent study funded by the National Heart, Lung, and Blood Institute concluded that frequent exposure to other children (and their germs), particularly in the first six months of life, reduces the chance of a child developing asthma later on.

Medication Advice

You shouldn't give a baby (or any child under two years) any cold medications. These medicines really don't work, and may make him hyperactive or cause other side effects rather than help your baby sleep better. Use a nasal aspirator to clear out his nose before feeding him, or whenever he seems particularly uncomfortable.

FIGURE 12-1: Using a nasal aspirator

Using a Nasal Aspirator

Hold your baby in a sitting position. Tilt his head back, put in a few drops of saline solution in each nostril, and wait a minute. First, squeeze the bulb of the aspirator, and then, with his head upright, place just the tip into one nostril, and hold his other nostril closed with your finger. Slowly let go of the bulb. Remove it from your baby's nose and squirt any mucus out onto a tissue. Repeat for the other nostril.

Saline Solution

You can also temporarily clear your baby's congestion with a few drops of saline solution placed in each nostril (wait a minute or two, and then use the aspirator). Saline solution is sold in special applicators for this purpose, or you can use any commercial saline solution and a standard eyedropper. You can also make your own saline with one-quarter teaspoon of table salt in eight ounces of warm tap water, just remember to make up a fresh batch every day or two and store it in a clean bottle. If his nose and lips are getting irritated, dab them with petroleum jelly.

Other Cold Strategies

At night, use a cool air vaporizer or humidifier in your baby's room to keep the nasal secretions from drying out. Elevate the head of your baby's crib by putting a pillow UNDER the mattress or blocks under the legs of the crib. (Don't put a pillow in the crib.)

Make sure your baby drinks plenty of liquids. Nurse frequently if you are breastfeeding, or offer a variety of liquids if your baby is on solid foods. A baby with a stuffy nose may prefer to drink from a cup since it's easier than from a bottle. Don't cut back on milk since it rarely increases the production of mucus and any liquids your baby will drink are beneficial.

Other Common Illnesses

Your baby's immune system is still developing and she is susceptible to a host of viruses. Here are some of the more common ones and their treatments.

Diarrhea

In babies, vomiting and diarrhea are usually caused by viruses. Wash your hands often as viral diarrhea is very contagious. If vomiting and diarrhea continue after several feedings, your baby risks dehydration.

If you are breastfeeding and your baby has diarrhea, nurse more frequently. If you are formula-feeding, switch to Pedialyte or a comparable non-prescription oral rehydration fluid that will replenish electrolytes in addition to lost fluids. (Don't use sports drinks; they contain too little sodium and oftentimes large amounts of sugar.) These rehydration fluids come plain or flavored and are available without a prescription. Stick to the plain; most babies find the flavored versions unpalatable. (You can also try freezing it in popsicle form.)

Try to get your baby to drink four ounces of the solution every time she has a watery movement. Switch back to formula if the diarrhea becomes less watery and your baby is peeing regularly. Some moms have had success treating diarrhea with barley or rice water (cook rice or barley until very soft, then strain out the grain and put the remaining liquid in a bottle, adding one-quarter teaspoon of salt to every two cups of water).

If your baby seems listless, is urinating a lot less than usual, cries with few tears, has a sunken fontanel (soft spot), or the diarrhea lasts longer than a few days, call your doctor.

Vomiting

Sometimes it's hard to tell the difference between normal spit-up and vomiting. It can seem like a lot of what you've just put into your baby has come back out and is all over you. Some babies spit up a lot because they gobble their food and inhale a lot of air that produces bubbles and gas.

Here's a basic rule of thumb: spit happens. It's a result of a weak and immature valve between the stomach and esophagus that usually resolves itself by the time your baby is a year old. The spit-up often comes with a burp.

Vomiting, on the other hand, is much more forceful, involves most, if not all, of the feeding, and can upset your baby. Your baby may run a fever.

FACT

On the far end of the spectrum is pyloric stenosis. In this rare condition (affecting up to 1 in 300 babies, primarily male and usually between three and five weeks old), there is a blockage of the stomach valve. This causes the baby to vomit the entire feeding within thirty minutes and often involves projectile vomiting. Talk to your doctor if you are concerned that your baby's spit-up is abnormal.

If your baby is vomiting, spread towels over vulnerable surfaces. Reduce nursing time, but not frequency, with your breastfed baby. If she vomits once or twice, nurse on only one side every hour or two; if she vomits more than twice, nurse for five minutes every thirty to sixty minutes. Return to your regular feeding pattern after eight hours without vomiting. For a formula-fed baby, switch to one of the rehydration fluids and give a teaspoonful of fluid every ten minutes, increasing the amount after four vomit-free hours. Resume normal feeding after eight hours (at which point you can start dealing with the piles of laundry).

Contact a physician if:

- There are signs of dehydration, such as no urine in over eight hours.
- Any blood appears in the vomit.
- There seems to be abdominal pain that lasts for more than four hours.
- The vomiting continues for more than twenty-four hours.
- Your baby just seems really, really sick.
- You are concerned and your instinct tells you something is wrong.

Ear Infections

Unlike stomach viruses that announce themselves clearly (and messily), ear infections are harder to identify, at least until your child is old enough to say "Hurts" as she points to her ear. She may pull on her ear or bat at it—but some babies do that anyway. She will probably be cranky, particularly when you try to lay her down, and may have trouble sleeping—but some babies are like that anyway. And she may eventually get a fever or have a runny nose for a few days.

Your doctor will look in your baby's ear and, if the ear is infected, will see a red ear drum that is bulging with the pressure of trapped fluid. If your doctor decides to prescribe antibiotics, the good news is that you'll often see a change in your baby's behavior within forty-eight hours. If the doctor wants to wait a day or two because signs of infection are minimal, don't push for unnecessary antibiotics.

To make your baby more comfortable in the meantime, give her acetaminophen or ibuprofen to dull the pain and soothe her ear with warm compresses. Wet a washcloth with warm tap water, wring it out, hold it over the ear, and keep her in a sitting position. Bring in her car seat and let her sleep in that or in the stroller. Pile pillows or books *under* the head end of the mattress if she's in her crib. (Lying horizontally increases the pressure on the ear.) Ask your doctor to prescribe anesthetic ear drops to numb the pain.

Some babies get ear infections constantly—whenever, it seems, they get a cold. This can be more than a nuisance since an ear infection may muffle your baby's hearing just when she is learning to speak. Children usually outgrow ear infections as their Eustachian tubes enlarge, become firmer, and have improved drainage.

FACT

If your baby gets ear infections constantly, you can ask your doctor to prescribe prophylactic antibiotics. These are low-dose antibiotics given every day during the worst of the cold season, or for seven days every time your baby gets a cold. In general, you should avoid giving your child unnecessary antibiotics, but this has been a proven deterrent if she is prone to infection.

Chronic ear infections can also be treated by a tympanostomy (insertion of drainage tubes in the eardrums) or the removal of tonsils or adenoids. Both procedures are performed under anesthesia, but at much lower levels than what's required for general surgery. A laser treatment that puts a hole in the eardrum for drainage and can be performed with just a topical anesthetic has been approved, but isn't in wide use.

A vaccine called Prevnar (or PCV, for pneumococcal conjugate vaccine), intended for prevention of bacterial meningitis, blood infections, and pneumonia, protects against some ear infections as well. This vaccine is universally recommended by the Centers for Disease Control and Prevention and the AAP for children at two, four, and six months, and again between twelve and fifteen months.

Croup

Croup is one of the scarier viruses, although it sounds much worse than it actually is. It seems to come on suddenly, usually in the middle of the night. You'll know croup when you hear it—your baby will sound like a seal barking. Croup usually lasts for five to six days, with the worst symptoms at night. Use a cool humidifier in the bedroom or hang up wet towels as dry air makes croup worse.

In severe cases you may hear a raspy, vibrating sound when your baby inhales between coughs, and breathing becomes difficult. If this happens, race her into the bathroom and stand *outside* the shower, turning it on full blast as hot as it can go. You want the steam that is generated, not the water. The steamy room should ease her breathing. Try to calm her down by singing or reading a story—whatever works best. The more upset she is, the worse her croup will be. If steam immersion works, put a humidifier in her room, crank it up, and put her back to bed You can also bring a quilt into the steamy bathroom and lie down with her on the floor. You can also take her outside—cool, damp air can help her breathing, and the change of scene may calm her down.

Call your doctor immediately if these efforts have no effect after twenty minutes, if she struggles to breathe even when she isn't coughing, or she can't cry because she can't get enough breath.

Asthma

Asthma is the leading cause of chronic illness in children. It can be triggered by allergies or by a virus that inflames the lining of the bronchioles, airway branches of the bronchi that are smaller than one millimeter in diameter. Often the attacks come on at night. The child wakes up, has trouble exhaling, and panics. You may hear wheezing as your baby exhales, or notice the center of her chest, between her breastbones, pull inward when she takes a breath. Call your doctor if the breathing problems seem severe, if she's breathing rapidly (more than forty breaths a minute), or if her lips or fingertips turn blue. Sit your baby up and try to calm her down while talking to the doctor, as crying only makes her struggles to breathe worse.

If allergies and asthma run in your family, talk to your doctor about medication like albuterol (to open airways) and prednisone (a steroid that reduces inflammation of the bronchial tubes). Never administer another family member's medication.

Infectious Rashes

A number of infectious diseases are accompanied by a characteristic, and often uncomfortable, rash. The good news is you probably won't have to take care of a child in itchy distress from measles, rubella, or chickenpox since your child will be vaccinated against those diseases when she turns one. Your antibodies will provide some protection as long as you breast-feed, and until about four months of age if you're bottle-feeding. Nevertheless, your child may still contract coxsackie, roseola, and fifth disease.

Coxsackie

In coxsackie, also called hand, foot, and mouth disease, spots appear inside the mouth and on the hands, feet, and butt. It usually comes with a fever, but the condition rarely causes long-term complications. Your baby will probably be miserable, as the mouth spots often blister making swallowing uncomfortable. Keep nursing your younger baby; you can give an older baby juice popsicles to help soothe her throat. She might be happier drinking from a cup than a bottle and for older babies you can try giving half a teaspoonful of a liquid antacid (like Maalox) before meals to coat the ulcers. A coxsackie bout can last as long as a week—and it makes for a very long week.

Coxsackie is very contagious from about two days before the rash appears until about seven days after, with a three- to six-day incubation period. Because it's hard to prevent spreading this one and it is generally harmless, pediatricians don't advise making yourself crazy quarantining your child.

Roseola

The first symptom of roseola that you'll notice will be a fever as high as 105°F. The fever lasts for three to four days, and there are rarely any other symptoms, so you may have no idea what is wrong. Then the fever will go away and faint pink-red spots appear on your baby's trunk, neck, and arms. This is good news—unlike the other rash diseases, the spots signify the end, not the beginning, of the virus. It is contagious until the rash is gone; the incubation period is about twelve days. Complications from roseola are rare, with the small possibility of a febrile seizure because the baby's temperature spikes fast and high.

Fifth Disease

In fifth disease, also called slapped-cheek disease, your baby's face will be bright red, as if her cheeks were sunburned. The rash travels to the arms and legs, then on to other parts of the body. It usually lasts for a few days but may go on for weeks, reappearing whenever she gets warmer than usual, like when taking a bath. Again, this is a fairly benign virus and causes complications only in pregnant women.

Fifth disease is mainly contagious for a week before the rash appears. Once the rash appears, she is no longer considered contagious. If you believe a pregnant woman has been exposed to your baby, tell her to see her obstetrician. The OB will order an antibody test to determine if the mother was previously protected from the disease or not. If she wasn't, the pregnancy will be monitored closely. Fifth disease doesn't cause birth defects, but some infected fetuses develop severe anemia, and a small percentage die.

Other Rashes

Babies also typically get blotchy, red pimples in their second or third week. This baby acne is normal and goes away on its own. Heat can also cause a rash, particularly around your baby's neck, armpits, or diaper area.

Be sure not to overdress her when the weather is hot and humid. To soothe heat-induced rashes, give your baby a cool bath every few hours, letting her skin air-dry. For small areas, lay a cool, damp washcloth over the region for ten minutes or so at a time.

Minor Ailments

The following are more of a nuisance than a crisis, but can cause problems if not treated:

- **Blocked tear duct.** A baby with a blocked tear duct (the little opening at the inside corner of the eye) looks like he is continually crying. Your baby's doctor will show you how to massage the area to open the duct. If this doesn't work after many weeks, the doctor may suggest having an ophthalmologist open the tear duct.
- **Eye infection.** If not kept open, blocked tear ducts can turn into eye infections. Sometimes, of course, eye infections can appear out of nowhere. You'll see a watery discharge that clumps in your baby's eyelashes and sometimes seems to glue his eye shut. First clean the eye by dipping a cotton ball in clean water and wiping from the inside corner to the outside. Repeat until the eye is clean, using a fresh cotton ball for each swipe. If the redness lasts more than seven days, or if the outer eyelids are swollen, call your doctor.
- **Pinkeye.** Babies with conjunctivitis, or pinkeye, have yellow discharge along with red, irritated-looking eyes. Call your doctor for antibiotic drops or ointment. You can apply cold compresses to soothe the eyes and reduce swelling. Pinkeye is highly contagious, so wash your hands frequently and thoroughly to avoid giving it to others.
- **Eczema.** These dry, red, and extremely itchy patches most commonly appear in the creases of the elbows, wrists, and knees, but can appear anywhere on the body. Eczema is often inherited, and flares up when the skin is irritated or as a result of food allergies. If your baby gets eczema, use soap infrequently and detergent sparingly. Avoid wool clothing, moisturize him frequently, and, when he's going through a severe bout, talk to your doctor about a prescription for steroid cream

to put on the scaly patches. Do not overuse over-the-counter steroid creams because they can thin your baby's skin.

Surviving Your Baby's Illnesses

Clear your calendar and put away the "to do" list. If you work, call in sick. Given the amount of sleep you're probably getting, this won't be a lie.

Your baby will want to be held most of the time. When she actually does fall asleep somewhere other than your arms, you'll need to lie down yourself and rest. You'll be getting a lot less sleep at night when your baby is sick, and will probably be fighting a bug yourself.

Use Your Energy Wisely

Don't clean, don't cook, and don't do laundry (except for anything that's been pooped or thrown up upon). Expect your baby to regress a stage. A baby who has been eating solids may only want to nurse; a baby who gave up her bottle for a cup a month ago may want her bottle again. Don't fight it—let her have what she wants now.

Your baby may wake several times a night, and will sometimes stay awake for hours. Don't pace the floor in the dark, bored and frustrated that you can't put her down and go back to sleep yourself. Discover late-night television. Find a trashy show that strikes your exhausted mind as funny (infomercials can be entertaining). Or make a nest of towels on the floor and lie down with your baby. This way, your bed won't get covered by snot or vomit, and maybe you'll both get some sleep.

ESSENTIAL

When your baby is sick and you feel sleep-deprived: use the telephone. Call your mother, and cry to her. Call a far-away friend and complain to her about how hard it all is. Call your nearby friends and tell them how miserable you are (maybe some of them will offer to drop off a meal).

Remember: even though your baby is up all night crying, every sheet and blanket in the house needs a good washing, and the only thing that calms her is you walking up and down the hall—this will pass and you will sleep again.

Vaccinations

In your child's first year of life, he will get a lot of shots, first at the hospital, and then at nearly every doctor's checkup. Please refer to the detailed list and chart in Appendix A to read up on standard vaccinations.

Your baby may also be vaccinated against diseases caused by Streptococcus pneumoniae, a bacterium that causes bloodstream infections and meningitis. Approved in early 2000, this pneumococcal conjugate vaccine (PCV), also known as Prevnar, can provide some protection against ear infections and pneumonia and is recommended for all children.

In 2006, a new vaccine for rotavirus, a disease characterized by severe diarrhea, was approved. Ask your doctor about vaccinating your child.

Side Effects

Some children will have a reaction to some of these vaccines. A low-grade fever, soreness at the injection site, and a mild rash with the rash-disease vaccines are typical. Serious reactions are few and are decreasing as vaccines are reformulated. The standard pertussis vaccine, given in combination with diphtheria and tetanus, was most likely to cause complications. Many doctors are now giving a reformulated vaccine, called "acellular," because it doesn't contain the complete pertussis bacteria. This version is much safer. The live-virus polio vaccine, administered orally, caused about ten cases of polio a year; the newer version, containing a killed virus and given by injection, removes the risk.

Getting the shot may actually be harder on you than your baby. He will probably let out a loud yell, but be soothed fairly easily. Try to stay calm yourself—he'll pick up on your reaction. Consider stripping your baby to his diaper and pulling your shirt up. A recent study has shown that babies who had whole-body, skin-to-skin contact when their heels were pricked for a blood test had lower heart rates and didn't cry as much as other babies.

If your baby seems uncomfortable, is particularly fussy, or runs a fever in the day or two following the vaccine, medicate with acetaminophen. (If your baby typically has a reaction to a certain shot, you may want to pre-medicate.) If he develops a high fever or high-pitched screaming, he may be having a serious reaction; call your doctor.

ALERT

WARNING: Get the dosage right. Double-check the dosage with your doctor, and make sure you are identifying the medicine correctly. Infant drops, for example, are much more potent than regular liquid medication. Acetaminophen, in particular, must be measured carefully, because an overdose (ten times the recommended dosage) can cause liver damage.

If you are concerned about the potential of vaccine-related complications, rare as they are, you should:

- Be sure that your doctor is using the acellular pertussis vaccine contained in DTaP rather than the whole-virus pertussis contained in DTP.
- Confirm that your doctor is administering the polio vaccine via injection instead of orally.
- Put off your moderately-to-seriously sick child's vaccinations until he is well. However, the AAP recommends that immunizations should not be delayed for children experiencing ordinary cold symptoms.

Autism-Vaccine Link?

Parents have raised concerns, based on anecdotal evidence, about a link between autism and the measles, mumps, and rubella (MMR) vaccine. To be clear, measles, mumps, and rubella are not mild childhood diseases. The potential complications from these diseases can be deadly, so protecting your child from contracting any of them is important.

Extensive studies have failed to prove a link between the MMR vaccine and autism. Attention also turned to thimerosol, the mercury-based preservative contained in some of the other vaccines. Mercury at high levels is a recognized neurotoxin. Infants simultaneously receiving several of those vaccines could potentially have blood levels of mercury higher than is considered safe, but actual occurrences have not been documented. Almost all of these vaccines have been reformulated; the remainder contain less mercury per shot than a half a can of tuna.

For more information on studies about autism and vaccines, go to: *www .cdc.gov/vaccinesafety/concerns/mmr_autism_factsheet.htm.*

Early Intervention

Babies develop at different rates. Some may walk at ten months while others may not reach that milestone until they're fourteen months old. Some babies crawl at seven months, while others are ten months or older. Some babies skip that step and go directly to walking. Some talk early, and some talk late. Parents, especially first-time parents, worry. Remember, there is a wide range to normal.

If your child was born very early, has been diagnosed with a developmental delay, has a visual or hearing impairment, motor problems, a language disorder, a chromosomal disorder, or any other serious condition, early intervention is critical. These first few years, from birth to three, is when the rate of learning and development is most rapid. Getting the right help for your baby can make a long-term difference.

You want to get a specific assessment of the issue(s) and a clear plan of therapy. Early intervention has been proven, both in long-term studies and on an anecdotal basis, to be effective. In fact, the earlier the intervention, the more effective it is.

Trust your instincts and talk to your doctor if your baby is not reaching developmental milestones or you suspect your baby has a hearing or vision problem. Be persistent and ask for a second opinion if you are not satisfied with your doctor's assessment.

CHAPTER 13

Returning to Work

More than 60 percent of women with children under the age of one are in the workforce. It's a constant juggling act to feel like you are doing a good job as a parent while still doing a good job at work. It requires you to be well-organized in both parts of your life, while at the same time being more flexible and creative than ever before.

Juggling Parenthood and Career

Returning to work is tough. There are times when you may feel that you're not doing a good job at either place—as a parent or as an employee. You may feel like your mind is always someplace else: worrying about your baby while at work; worrying about job demands while caring for your baby.

Let's get the guilt out of the way. You are a good mother if you love your child with every fiber of your being *and* you leave her to go to work every day. While it's true that being a parent is a 24/7 job, that doesn't mean you have to be with your child every moment of every day. The key is to find good child care so you know your baby is safe, happy, and loved.

But will you feel conflicted? Will you worry? Will you sometimes wish you were at home rather than at work? Of course you will. On the other hand, there will be days when you're home with the baby that you'll wish you were with other adults or talking about something other than baby poop or sleep schedules.

Realistically, you'll feel a full range of emotions. Be good to yourself and remember that emotions aren't good or bad, they just are. Some days you'll barely get through the day and wonder how you'll ever pull it all off. Other times, you'll feel like Wonder Woman—able to be a super mom and super-career gal.

ESSENTIAL

On your way to work, drop off the dry cleaning or stop at the post office. Try to plan ahead so that you multitask, combining trips to save time (and gas).

Here are some tips to ease the return to work. Finding a work-life balance takes planning and a readiness to give yourself a break. You've got a lot on your plate, so how can you make your life easier and smoother?

- **Divide the chores.** If both you and your partner work outside the home, the household chores should be evenly shared. Don't get trapped into gender stereotypes. If he's a better cook and you're better at repairing toilets—then do what needs to be done and don't buy into women's versus men's work. Establish a list of responsibilities, then step away. No criticizing how a household chore is done, just as long as it's finished.

- **Simplify.** Eliminate, at least at first, outside responsibilities like church committees, professional associations, and even family obligations. You need the time outside of work for yourself, your partner, and your baby. You'll be able to add back outside responsibilities when you've established a rhythm to work and family.

- **Unclutter your home.** Donate or toss what you don't use or wear. It will be less to clean.

- **Let it go.** Ease up on your standards for keeping the house clean. If you can afford to hire someone to clean your home, it may be worth it (even if it's just a couple of times a year for a thorough cleaning). If not, clean what you can and ignore the rest. If you can afford it, buy extra baby clothes in order to reduce how often you have to do laundry.

- **Eat healthy, but simply.** Buy prepared foods (healthy ones) or cook ahead on the weekends.

- **Shop online.** Save time and money by using the Internet to compare prices and purchase most items. In many areas, you can even do your grocery shopping online.

- **Time versus money.** Sometimes it's worth it to spend a little more money at a local store that is convenient to save yourself time that you can spend with your baby.

Maximizing Your Maternity Leave

Whether you are returning to the same job you held before giving birth—or hunting for a new one—you need to plan ahead to smooth the transition back to work. But first, give yourself some time to: recuperate from the physical and emotional effects of delivery; learn your new job as a mother; or just enjoy your wonderful new baby. Turn off the phone(s), your BlackBerry, and computer and declare a "no work" zone for a few weeks.

Once you are feeling a little more yourself, and can see a pattern to your baby's day, you can begin to carefully consider your options. You may have already considered child care options before you delivered, but you want to finalize those plans at least a month before you return to work. You will want to start using the caregiver or program a few weeks before your first day back at work so that, if necessary, you can refine or change your plans.

ESSENTIAL

Don't worry that your baby won't bond with you if you go back to work. A study of more than 1,000 infants and their mothers found that the sense of trust felt by fifteen-month-old children for their mothers was not affected by whether or not they were in day care or by how many hours they spent there. It's a mother's sensitivity and responsiveness to her child that is the foundation for strong attachment and trust.

The Most Important Question

Regardless of what kind of child care you select, your choice is based first and foremost on the quality of attention given to your baby. Here's the bottom line question: is the person or day care center you have chosen to watch your child loving, responsive, and skillful at interacting with your baby?

You may find only one situation to which you can confidently answer "yes" to the basic question, in which case your choice is easy and you will make your arrangements based on that decision. But more likely, you'll have a variety of options and then you have to decide which one best meets your other criteria of cost and convenience.

Don't assume that a higher cost will give you better care. You will need to carefully interview the caregiver(s), as well as inspect the facilities. You will want current references and you want to personally interview other families who have hired the caregiver or enrolled in the program.

There are three basic child care options:

- **A day care center.** An institution, private or public, that operates a full-workday schedule.
- **A family day care home.** Typically a woman who watches a few children in her home.
- **In-home child care.** This is a sitter (nanny, au pair, grandparent, etc.) who comes into your home. She may live-in or come in as a daily worker. She may also be responsible for household chores.

Day Care Centers

Day care centers may have as few as thirty children or as many as several hundred. Some are nonprofit programs run by churches, community centers, local government, etc. Some corporations run their own on-site day care programs—others outsource child care to another organization. There are also for-profit day care programs. Who "owns" the day care program is less important than how it is administered. There are advantages and disadvantages to using a day care center.

ADVANTAGES TO DAY CARE CENTERS

- **Coverage.** Many day care centers have longer hours than family day care, and you don't have to worry about staff absenteeism. If a caregiver becomes ill, it's up to the day care center to figure out coverage.
- **Standards.** There are clear licensing requirements for day care centers. According to a survey by the AAP, day care centers "have better regulations for health, safety, sanitation, and nutrition than family day care homes." But keep in mind that the licensing requirements are usually the minimum standards that are professionally approved. Preferably, any center you choose should exceed those standards.
- **Training.** Day care center workers, especially directors and teachers, have more training in child development and more opportunities for training.
- **Backup.** There is some research to suggest that day care staff are better able to cope with a larger number of children than an in-home sitter or family day care operator because they have backup in case of an emergency, or if they are simply stressed out.

DISADVANTAGES TO DAY CARE CENTERS

- **High turnover.** The pay is low and the hours are long, so is it any wonder that more than 40 percent of day care staff will change jobs each year? Ask the director what the turnover rate is for her staff and what she does to retain them. Ask how the director helps ease the transition for the children when there is a turnover. It's a good sign if you find a center with a low turnover rate.

- **Institutional feel.** The day care center may feel less like a home. It may be busier and have the strict rules necessary to make the program run smoothly.
- **Group size.** Your baby may be with other infants, which can be a wonderful source of stimulation for him, but can also mean not as much one-on-one, adult-baby interaction. Experts recommend a maximum of six babies in a room, with a 3:1 child-to-staff ratio.

Family Day Care

While one study suggests that over 3.6 million children are in family day care situations, the actual number is unknown. Probably two out of three youngsters are cared for by unlicensed day care providers.

ADVANTAGES TO FAMILY DAY CARE

- **Homelike atmosphere.** When it's good, family day care mimics your home. It's a personalized, caring, and thoughtful approach.
- **Less expensive.** Generally, though not always, family day care is less expensive than day care centers or an in-home sitter.
- **Sick days.** A family day care provider may be more flexible about caring for your baby when she is sick. Being around other kids, while fun for baby, is also a constant source of exposure to viruses. Expect your baby to come down with colds and other viral illnesses. A family day care provider may be more willing to watch your child when she's slightly ill.
- **Flexibility.** A family day care provider may be more flexible about your work hours, if you have to stay late, or work on weekends. She might also be available for baby sitting during non-work events.

DISADVANTAGES TO FAMILY DAY CARE

- **Burnout.** With no adult backup on site, a family day care provider is under greater stress when dealing with a group of children. If she decides to quit her job, you've got to make new arrangements and your baby will have to adjust to a new environment.

- **Coverage.** If your family day care provider gets sick or wants to take a vacation, you may be responsible for finding other arrangements regardless of whether or not it's convenient for you.
- **Standards.** If the family day care you use is not licensed, the recommended health and safety standards and adult-to-child ratio may not be met. Furthermore, the provider may not have formal training in early childhood development.

ESSENTIAL

Decide how you are going to handle days when your baby has a mild illness. Have a backup plan in place before you return to work. For example: Who will stay home with her? Can you use your sick leave or personal days to care for an ill baby? Is there flexibility in your job for you to work at home on those days when your baby is sick and can't go to day care?

In-Home sitter

Nanny, babysitter, au pair, livein, live out; there are several options when you decide to hire someone to come to your house and care for your baby while you work. This is usually the most expensive option, but it may offer you more flexibility in terms of meeting your work schedule.

ADVANTAGES TO IN-HOME CARE
- **One-on-one care.** Your sitter can focus on your baby's needs and not have to juggle the needs of other infants at the same time.
- **Flexibility.** You can adapt the sitter's schedule to your work schedule. If you're going to be late, your baby is already at home and can stay on his eating/sleeping schedule.
- **Convenience.** You don't have to make an extra stop on your way to or from work.
- **Less exposure to contagious diseases.** While your baby will still get his share of colds, he will have less exposure to germs and viruses.
- **Household chores.** If negotiated, the sitter may also be able to help with cleaning, cooking, and laundry. But make clear that the first priority is the care of your baby.

DISADVANTAGES TO IN-HOME CARE

- **Supervision.** Even with nanny-cams and careful reference checks, you have a sitter alone with your baby with no on-site supervision.
- **Coverage.** If your sitter becomes ill or needs a day off, you will have to make other arrangements. There is no on-site backup.
- **Training.** Most in-home sitters don't have formal child development training.
- **Privacy.** If you choose to have someone live in your home, you will give up some of your family's privacy. If you choose to use a family member as your sitter (e.g., grandparent, aunt), you have to straddle the line between family relationship and employee.

Checklist for Choosing Child Care

Whether you've decided to use a day care facility, a family day care program, or an in-home sitter, here is a list of points to consider:

- While a licensed facility or home-care business does not guarantee quality, it does mean that the center or home has met minimum standards. If possible, go with a licensed facility or individual.
- Personally check references for the day care center or home day care provider—and also check how the day care center checks the background and references of its employees.
- Ask about the turnover rate, both of employees and of families. How many of the same families continue to use the facility or home day care provider from year-to-year?
- Ask whether parents can visit the center or home without prior notice. If unscheduled visits are not allowed, choose another facility.
- Check the staff-to-child ratio. For children under two, there should be a maximum of six children in the room and one adult for every three children.
- Discuss childproofing and safety issues, and visually inspect the rooms in which your child will be. Are they as safe as if your child were in your own home?
- Ask about the center or day care provider's policies on immunizations, infection control, and exclusion criteria for sick children. Will

the center notify you if another child becomes ill with a contagious disease?

- Look at the toys to see if they are age appropriate.
- Discuss the center or day care provider's policies on meals (who provides what and what is the menu); diapers (who provides and how many); and support for breastfeeding mothers.
- Ask about napping arrangements (where and how often), as well as what will be done if your baby doesn't want to take a nap that day or time.
- Ask if the staff/sitter is certified in infant CPR, trained in basic first-aid, and has in place a plan for emergencies.
- Discuss how you will get feedback on your child each day? Is it formal or just a quick discussion at the end of the day (which may be difficult since you and your baby may both be tired)?

A Smooth Transition

Getting organized before you return to work will ease the transition. Settle on the child care you will use and begin using it a few weeks before you return to work. Make some meals ahead. Be prepared for any and all emotions. You may or may not feel guilty. You may feel a sense of relief. Remember: you're a good mother.

Here are some other tips that will help:

- **Stay in touch.** While you are on maternity leave, keep in touch with work colleagues. Call, e-mail, or even go out to lunch with some work friends to keep up with office politics and changes. You don't have to take on any projects, but staying in touch will ease the transition.
- **Do some practice runs.** Even before you return to work, try and follow the morning schedule you'll have so you can know exactly how much time and what you need to get you and your baby ready and out the door.
- **Check your wardrobe.** You want clothes that are comfortable and fit. Don't be discouraged if you haven't lost all the pregnancy weight or your body and feet have changed sizes. Buy what you need so you return to work in appropriate, well-fitted clothes.

- **Make a decision on how your baby will be fed when you are at work.** You don't have to stop breastfeeding if you return to work. You can pump and freeze breastmilk that your child care provider will give him. If you want to continue breastfeeding, start pumping and freezing milk weeks in advance of your return to work. Make arrangements to pump at work. If you decide to wean your baby, do it slowly so the transition to formula is easy on both you and your infant.
- **Start off slow.** If possible, return to work on a Thursday, so your first work week is short. Ask if you can work shorter hours the first week or two. It's already a big adjustment, so it's better if you don't feel overwhelmed immediately.
- **Prepare for mixed staff reactions.** You may return to a warm welcome and offers of help and support. Or you may find some coworkers who resent your time off and check your workload against their own. Do your job, take care of yourself and your family, and don't worry about the negative vibes sent your way.
- **Eat a healthy snack at work.** Before you race out the office door, eat a snack so that you're not overwhelmed by hunger while trying to take care of your baby at the end of the day. You can eat a meal with or without your partner later in the evening.

Adjust your expectations and perhaps your job. After a few weeks, evaluate how your return to work is going. Are there ways to streamline the process or ease the transition for you and your baby? Do you want to consider changing jobs? Can you work less hours? Can you arrange for flextime? Can your partner work different hours to care for the baby?

None of it is written in stone, and you will need to make adjustments at work and at home as your baby grows.

CHAPTER 14

Playtime

You'll find that most of your baby's early fusses will have to do with either being hungry, tired, or needing to be changed. Then, after she's a few weeks old, you may find that she's not tired, hungry, or wet and yet she's still fussing. Why? Simply put, she's bored. Once your baby tells you she's bored, it's time to introduce her to the concept of playtime even though she's only a month old and doesn't seem able to do much of anything. Work with what she's got—hearing, sight, touch, smell, and some muscle control. Play that appeals to these abilities will entertain your baby and enable her to develop her mind and body.

Why Play?

Play is actually necessary for development. Play with others gives babies a chance to connect with them. Play with objects gives babies a chance to discover that they are powerful and that they can act on their environments. Solo play gives babies a chance to connect with themselves, and it will give you a few minutes while your baby happily entertains himself.

Let your child learn to entertain himself—it will pay off down the line. But that doesn't mean that you abandon him. Instead, set up a series of play stations in your house and move him from one to another, letting him explore something new. For example, position the infant swing so your baby can look outside; place the baby chair on the counter (back from the edge) but with a view of the kitchen and you working in there; put a quilt on the floor and scatter a few toys on it. Moving your baby from station to station will keep him happy and amused for as much as an hour.

The Toy Box

You don't need a lot of store-bought, primary-colored plastic objects to entertain your baby. Besides, whether or not you fill a shopping cart at the toy store, you'll soon find out that you have more of those toys than you ever wanted. Some of the best baby toys are things you already have around the house.

Once your baby can sit, she'll love playing with containers. Plastic food storage containers work just as well as primary-colored ones sold in toy stores. She'll play with them empty, but will like them even better with something to dump out of them—water, sand, oatmeal, and birdseed all have great dumping potential.

ESSENTIAL

Your baby will want your television remote control. She sees other people in the family jockeying for its possession—she'll know it's important. She won't be placated with a toy one, with its chunky buttons and bright colors. Dig up an old remote (you know you have one somewhere), remove the batteries, and tape the battery cover on.

She'll like to empty your kitchen cabinets. Don't childproof everything. Instead, make sure one or more drawers or cabinets are filled with things she can safely empty out.

Stick to the classics when you do buy toys. Some baby toys you remember from your childhood are still around—there's a reason for that. These toys typically can be played with in a variety of ways and will interest your baby for years.

The Basics

Here are some of the toys that have entertained generations of babies:

- **Rattles.** Even a very young baby, who instinctively grasps anything put into his hand, can wave a rattle. After you've used it yourself to teach him to follow sounds, it will be a great entertainer during diaper changes.
- **Nesting cups that fit inside each other.** This will be your baby's first puzzle. These cups can also stack, pour, be sorted into colors, and be counted. They let him experiment with the ideas of inside and outside and bigger and smaller.
- **Stacking toys**—plastic or wooden rings that stack up on a post, preferably not in graduated sizes until he's older. In the first year, he's mastering control of his hands and will be frustrated if he can't put a ring on a post because its diameter is too small. You'll also need lots of blocks—for touching, tasting, and banging together. Eventually, they might even be used for stacking.
- **Toys that react when a button or lever is pushed** (a train spins around, a funny man pops up). These break the classic rule about toy flexibility, but they teach cause and effect, and babies love them. (A light switch fits into this category, but just how long do you want to hold your baby up so he can turn the overhead light on and off?)
- **Toys that imitate your activities**—bowls, spoons (if you don't want to sacrifice your own), a little stove, a toy telephone, dolls, a mop, a toddler-sized stroller or shopping cart are all good choices.

What you don't need are "educational" toys designed to turn your baby into a child genius. Your baby has a huge curriculum he's covering in his first year as it is. Your job is to simply expose him to life, not drill him in his numbers. Sometimes it is hard to resist, so go ahead and teach. Just remember that he'll be better off learning his academics at a more developmentally appropriate time. Brain growth, recent research shows, does not stop in early childhood, as used to be thought. It continues throughout life, so there really is no rush.

QUESTION

Are there any concerns about chemicals used in plastics?
As an optional safety measure, avoid phthalates. (Phthalates are used in plastic toys, particularly teethers, to make the plastic soft.) Although public interest groups raised a concern about the use of the chemical diisononyl phthalate in baby toys, an independent panel of experts, as well as the Consumer Product Safety Commission, reported that concerns over phthalates are unwarranted. However, many major toy manufacturers have, since 1999, removed phthalates from their products.

Toys You Already Have

Look around the house; you are well stocked with infant toys, you just may not realize it yet. Babies like things that go inside other things, things with lids to open and close, and things that can be stacked or dumped. They like things with interesting textures or ones that make interesting sounds. Some of the best are:

- **From the kitchen:** Wooden spoons, measuring cups and spoons, pots and pans, plastic containers with lids, balls of waxed paper or aluminum foil (bigger than your baby's fist).
- **From the bathroom:** Clean makeup brushes, cloth diapers, empty tissue box filled with light scarves, empty baby wipe container, nylon net bath puff.
- **Just stuff:** Coasters, napkin rings, socks rolled into balls or used as puppets, clean feather dusters, shoes, old wallets and credit cards.

- **Filled clear plastic bottles:** Clear or colored water, liquid soap, dry pasta, feathers, rice, or anything else that fits, makes noise and looks fun (glue or tape the top on to prevent choking hazards and messes).

Toy Safety

To be safe, be sure your baby's playthings meet these criteria:

- The paint is non-toxic.
- It has no small detachable parts.
- None of the edges or corners are sharp.
- No bells and whistles are at excessive decibels (some toy trucks emit siren noises that rival those from real fire trucks).
- No "bean-bag" stuffing (the pellets that stuff them are a choking hazard so stick to cuddlers stuffed with fluff).
- The toy doesn't have long or loose cords, strings, or ribbons (avoid anything, including necklaces, that your baby can get tangled around herself—especially her throat).
- No cords are more than twelve inches long.
- The toy, and any detachable parts, should be too large to fit inside a toilet-paper tube (smaller pieces are choking hazards).
- The toy has no lead in it.
- No recall has been announced for that version of the toy.

ALERT

Avoid giving your child empty film containers. While babies love them— they are the perfect size to clutch in a baby fist and can be filled with interesting things to dump or shake—film containers absorb chemicals from film that your child should not be ingesting. Also avoid giving your baby coins, which are a choking hazard.

Organizing the Mess

Toys seem to multiply at night, especially when you've just tripped over them, so developing a system for organizing and storing all the baby toys is important. While there is a temptation to buy a big toy box and heave everything in it, it's neither safe nor practical.

Toy boxes, especially those with heavy lids, are especially dangerous to exploring children. Even if the lid doesn't seem heavy to you, it can cause serious injury if it drops on a little one peering into the toy box. A child can even suffocate to death if he crawls into the box, the lid slams shut, and there isn't enough ventilation.

A better system is open baskets, preferably organized by the type of toy. This makes cleanup easier for you (a place for everything, everything in its place) and it also will help your baby learn about classification and sorting as he helps you put all the stuffed animals in one basket, all the blocks in another.

Multi-Purpose Baby Games

Use playtime to encourage development by providing lots of opportunity for practice. Get her out of her infant seat and onto the floor, give her interesting objects to look at and reach for, or take her out into the world and tell her about what she's seeing. Use baby games that combine several of the senses and teach important lessons.

- **Peek-a-boo.** Everybody likes to play peek-a-boo with a baby—probably because it gets such a great reaction. Cover your face with a baby blanket or burp cloth and whisk the cloth away, saying "Peek-a-boo!" You can also cover a toy with the blanket and then make it reappear with a flourish or cover your baby's head and let her pull off the blanket and say peek-a-boo to you. This teaches object permanence— that when things are gone, they aren't gone forever.
- **Hide and seek.** Lay your month-old baby down in the middle of the floor and move around the room, talking to her. As she hunts for the source of the sound of your voice, she starts to associate sights and sounds. Once your baby is crawling, partially hide behind a couch or doorway and call her to find you. When she gets good at this game, hide completely, but still call out. Eventually your baby will be able to hunt you down without the help of your voice. This also teaches object permanence—when mom is gone, she will come back.

- **Ah boo.** Put your baby, facing you, on your lap. Look her in the eyes, say "AAAhhh" then lean forward, gently bump foreheads and say, "Boo!" This teaches her to anticipate you—she'll soon join in by leaning forward to meet you.
- **Ankle or knee rides.** Sit down and put your baby on your knees, facing you, or straddling your ankles, lying forward against your legs. Support her firmly under the arms as you bounce her gently (she shouldn't pop off of your leg) to the rhythm of a favorite rhyme. This teaches her balance, rhythm, and anticipation as she hears the same rhyme over and over and learns to expect her favorite part ("had a great fall"). A variation (and a great exercise for parents) is inverted knee rides. Lie down on a rug, and bring your knees up above your chest, holding your calves parallel to the floor. Put your baby's stomach down on your calves, head peeking over your knees. You can bounce her with your legs, or rock her from side to side (again, make sure you hold her firmly and bounce gently).

Keep in mind that unless her muscles, brain, and nervous system have matured to the required level, no amount of practice will get her to a milestone before she's ready. Don't make yourself—or your baby—crazy by trying to push her to achieve every milestone as soon as possible.

Social Butterfly

Child development may be most visible when it comes to physical growth and mobility, but along with strengthening muscles and improving coordination, your baby is developing in other ways. He's figuring out his feelings about his world and about other people. Your baby needs friends his own age to encourage that exploration. Although he may not be old enough to do more than lie on a blanket and kick his legs, getting him together regularly with other babies is important.

It's also important for parents to meet other parents. You learn from each other; support each other; and commiserate with each other. Only another new mom understands how you haven't slept in a month, haven't combed your hair in days, and why you consider showering without a baby in a bounce seat in the room an absolute indulgence.

Playmates

Researchers used to think young babies didn't really interact and that all two-year-olds did was parallel-play (sit near and imitate each other, but not really play together). Researchers have now shown that even three-month-old babies look with interest at other infants. By six months, you'll see the beginnings of rudimentary games, such as one baby squealing and the second baby answering back.

Research has caught up with what a lot of parents know from observations. Peer relationships start early and are different from parental or sibling relationships. At two months those two babies on a blanket will probably just look at each other; at three months they may try to touch each other; at seven or eight months one may crawl over to the other (or over the other) and try to hand him a toy. In fact, for a while you'll think your child is wonderful at sharing as he tries to give toys to everyone (the "No, mine!" stage comes later).

Playgroups

If you do need encouragement to start socializing, there are two things to keep in mind. You'll stay a lot saner if you spend some time with moms of children the same age, and long-term studies have shown that children who form good friendships early do better in school later on.

Start a playgroup. Find out if there is a mothers' or newcomers' club in your area—most mothers' clubs sponsor playgroups. Attend a parenting class sponsored by your local hospital—"graduates" of some of these classes form playgroups. Take a lot of walks, get the phone numbers of other baby-toting mothers that you meet, and organize your own. Post a notice on the community bulletin board in the supermarket or in your synagogue or church.

ESSENTIAL

While many playgroups successfully meet at parks, most kids—and moms—interact best at playgroups hosted at the members' houses. The group is less easily scattered (and your baby will get the idea of sharing his toys before he even knows that they are his toys).

Try to start out with at least five or six other mothers—that way you'll still have a quorum if one or two miss a session. Schedule your meetings at least weekly (you'll probably find that early morning hours are best for infants, but you'll shift the time as the babies get older and nap schedules evolve).

These early friendships may last for years, or they could be transitory. The moms may become close friends, while the kids drift apart. For right now, you're looking for a comfortable group of kids and mothers to share the experience of that first year. Even if you work full-time, look for (or organize) a playgroup that meets on weekends. The benefits for mom and baby are enormous.

Social Milestones

As a newborn, your baby will be able to recognize her parents' voices and the voices of other people that surrounded her mother during pregnancy, from siblings (if she has them) to the cast of her mother's favorite television show. She will also be sensitive to the feelings of others, particularly her mother. She'll notice if mom is feeling tense and will quickly become tense herself. (You may come to believe that your baby will wake up on cue if you even think about having sex with your husband.)

By four to eight weeks your baby will probably be actively smiling in response to things that make her happy. Around two months she will probably turn her head in the direction of a parent's voice and spend many happy moments gazing directly into your eyes.

You'll hear her first laugh when your baby is around four months old, and will put yourself through all sorts of crazy antics trying to get her to repeat it. Also around four months, you'll be able to tell when she's excited—she'll squeal, wriggle, or breathe heavily.

At around six months another emotion will emerge: anger. You'll discover that your baby's angry cry is much different from her tired or hungry cry. This one won't be as much fun for you as joy and excitement, but it's an important one for your baby because anger is motivating. A child who is mad that her favorite toy has rolled out of reach is motivated to wriggle over to it, developing her motor skills. Around the same time your baby will also begin to recognize the difference between an angry voice and a friendly voice, and react accordingly.

Stranger Anxiety

Sometime around the six-month mark, but perhaps as early as four months or as late as eight, your baby will, for the first time, get upset when you try to hand him over to a stranger. Stranger anxiety will make your life more difficult for a while, but it is an important developmental step. It means that your baby has figured out that his mommy, daddy, and the other people he sees every day are different from everybody else in the world. He knows that food, comfort, and fun come from these people and he doesn't want a substitute.

You can get through stranger anxiety best by giving in to it. Warn people whom your baby doesn't see often to approach him slowly, or recommend that they sit across the room, ignore him for a while, and wait until he approaches them (or, if he's not mobile, shows interest in them) before coming closer.

You also need to monitor your emotions to make sure you're not sending the wrong message. When a stranger approaches you in the grocery store to comment on your beautiful baby, do you clutch him tighter, or do you smile and tell your baby, "That nice lady thinks you're sweet?" When you hand your baby over to a sitter, make sure it's a sitter you feel comfortable with. Always say good-bye if you're leaving your baby in someone else's care. If you sneak out, you might get away easy that one time, but you'll pay for it for months. After your baby comes to trust that you are not going to give him to a stranger and realizes instead that these people are just more fun faces to gaze at, stranger anxiety will pass.

Don't Leave Me!

Separation anxiety is different from stranger anxiety and usually strikes at around eight months. It starts when your baby first falls deeply in love with her primary caregiver, the person most often feeding and cuddling her. This person will be showered with adoring looks and joyous greetings. The baby seems miserable whenever this special person is out of sight.

Like most other species, human babies develop this passionate attachment just before they are about to move independently. (Want a duckling to follow you everywhere? Adopt it just as it's about to waddle.) Your baby realizes that she can be independent from you and is therefore afraid that you'll move away from her. And, frustrating as it can be, separation anxiety is a plus—it makes it less likely that your newly mobile baby will be moving herself out of your sight.

The best way of dealing with separation anxiety is to simply go along with it. If your baby is clingy, pick her up and cuddle her. If she wants to explore, smile and nod at her explorations from across the room. If she doesn't want to leave you, pick her up and move her from room to room as you go.

Once she's moving on her own, move slowly so she can catch up with you. In a couple of weeks her speed will have picked up, so she'll be more confident of her ability to follow you and less panicked when you move. You can also keep up a constant conversation if you step out of the room because she may not be so worried if she can hear your voice. You can play hide and seek (peek out from your hiding place and call her) to get her used to you appearing and disappearing.

A "lovey"—a special blanket or toy—might help you and your baby through this phase. The lovey will remind your baby of you when you're not around. Some kids never become attached to a lovey and have to struggle through most separations unaided.

In short, don't count on going to the bathroom alone any time soon.

Separation anxiety will come and go for years, so get used to it. It doesn't mean that you should never leave your baby or that she's miserable the whole time you are gone. Find a babysitter you trust, someone who is willing to actively work to calm your baby down when you leave, and know that the tears don't leave a permanent scar on her psyche. Usually, if it's a familiar babysitter, your child will calm down and enjoy herself after a few minutes.

CHAPTER 15

Watch Your Language

You've been communicating with your baby since you found out you were pregnant. Now that he's here in the world with you, don't stop talking. The sound of your voice will comfort him as a newborn and guide him as he grows. Reading, singing, and telling stories to your baby are critical for language development. He'll practice imitating what he hears and will watch and feel the way your mouth moves. You may even teach him a few simple words in sign language. Eventually, of course, he'll understand what he hears and be able to communicate back. Before you know it, he'll tell you exactly what he thinks.

Life of the Mind

Even though babies aren't quite ready to fill out I.Q. tests, researchers still know quite a bit about what is going on in their minds. Babies start to recognize their mothers' faces by one to two months.

At two months or so they become interested in things besides themselves and their mothers—this is the time to get out the toys. (This is a useful development, because it means your baby can be distracted when he is fussy.)

Between the ages of three and four months your baby can understand that three objects are more than two. At around four months she learns to anticipate regular events. For example, she may open her mouth when she sees you getting out your nursing pillow or taking a bottle out of the refrigerator.

At around four months she will also start preferring certain people or certain toys to others. At five months or so she'll learn to follow another person's gaze—if you look up at an airplane, your baby will probably look up, too. Somewhere between six and nine months she'll recognize that a face that she sees in a mirror is her reflection, not another baby, and may spend hours exploring that phenomenon.

At around eight to nine months she'll understand object permanence— that when you leave the room or a toy is hidden out of sight, it continues to exist. (You can test this understanding by hiding a toy under a blanket. Until your baby understands object permanence, she won't bother to look for it, but may cry because it's gone.) By eight or nine months, your baby will be able to set a goal (get a toy), make a plan to carry it out (crawl around the table), and ignore distractions (you calling her in the other direction) while she carries out her plan. Here is a listing of some major intellectual milestones:

▼ INTELLECTUAL MILESTONES

Age	Milestone
1–2 months	recognizes his mother or primary caregiver
2 months	interested in things besides himself and caregiver
3 months	can discriminate between the possible (block sits on table) and the impossible (block floats in air)
3–4 months	understands that three objects are more than two
4 months	demonstrates preferences

Age	Milestone
4 months	anticipates events
5 months	follows another person's gaze
6–9 months	recognizes that his face in a mirror is a reflection
8-9 months	understands object permanence
8–9 months	can set a goal and ignore distraction while pursuing it

Talking for Two

In your baby's first year, her senses and muscles are programmed for quick development. But they can't develop without stimulation. In a famous experiment, kittens were blindfolded at birth. Some time later the blindfolds were removed. Though the kittens had physically normal eyes, they were never able to see because their vision was not stimulated during a developmentally critical period.

Of your baby's senses, the sense of hearing is most developed at birth. She began listening before she was born. She's used to the sound of your voice—and she likes it a lot. You'll find that you'll naturally raise the pitch of your voice and talk in a sing-song pattern—these are the sounds she wants to hear and you automatically know how to make them.

ALERT

As many as 4 in 1,000 infants have some form of hearing impairment. Those who get help before six months of age are more likely to develop language normally. A simple test that measures brain activity in response to tones and sound is available. In some hospitals this test is performed routinely, so ask for one before you take your newborn home from the hospital. The test typically costs between $30 and $150 and is covered by many insurance plans.

You won't necessarily know what to say at first. You might even feel pretty silly talking to someone who doesn't talk back, but you'll get used to it. You shouldn't use baby talk. You're better off saying blanket than "blankie," for example, to allow your baby to hear all of the sounds of the language she will soon be speaking. You do, however, need to forget about pronouns for a while. Instead of "I, you, he" say "Mama, Susie, Daddy." Right now Susie's finding out that everything has a name; later she'll figure out that lots of people can be called "she" or "you."

Pretend you're the narrator of a show starring your baby. Whatever you're doing, describe it. "Mama is taking off Susie's pajamas. One snap, two snaps, three snaps, four snaps. Ohh! There's Susie's tummy. Mama gives Susie's tummy a kiss. Kiss! Now Susie needs a new diaper. Okay, here's the diaper now."

If your baby responds with any kind of noise, act like she's talking back. Pause to let her finish her comment, and then respond. You can have great conversations and your baby will agree with anything you say (for now). Savor this!

Goo-Goo, Ga-Ga

A newborn communicates through crying, which will quickly turn into a vocabulary. If you've been listening attentively, you will probably be able to distinguish cries of pain, hunger, and exhaustion. At around a month you may find your baby imitating you by opening and closing his mouth when you speak.

Around six weeks or so, you'll begin to hear classic baby coos. These are strings of vowel sounds, like aahh, eeeh, uhh.

▼ **LANGUAGE MILESTONES**

Age	Milestone
Newborn	cries
1–2 months	cries differently to communicate pain, hunger, and exhaustion
6 weeks–2 months	coos or oohs (vowels)
4–5 months	understands his name
4–8 months	babbles (consonants)
9 months	understands "no"
10–12 months	babbles without repeating syllables
8–14 months	points
10 months	responds to a spoken request
10–18 months	says first words

Somewhere between four and eight months your baby will add consonants, like gagaga and dadada. Since the most common first consonants are g, k, l, and d, he won't, however, be saying "mama" yet, unfair as that may seem. By ten months or so he'll progress from repeating the same syllable to babbling strings of different syllables in a cadence that sounds a lot like talking.

Meanwhile, he's learned to understand his name, the word no, and a few other simple words. Between ten and twelve months he will respond to a simple, spoken request, such as "wave bye-bye," or "give me the ball." (Enjoy this phase; in about another year he'll quite gleefully do the opposite of what you ask.)

Between eight and fourteen months he'll begin to point. That's a recognizable attempt at sign language and, if you're interested in signing with your baby, a signal that he's ready to learn more signs (see page 197).

Sometime between ten and eighteen months he'll say his first words.

QUESTION

Should I worry if my baby is slow to talk?
Babies can't do everything at once. Some babies focus on motor skills first, and may get around to working on language later than a more sedentary baby. As long as he's hearing language, your baby is probably learning to talk, whether he demonstrates it at ten months or eighteen months.

Rhymes and Rhythm

Sometimes you'll feel like you've completely run out of things to talk about. That's why we have nursery rhymes. Babies love the rhythm of rhymes. They also like hearing the same rhyme over and over again, and come to anticipate what you'll say next. You don't need to know a lot of them; a few basic ones are sufficient. You can also get a Mother Goose book from the library and learn a few of the more obscure rhymes just for fun.

Nursery Rhyme Refresher Course

Here are some favorite rhymes to share with your baby:

Jack and Jill
Went up the hill
To fetch a pail of water.
Jack fell down
And broke his crown
And Jill came tumbling after.

Little Miss Muffet
Sat on a tuffet
Eating her curds and whey.
Along came a spider
Who sat down beside her
And frightened Miss Muffet away.

Hey diddle diddle
The cat and the fiddle
The cow jumped over the moon.
The little dog laughed
To see such sport
And the dish ran away with the spoon.

Bouncing and Movement Rhymes

Gently bounce or move your baby on your knees to the rhythm of these poems:

As I was walking down the street,
down the street,
down the street
A bumblebee (refrigerator, flower, teakettle—name anything)
I chanced to meet,
Chanced to meet,
Chanced to meet.
Hi Ho Hi Ho Hi Ho
Riga-jig-jig and away we go, away we go, away we go
Riga-jig-jig and away we go
Hi Ho Hi Ho Hi Ho
(Repeat using another object)

To market, to market, to buy a fat pig
Home again, home again, jiggety-jig.
To market, to market, to buy a fat hog
Home again, home again, jiggety-jog.

Humpty Dumpty sat on a wall
Humpty Dumpty had a great fall
All the king's horses and all the king's men
Couldn't put Humpty together again.

Row, row, row, your boat
Gently down the stream.
Merrily, merrily, merrily, merrily
Life is but a dream.

Finger (or Toe) Play Rhymes

Here are some fun rhymes that you can do with your baby using her digits:

These are baby's fingers (touch fingers)
These are baby's toes (touch toes)
This is baby's bellybutton (touch bellybutton)
Round and round it goes (draw circles on belly)

This little piggy went to market
This little piggy stayed home
This little piggy had roast beef
This little piggy had none
And this little piggy went wee-wee-wee-wee
All the way home

Pat-a-cake, pat-a-cake
Baker's man
Bake me a cake!
As fast as you can
Roll it, and fold it,
and mark it with a B,
And put it in the oven
for Baby and me.

Here sits the Lord Mayor (touch forehead)
Here sits his two men (touch eyebrows)
Here sit the ladies (touch cheeks)
And here sits the hen (touch nose)
Here sit the little chickens (touch chin)
And here they run in (touch mouth).

Baby Sign Language Basics

Introduce basic sign language as early as you'd like. When your baby is seven or eight months old, you can teach her a few simple signs at dinner time, when she is sitting in her highchair and her hands are free. Research has demonstrated that early use of sign language may encourage the development of spoken language. But the big bonus of a baby who signs is the potential reduction in frustration—and accompanying tantrums—because she can tell you what is bothering her.

Exactly what sign you use for a particular word isn't important, as long as you are consistent. You can make up your own, get a book of simple signs intended to be used with babies, use American Sign Language standard signage (animated tutorials are easy to find on the web, and a host of books are also available), or use a mixture of all three.

Here are a few basic ones:

FIGURE 15-1:
All Gone/empty

FIGURE 15-2:
Down

Sweep your right hand over your down-turned left hand.

Point your index finger downward. Lower your finger a few inches.

FIGURE 15-3:
Drink

FIGURE 15-4:
Eat

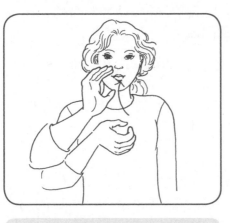

Cup your hand as if holding an invisible glass. Raise it up to your mouth as if drinking.

Draw the tips of all of your fingers and thumb together as if operating a hand puppet with its mouth closed. Bring your hand up to your mouth and touch your fingertips twice to your lips.

FIGURE 15-5:
More

FIGURE 15-6:
Scared

Hold both hands in front of you, fingers on each hand held together and thumbs tucked in, forming a loose "O" shape. Bring the fingertips of both hands together in front of you twice.

Place your hands open, fingers spread wide, against the front of your chest.

FIGURE 15-7:
Sit

FIGURE 15-8:
Tired

Extend the index and middle fingers of your left hand horizontally in front of your body, palm down. Raise the same fingers on your right hand and bring them down to rest on your left fingers.

Use the sign for bed as shown: Tilt your head to one side. Bring the palm of one hand up to your cheek. Rest your head against your open palm. Or you place your hands palms in, on your shoulders and move them down from your shoulders as you slump.

Reading Lessons

You should also read aloud. Besides helping to develop your baby's language skills, it also establishes very early the importance of books and learning. Plus, reading a book can be a part of your bedtime routine that helps to settle your baby down before she goes to sleep.

Read from baby books, or from whatever magazine or newspaper you'd like. Remember that you're reading, seeing, and interpreting for two when reading to your baby. This is your best opportunity to provide editorial commentary!

Discuss the story as you go, pointing out pictures that relate directly to the story, or to familiar things. "See the cat? That's just like Suzie's cat!" Ask questions about how or why things are happening in the story, and speculate as to what the answers might be. Really, just verbalize your own observations and thought processes.

Read the same book over and over if that's what your child wants. Even if you're bored and ready to move on—he's not. On the most basic levels, repetition develops memory and comprehension.

Reading out loud is a one-man show. Change your voice for different characters, act out noises and sounds, and exaggerate the pitch of your voice. The more animated you are, the more your baby will focus.

Finally, improvise. Your baby's favorite part may be something that you add. This could be your big chance to explore your wild theatrical or literary side.

ESSENTIAL

Don't prevent your child from turning back in the book, even if you read the same page all night. And don't rush. It may take a while for your baby to settle into a story.

Beyond Lullabies

Babies love music, so, no matter how poorly you do it, sing—you will have an appreciative audience. Turn on the stereo to music you like. Your baby will probably like it too, whether it's rock or reggae or classical. You don't need to buy special tapes of baby music (unless you have a particular fondness for the sounds *of Sesame Street* or the *Barney* song). Down the road you'll be listening to your kid's favorite music often enough, so now's your chance to get her to listen to your favorites.

If you have a wind-up music box (on a mobile, in a stuffed animal, or freestanding) you'll use it a lot. You'll use it now to entertain your baby in the crib or on the changing table, and later when your baby figures out how to wind it up herself.

You'll also be using musical instruments for a long time. Your baby's first instrument will be a rattle, and initially you'll shake it for her. Try shaking it on one side of her head and then the other. After a while she'll start looking around, trying to figure out what is making the sound. At about four months she'll be ready to hold the rattle for herself. At six months or so she'll start banging rattles together to hear the different sounds that makes. At this point she'll be ready for more complex musical instruments—like drums or tambourines.

Besides music, introduce your baby to animal sounds. If you hear a bird or a dog outside, imitate it. If you look at a book about animals, make all the sounds yourself.

CHAPTER 16

Movin' and Groovin'

Your baby is only three days old, but clearly he's a genius. He already knows how to grab your finger and move his feet like he's walking. Well, okay, those are just reflexes. But hey, wasn't that a smile? Although babies don't smile in response to your smile until two months or so, you may catch a few smiles from a newborn. Your mother might tell you that it's only gas, but these are real smiles. Child development specialists used to say that a newborn's smile was random, not a sign of emotion. But now some experts are contending that even newborns can feel happy—and smile to show it. So break out the baby book and record that smile; it's one of your baby's first milestones.

What's "Normal"?

If this is your first child, you'll be eager to fill in that list, noting when he first rolls over, sits up, and crawls. If this is your second or third baby, you'll probably have mixed feelings when he hits a milestone. You'll be applauding his achievement, but will be aware of how much it will change your life. (A baby who turns over is no longer easy to diaper; a baby who crawls needs a childproofed house.) And you may be mourning the passing of an earlier stage.

ESSENTIAL

Remember: Enjoy today's stage of development (and take pictures); it may not last until tomorrow. And don't compare your child to anybody else's. Such competitions can be annoying at best, damaging to friendships, and potentially, harmful to your child's self-esteem.

First-time mom or experienced mom, you'll be noting your baby's developmental milestones, and, whether you plan to or not, comparing them to those of your baby's peers. Odds are he'll do some things earlier than others, some things later, and once in a while will hit the median. You may be running to Home Depot for safety gates months earlier than you expected or wondering why your baby hasn't taken a step while other babies his age are jogging. Your child may be focused on learning to talk and will get to walking later. However he's progressing, don't forget that there is a wide range of "normal."

Now You See It

At birth, sight is the least developed of the senses. Babies are nearsighted, and the world is pretty much out of focus. They focus best about eight inches from their noses, and can't see much beyond eighteen inches from their nose. Babies' vision develops at different rates, so your baby may have nearly normal vision by six months or it may take years.

In the beginning, babies prefer to look at faces—particularly their mother's face—more than anything else. So give your baby plenty of face time.

Hold her on your lap and gaze at her; sit her in her chair and make faces at her. Here are some vision games you can play with your newborn:

- While baby toys are often brightly colored, infants enjoy black and white objects best in the first few months because the colors contrast so well. Look for mobiles and other toys that are black and white.

  Give her other things to look at as well, factoring in that critical eight-inch distance for the first two months or so. You've probably hung a mobile over the changing table and maybe another one over the crib. But babies would rather look at something new than something they've seen before, so change these mobiles regularly (simple cutout shapes or pictures from magazines are fine).

- Take your baby on a flying tour. Steve Wozniak, cofounder of Apple Computer Inc., has this great idea. You can do this as soon as your baby is strong enough to hold her head up on her own, while she's still light enough for you to carry easily on outstretched arms. Put one hand under her chest, fingers splayed wide so you can feel her muscles. Use the other hand to support her pelvis. Start near an interesting spot and hold your baby in the air, then try to sense which way her muscles are trying to tug her. It may take you a few minutes, but you'll begin to be able to tell which way she wants to go. (Resist the urge to take her to where you see her looking; let her muscles guide you instead.) For people who didn't believe babies have minds of their own, Woz has said that he used to do a trick—he'd have someone blindfold him, and throw a handkerchief on the floor. He'd then let the baby direct him to the handkerchief.

- Stock up on bubble soap. Bubbles move slowly, float in interesting patterns, and catch the light. They'll give your baby lots of eye-tracking practice early and develop her hand-eye coordination later on when she begins to try catching the bubbles.

- Use the mirrors in your house, or buy an unbreakable mirror for your baby to play with. Look in a mirror with your baby, make faces, and label your expression (happy, sad, angry). Encourage her to touch the baby in the mirror—one day she'll figure out that it's her and will be amazed. Act as a mirror for your baby. When she makes a face, you make the same face. She'll be thrilled with her new power!

Protecting Your Baby's Vision

Your baby may appear to be cross-eyed. Often it's just an illusion caused by the combination of the broad bridge of her nose and the folds near the inside corner of her eyes, making it look like her eyes are turning in. Sometimes your baby's eyes may actually cross temporarily as she looks around. This happens because the inner muscles are stronger, but be sure to talk to your doctor if her eyes stay crossed.

Make sure you protect your baby's eyes from bright light (sunlight and reflected glare). Keep her in the shade, have her wear a brimmed hat, and keep her under an umbrella. If you're going to put sunglasses on your baby, make sure that they have 100 percent ultraviolet filtration.

Here are some warning signs that might indicate a vision problem. Talk to your doctor if you have any concerns.

- Doesn't see objects unless they are held close.
- Turns sideways or tilts head at an unusual angle to look at objects.
- Has persistent redness in or around eyes, or swelling or a discharge from eyes.
- One or both eyelids droop.
- The colored part of one or both eyes appears cloudy.
- Shows excessive tearing, light sensitivity, squinting, or blinking.
- Rubs eyes frequently.
- An eye flutters.
- Appears to be groping when offered a bottle.

Reach Out and Touch

You'll be doing most of the touching when your baby is a newborn, so remember that it's not just hands that can feel things. Sensitivity to touch develops from the top down—your baby's face will be able to distinguish different sensations sooner than his hands will. Use a makeup brush or large paintbrush to pretend-paint your child, talking about the parts of his body as you do it. Or stroke him with a cotton ball or even a cloth diaper or blanket. You can keep a clean feather duster near your changing table, and "dust" your baby when you change him. Blow gently on your baby's stomach, or kiss his toes.

Self-Discovery

By two or three months, your baby will have figured out that his hands belong to him and will watch them as he's playing with them, trying to reach out and touch objects. For a while his hands will be his favorite toy. You can vary this game by putting a brightly colored sock or wrist rattle on one of his hands.

Once he's figured out that he has hands, it's time for batting practice. You can buy an official cradle gym (straps over the crib), baby gym (self-supporting and can be placed over your baby when he's lying on the floor), or a bouncy chair with a toy bar. These toys provide babies good practice in entertaining themselves, and give you a few moments for yourself.

By four months or so your baby will be tired of hitting things and will want to take them in his hands—and bring them to his mouth.

Put a toy in your hand and hold it out to your baby—then be patient. It will take him a while to calculate the path from his hand to the object, and you'll interrupt this process if you rush to put the toy in his hand.

Massage 101

Massage is a great way to relax some babies. (A few just don't like it; don't force it if yours falls in that category.) Luckily it is easy to do—you don't need special classes (although such classes abound).

For your baby's first few massages, just do his arms, hands, legs, and feet (the face and chest are a lot more sensitive). Use a cold-pressed vegetable oil and warm it first by rubbing it between your palms. Avoid baby oil; it's made of petroleum and you don't want your baby sucking it off of his arm.

You might start with your baby's hand, perhaps with a finger-play poem. Then rub his palm gently, starting with your thumbs in the center and moving them out along the fingers. Do both hands and, if he approves, move on to his feet. Remember to stroke very slowly, moving down away from his head.

For his chest, start with your hands in the center, and move them away from each other, down to his sides, following the line of his rib cage. On his stomach, move your hands clockwise around his bellybutton (this is the direction the large intestine turns). (Caution: Don't massage his stomach until his umbilical cord falls off and there is no redness in the area.) You can even do a gentle face massage, making small circles with your fingers around your baby's cheeks, stroking behind the ears, and smoothing his forehead from the center outward.

You don't need to know any fancy massage moves—slow, gentle stroking is really all it takes. If you want a few advanced moves, try:

- Milking—Gently tighten your hand around his leg as you pull down toward his foot.
- Criss-cross—Put one hand on each of his shoulders, stroke one hand down toward his opposite hip, and repeat with the other hand. Then reverse this motion and go back up to the shoulders.
- Rock-a-bye—Put your hands gently on his stomach and rock him from side to side.
- Bread dough—Hold his arm between your two palms and roll it back and forth.
- This little piggy—Rotate each toe on your baby's foot, then gently massage the sole of the foot with your thumbs.

Dexterity Begins

At eight or nine months your baby will begin to use his fingers and thumbs separately, developing the pincer grasp (thumb and forefinger). He can be happily entertained for long stretches (long in baby time, anyway), trying to pick up Cheerios and put them into his mouth. At this stage he'll begin to feel things by rubbing them between his thumb and forefinger. Try making a toy for the car by securely sewing scraps of different types of fabric—silk, velvet, corduroy, lace—together.

He also will want to poke his index finger into things. A set of wooden rings, meant to be stacked on a rod, can be fascinating to a baby—they can hook their fingers through one in each hand and carry them as they crawl.

Soon after this stage your baby will start to learn how to let go of things ("testing gravity"). You'll first notice it in the highchair, as your baby deliberately drops things off the side and expects you to pick them up—again and again and again. He acts like it's a game, and it is. If you don't want him playing it with his food, give him other opportunities to practice with beanbags, balls, or blocks. (Place a basket under his highchair and encourage him to drop the toys in it—it will make cleanup easier.)

By nine months or so, your baby may be ready to start scribbling. Readiness for this game doesn't hinge so much on whether your baby can hold a fat crayon or chalk and use it to make marks on paper, but on whether or not he still insists on eating the crayon or chalk. Try white chalk on black paper; it takes a lot less pressure to get a piece of chalk to make a mark than it does a crayon, and white chalk is about as mess-free as it gets. (If you want to save these first scribbles, spray the paper with hair spray; just don't do the spraying anywhere near your baby.)

Pump It Up

Get double duty from playtime. Your baby should have plenty of opportunities to kick on his back (you can hold a beach ball over him and encourage him to kick it). In fact the more time he has on the floor, in all positions, the better. Unlike car seats, swings, and infant carriers, when he's on the floor he's in charge of how he moves.

Tummy time is important from the beginning. A newborn placed on his stomach will try to lift and turn his head. He'll do little pushups and, as the months go by and his muscles develop, rock up onto his knees. Eventually, tummy time typically turns into crawling.

When your baby is awake and ready to play, you don't always need to recline him in an infant chair or lay him down on his back. The AAP recommends that babies spend some time every day on their tummies, with an adult nearby.

If you have a quilt (not a fluffy comforter, but a cotton quilt that easily lies flat), use it for tummy time. A bare floor is too hard, and a carpet sheds fibers that end up being inhaled and swallowed. Lie down face-to-face with your baby, or put some toys in front of him to encourage him to pick his head up and look around.

Once your baby is crawling, use a bunch of couch cushions to create an obstacle course that he'll crawl around or over. Scatter a few toys around the room a short crawl from your baby. Give him things that scoot out of his reach and beg to be chased—balls or light toys on wheels. Get down on your hands and knees and let him chase you, and then chase him back.

Bicycle your baby's legs from the time he is an infant. Initially, you'll do all the work, but after a few months he'll push against your hands as you move his feet. Eventually, the two of you can bicycle side by side.

Let him jump. Hold him under his arms and with the soles of his feet on your lap, lower him to bend his knees, and then lift him up into the air. Pretty soon he'll bend and straighten his legs himself. He'll technically be jumping, though you'll support much of his weight. When he is four months old or so, he can start jumping in a spring-loaded baby seat that hangs from a door-frame—adjust it so he can touch the floor lightly with his legs. He may just hang there the first few times you try it, but in a few days will push himself up and down.

By the Numbers

No milestone chart can tell you what your baby will, or should, be doing at a particular age. Indeed, child development experts differ in their opinions of when milestones can occur, and those opinions change. Most babies do roll over between four and six months of age. Less than ten years ago more rolled over in the earlier part of that range than today. Today's babies sleep more on their backs and get less practice pushing up on their arms and lifting their torsos than the stomach-sleepers of the past.

Hitting a single milestone late or early doesn't mean much in the grand scheme of things. It doesn't correlate with intelligence and rarely indicates a problem, although falling behind normal ranges in many milestones may indicate that something is up and you should consult your pediatrician.

ALERT

Tell your doctor if: Your baby consistently falls outside the normal milestone ranges; doesn't seem to use one side of her body; doesn't react to loud noises; doesn't react to bright light; or doesn't realize the difference between familiar people and strangers by ten months.

Slower development may simply be a sign of your child's personality. Some children have more cautious personalities than others, and some learn by watching rather than doing. A doer may walk sooner but take a lot of spills, while a watcher may walk later with hardly a wobble. Your baby may hit a milestone sooner if she's around slightly older babies—there's nothing like peer pressure to get a kid motivated. Don't obsess about whether or not your baby is on some expert's schedule. The only schedule she's likely to be following is her own. Be sure to applaud her every step of the way regardless—babies thrive on enthusiastic audiences.

The Motor Skills Milestones

The first voluntary muscle movement a baby usually makes is turning his head. The head turn, which you'll usually see in your baby's first few weeks, develops the neck muscles and starts the progression of muscle movements that several months down the line will allow your baby to flip over.

To encourage your baby's attempt at a side-to-side head turn, lie down next to him until he looks at you. Then jump up and run around him, and lie down on his other side until he looks your way again. This move is great for getting parents in shape, but put a toy or a mirror on one side of him and switch its position if it's too much for you these days.

After the head turn comes the mini push-up, a move that takes a little bit of shoulder muscle to pull off. In the mini-push up, which your baby will probably conquer between the ages of two and four months, he uses his arms to lift his shoulders and chest (but not that big baby belly) off of the ground. He may be late reaching this milestone if he spends a lot of time on his back or sitting in an infant seat. For push-up practice, put him on his belly on the floor and hold a toy in front of and slightly above his head so he lifts himself up for a good look.

▼ **MOTOR MILESTONES**

Age	Milestone	Age	Milestone
Birth–1 month	side-to-side head turn	3–7 months	grasps objects
2–4 months	mini-push-up	5–9 months	sits unsupported
2–5 months	swipes at object	6–12 months	crawls (or somehow travels on four limbs)
2–5 months	brings both hands together	7–13 months	pulls up to a stand
3–7 months	rolls over	8–16 months	walks

The Swipe and Grab

Two early motor milestones that seem simple actually require developmental prowess to achieve: the swipe and the grab. You'll usually see these between the ages of two and five months. To perform both the swipe and grab your baby needs to overcome one reflex he was born with: the tonic neck reflex. This reflex puts his arms in a fencing position—one arm extended, the other arm bent—whenever he is placed on his back with his head to one side. He can't get control of his hands until he can suppress this reflex and get both hands in front of him. Then he'll need to recognize his hands as something he can control and bring toward other objects he can see.

To encourage him to swipe, use a baby gym. These are available for cribs, floor play, and infant seats. To encourage him to bring both hands together in a baby version of a clap, sit him in his baby chair and play pattycake, clapping the rhyme with your own hands and then with his.

The next obvious step after batting at objects is grabbing them, and babies usually reach this milestone between three and five months. To voluntarily grab something, your baby needs to override the grasp reflex that makes him close his hands tightly whenever something touches his palms.

ALERT

Never throw your baby into the air and catch him. Doing this repeatedly can cause Shaken Baby Syndrome—a bleeding in the brain that can cause permanent damage.

Roll Over

The roll is not only a very noticeable milestone, but for many babies is their first attempt at independent motion. You'll see it sometime between three to seven months. A baby that spends a lot of time on his stomach may roll sooner rather than later, using the front-to-back roll. This is a fairly simple movement compared to the back-to-front roll. Babies who spend most of their days on their backs will likely roll later and start with the back-to-front roll. Once your baby masters both rolls, you may be surprised one afternoon when you put him down in the middle of the rug for a little playtime, leave the room for half a minute, and come back to find him hiding under the coffee table.

To encourage your baby to roll make sure he gets plenty of tummy time. If he's willing, roll him across the room like a rolling pin. You can also use a pillow or rolled blanket to prop your baby on his side, lie down on his other side, and tempt him to reach for you or a toy you're holding. If he stretches his arm out enough, he probably will topple over. The roll will impress friends and grandparents, but will make your life a little more difficult since you'll no longer be able to count on your baby staying where you put him.

Sit!

The sit, which appears at an average of five to nine months and may arrive before or after the roll, will make your life a lot easier. A sitting baby has free hands and can entertain himself by picking up and dropping toys while you entertain yourself by, oh, doing laundry or putting away dishes. (When you've had to do both with a baby on your hip for six months or so, it is a thrill to do them with both arms free.)

For sitting practice, surround him with pillows for him to keep his balance. Stay close by, as he'll tip over and need rescuing regularly. Or sit behind him, with him leaning back against you, and use his hands to pull him gently up into a sitting position.

On the Move

The next big milestone for your baby, and a major life change for you, is the crawl. It's followed by one of the biggest milestones, walking. While a rolling baby can travel only a few yards at a time, a crawling baby can go just about anywhere—and doesn't like to be stopped.

Crawling Along

This is the time to start serious childproofing. Start out by getting down on your hands and knees and crawling around the room, thinking about what might hurt your baby. You'll see electrical outlets, tangles of cords, sharp corners of tables, the door to the broiler, knickknacks on the bookshelf, and oven cleaner under the sink. You may see upholstery nails sticking out of the underside of a chair, or tacks coming loose from under a couch.

Your baby may scoot about in a sitting position, creep or "commando crawl" (move around on her stomach, using her hands, elbows, knees, and feet for propulsion, looking like a soldier scurrying under barbed wire), or "elephant walk" (move around on all fours, but support herself on her feet instead of her knees). Not all babies do an official hand-and-knee crawl, and the fear that a failure to crawl means reading difficulties later on has been put to rest.

Your baby may skip the crawling stage altogether and focus on learning to walk upright. In fact, this is becoming more common, with an increasing number of babies going directly from sitting to walking because they spend so little time on their stomachs. There seems to be no medical consequence to this change.

If you want to encourage your baby to crawl, put her in soft, long pants to make crawling comfortable (she'll just get tangled in dresses or loose, long pants) and give her a beach ball or wheeled toy that easily rolls out of reach.

Upstanding Citizen

Once your baby starts pulling herself upright, she'll be pulling up on every object in sight, even at night. Sometimes even babies who are great sleepers have a spate of interrupted nights when, barely half-awake, they pull up in their cribs and discover they don't know how to get down. This is the time to lower the crib mattress down to the lowest rung in the crib frame so that your baby doesn't tumble out when she stands up and bends over the railing.

Once your baby starts pulling up, begin teaching her how to bend her knees and sit down again. Standing supported, a skill your baby will probably demonstrate between the ages of seven to thirteen months, takes the development of the muscles around her joints, general muscle strength in her legs and arms, some coordination, and a sense of balance.

To help your baby in her standing attempts, keep her barefoot as much as possible: she'll be more confident about standing if she can feel the floor. Forget about shoes. Your baby doesn't need them to support her feet, and they get in the way rather than help when she's starting to stand and walk.

If it's cold, put her in well-fitting socks with non-skid bottoms. Thick carpeting may give her trouble (even though it reassures you about falls), so let her practice on wood or linoleum floors. Make sure she has plenty of solid, safe objects to pull up on. (You might temporarily replace your glass-topped coffee table with an ottoman) Play games with her—start with her on her back, hold her hands, and slowly pull her to a stand.

Don't put your baby in a walker. It won't make her learn to walk faster, and some studies show that it may delay independent walking. Walkers, even newer models, pose a significant safety hazard, especially around steps. In fact, The AAP recommended that the U.S. government ban wheeled walkers. Instead, consider a stationary activity center. These devices resemble traditional walkers, but their lack of wheels makes them much safer. You want one that has a solid frame, no accessible sharp edges or sharp hardware underneath or on top, and comfortable, soft fabric edging on the sides and legs of the seat cushions. Take your baby to the store to "test drive" different models.

Walk This Way

After standing comes walking, and this usually occurs at eight to sixteen months. Heavy babies may fall to the late end of that spectrum, while adventurous babies may walk on the early side. The level of parental protectiveness plays a role, so try to rein in your fears. Early walkers may fall more often than their later-walking peers, but are unlikely to get seriously injured.

QUESTION

What if my baby's walking funny?
The duck-walk (legs spread wide apart and toes turned out like a duck) helps a shaky walker keep his balance. Most babies are naturally pigeon-toed, and some have shins or thighs that just tilt a bit. Other babies seem to always walk on their tiptoes. Have your pediatrician check her for tight muscles if you have a tip-toeing baby, but the odds are it's simply a matter of her personal style.

To encourage your baby to walk, simply move just out of reach, hold out your arms, and call her toward you. Some babies learn to walk by wheeling push-toys around. If you think all your baby needs is a little confidence, hand her a toy when she is standing. She may think that she is holding on to something supportive and take a step.

Try This

Here are some fun activities you can do with your baby to help develop his senses:

- **One month:** Place your face about a foot from your baby's face and move slowly from left to right, letting your baby's eyes track your movement.
- **Two months:** Purchase a wrist rattle. Put the rattle on your baby's hand and watch as he discovers the connection between his hand movements and the sound the bell or rattle makes.
- **Two months:** Say hello to your baby every time you enter a room. He'll recognize your voice and soon come to anticipate your arrival.
- **Four months:** Put a toy just out of your baby's reach—you may find that he can somehow wriggle or roll his way to it. (But don't make him crazy; hand it to him if he doesn't get it in fifteen seconds or so.)
- **Five months:** Whenever you're about to pick up your baby, hold out your hands and say "up." Pretty soon, he'll be reaching toward you as soon as you say the word.
- **Five months:** Draw a picture of a simple smiling face on one side of a paper plate—and a mixed-up, Picasso-esque, face on the other. Hand your child the plate; he'll quickly figure out which side he prefers to look at.
- **Six months:** Drape a blanket or cloth diaper over a favorite toy, leaving a bit of the toy peeking out. Your baby will be thrilled when he "finds" his toy.
- **Six months:** If your baby is crawling confidently, make him an obstacle course of pillows and couch cushions to crawl over and around, always under adult supervision.
- **Eight months:** Let your baby watch you as you hide a toy under a blanket for him to find.
- **Eight months:** Show your baby how to put a lid on a pot. After he masters this puzzle, give him two lids and two pots.

- **Nine months:** Put several simple but distinct toys in front of your baby. Ask him to hand you one by name. "Give Mama the ball," holding your hand out. You may be surprised that he gets it right.
- **Ten months:** Hand your baby a toy for each hand. Then hold out a third toy to him and see what he does. Will he try to somehow hold all three toys, or drop one of the two in order to pick up the third?
- **Twelve months:** If your baby is walking, give him a barefoot tour of different surfaces such as carpet, floor, grass, and sand.

CHAPTER 17

Childproofing and Safety

In addition to coughs, sniffles, and sneezes, you'll also have to deal with the bumps and bruises your baby will encounter in spite of your best efforts. Certainly she'll increase her exposure once she's mobile, but even infants can get bumped, burned, or scratched. You'll find a hundred things to do to childproof your home, and your baby will probably find a hundred more things to get into. Prevent what you can, and know how to treat the rest.

First Things First

Before you buy a lot of childproofing gear, do the simple things. If you don't want your books all over the floor, replace the books on the lower shelves with your baby's books or stuff extra books in each row until they're jammed in too tight to move. Gather up any poisonous items, from detergent to vitamins, and put them on your highest shelves (locking a cabinet works only if you always close the lock). Knot looped blind cords up out of reach.

If you have glass-topped coffee tables, put them away. Put away your tablecloth and invest in a set of place mats. If you sew, put your sewing basket on a high shelf, and make sure you unplug your sewing machine and put it away every time you use it. Put your knitting needles on a high shelf, as well. Make sure you can identify all your houseplants (if you have to, take a leaf to a local garden center) and confirm that they are nontoxic. Turn your water heater down to the lowest setting if you haven't already. Put at least one trash can in a locked cabinet, and think before you throw things into accessible trash cans (avoid things like empty containers of cleaning products or used disposable razors). Make a list of the childproofing gear you need to get.

The most important childproofing element, however, is adult supervision. Babies are curious and inventive. Despite all the childproofing gear, they can get themselves into trouble, fast. The bottom line is that you need to childproof your house so they can explore, but you also need to keep a watchful eye on your little one and never leave her alone in a room for an extended period of time.

ESSENTIAL

Don't childproof absolutely everything in every room. Remove the hazards, but leave a few things out that would be inconvenient (a torn magazine cover, for example) but not disastrous if your baby got into them. Use them as tools to teach your baby that some things are okay for her to play with and some things are not. You don't want to make your baby crazy by telling her "No, No, No" all day, but she needs to understand the concept or you won't be able to take her out much.

The stairs will probably need to be gated, as will any rooms that you plan to keep off-limits. Gates that screw into the walls are better than pressure gates, particularly at the top of the stairs. (You don't want a pressure gate giving way when your baby flings herself against it—and she will.)

You'll probably also want to get outlet covers, either caps for unused outlets or covers that block access to the plug for outlets you use frequently. You don't need cord shorteners or guards—just use twist ties and wide masking tape. (Buy the more expensive type that is less likely to damage your paint.) If your child is tall enough to reach the doorknobs, consider installing a chain or latch, high out of reach, on the doors that lead outside.

Basic Childproofing

FOR CRAWLERS:

- Cover electrical outlets.
- Remove or block access to furniture that is easily tipped over (like floor lamps).
- Move breakables or other dangerous knickknacks out of reach.
- Regularly hunt for dropped coins or other potential choking hazards.
- Hide, coil, cover, or block access to electrical cords.
- Knot blind cords out of reach, or cut through loop and shorten strings.
- Gate stairs.
- Don't put your baby in a walker, but if you do, never use a walker around stairs.
- Make sure your pool, if you have one, is solidly fenced and the gate is kept closed and locked. Hot tubs should be kept closed and locked when not in use, and toilets should be locked. Don't even leave a pail of water unattended.
- Cede the lower shelves of your bookcases to your child; move your books out of reach, and restock shelves with baby books.

ADDITIONAL CHILDPROOFING FOR CRUISERS AND WALKERS:

- Install window guards.
- Lock kitchen cabinets and drawers that contain anything dangerous (knives, etc.).

- Turn pot handles toward the back of the stove when cooking.
- Make sure bookcases will not topple over.
- Secure the TV so it won't fall if tugged on or pushed.

Your Shopping List

Whether or not you need these items depends on the layout of your home and your childproofing decisions. For example, do you want to latch your kitchen cabinets, or do you want to rearrange the contents so that all hazardous and breakable items are stowed high out of reach with only child-safe items (pots and pans, Tupperware) in the lower cabinets?

- Outlet covers or caps
- Gates
- Drawer and cabinet latches
- Toilet locks
- Foam strips or corners for table edges
- Window guards
- Window latches
- Oven locks
- Doorknob covers
- Stove knob covers
- Bathtub faucet covers

So, You Think It's Safe . . .

When you think you've thought of everything, watch your child to see what hazards she discovers. Is she fascinated by the oven door? You may have to strap it closed. Does she like to throw toys in the toilet? You may want a toilet lock, but since these are difficult for older siblings or uniniti-ated guests to operate you may prefer just to keep the bathroom door shut. Is she climbing the bookshelves? Make sure they are bolted to the wall. Some babies simply require more childproofing than others. You'll soon discover what kind of adventurer lives at your house.

▼ **TOP TEN HOUSEHOLD DANGERS**

10.	Poisonous plants
9.	Venetian blind cords
8.	Electrical cords
7.	Electrical outlets
6.	Stoves, heaters, and other hot appliances
5.	Poisonous household products
4.	Medicine
3.	Water (even water in a bucket used to mop the floor is a hazard)
2.	Coins or other small objects (choking hazard)
1.	Stairs

Poisonous Plants

The following plants can cause severe poisoning (this is not a complete listing):

- Avocado leaves
- Larkspur
- Azalea
- Mistletoe
- English ivy
- Nightshade
- Foxglove
- Oleander
- Hemlock
- Rhododendron
- Hydrangea
- Sweet pea

The following plants cause uncomfortable, though usually not life-threatening, reactions (this is not a complete listing):

- Calla lily
- Philodendron
- Daffodil bulb
- Poinsettia

- Dieffenbachia
- Tomato leaves
- Holly
- Wisteria
- Hyacinth
- Yellow jasmine
- Iris
- Yew
- Laurel

Warning! Lead Paint

Lead can be toxic to people of any age, but is particularly dangerous to young children. It damages the central nervous system, kidneys, and other organs and causes developmental delays, learning disabilities, and even permanent brain damage.

If your home was built before 1978, it may have been painted on the interior or exterior with lead-containing paint. On the interior, it may have several coats of safe paint over it, but it may chip (if, for example, your toddler rams her toy truck into a baseboard) or flake (as often happens when windows are raised and lowered). You may consider chemically stripping window areas, and putting an extra coat of paint on areas that may chip. If the exterior was painted using lead-based paint, lead can seep into the surrounding ground. Have the soil tested before you let your child play in the dirt (and before you decide to plant a vegetable garden). Think twice about doing any renovation that disturbs old paint.

Lead can also be present in old pipes and can leech into the water (the local water department, upon request, may be willing to test your water free of charge; inexpensive test kits are also available). Also check certain brands of plastic blinds, ceramic dishes, and even some toys manufactured outside the United States. (Test these items with lead-check swabs, available at most hardware stores.)

Childproofing on the Go

Once your baby is crawling, you'll need to make sure that anyplace you visit with him is safe and, when necessary, make temporary childproofing changes. You'll need to be on high alert when you visit other homes and hotels since they haven't been custom-childproofed to protect against your infant's specific habits.

Before you put your baby down on the floor to start exploring:

- Check for exposed electrical sockets.
- Move out of reach any breakable objects from coffee tables and bookshelves.
- Check for sharp corners on tables and wobbly furniture or lamps and move if necessary.
- Close sliding doors and open windows, and never allow your baby on a balcony unless there is constant adult supervision.
- Close the door to any bathrooms, ask if there are any dangers in lower kitchen cabinets, and, if necessary, temporarily lock with twist-ties or rubber bands.

ALERT

Keep in mind that houseguests may not be as aware of childproofing as you are. Remind them to keep jewelry, makeup bags, shaving kits, and medications out of your baby's reach. Elderly relatives, in particular, may not keep their medication in childproof containers.

Childproofing for the Holidays

Holiday decorations are bright, colorful, and often sparkly and dangly—all perfect to engage your child's curiosity. So go ahead and decorate for the holidays, but make sure that you also make it safe for your baby. You'll need to be on high alert during the holiday season.

- Put a baby-gate around the Christmas tree to keep your baby from getting too close and trying to pull off any ornaments or use a branch to pull herself up to stand.

- If you don't close off the tree, don't put any ornaments or lights on lower branches and put breakable, precious ornaments on higher branches.
- Don't put nuts or hard candies within reach on a coffee or side table. Choking is a major hazard for small children.
- Place candles and Menorahs out of reach to avoid burns or tipping over.
- Don't put any holiday greenery, especially those with berries like poinsettias and holly, within reach of little fingers. Much of it is poisonous if swallowed.
- Make sure your fireplace is properly screened and never leave a baby alone in a room where there has recently been a fire. Ashes can burn if touched.
- Check your tinsel—older versions were made with lead and shouldn't be used.
- Make sure that any alcoholic drinks are kept at adult height. Even a small amount of alcohol can be toxic if sipped by a baby.

Pets and Your Baby

Just like human siblings, your pets need to adjust to a new baby in the house. Having a pet is a wonderful experience for children, but you want to keep both your infant and your pet safe. Here are some tips to ease the transition.

- Make sure your pet's vaccinations are up-to-date and his nails are trimmed.
- Address any pet behavioral problems *before* your baby is born. You won't have the time or patience to deal with them in the first few months after your baby comes home. Lovingly, but firmly, practice training techniques so that you can control your dog or cat's behavior.
- If the baby's room is to be off-limits, install a gate or even a screen door (before the baby comes home). Be consistent in training the animal not to enter the room.

- While you are holding the baby, let your pet sniff him and become accustomed to the new smells. Reward your pet with treats for appropriate behavior.
- As your baby gets older, teach him how to treat and play with the pet safely and appropriately. Use words to describe what you want your baby to do ("let's pet the dog softly on her back; "can you throw the ball for the kitty?"). You will need to teach your child how to be gentle and kind to an animal.
- If your pet exhibits any aggressive behavior, consult your veterinarian or an animal behaviorist for techniques to handle the problem.

First Aid

As the parent of a small child, you'll be administering a lot of first aid—particularly once your child is getting around on her own. You can minimize hazards by childproofing, but your baby will still get her fair share of "owies" the first year.

The First Aid Kit

Once your baby becomes mobile, you'll be patching up scrapes and bumps, pulling out splinters, and administering other forms of first aid. You'll need:

- First aid manual
- Telephone number for Poison Control
- Sterile gauze
- Steristrips or butterfly bandages
- Soap
- Adhesive strip bandages (Band-Aids)
- Adhesive tape
- Antiseptic wipes
- Elastic bandage
- Papain (this natural meat tenderizer soothes bee stings)
- Antibiotic ointment such as Bacitracin
- Hydrocortisone cream

- Tweezers
- Old credit card (to scrape bee stings)
- Calamine lotion
- Cold packs (instant, or keep one in the freezer; use a bag of frozen vegetables in a pinch)
- Cotton balls
- Scissors

ESSENTIAL

When your baby does get hurt, how you react will influence her reaction. If you are matter-of-fact about the injury ("Oh, you scraped your knee. Come on, let's get a bandage"), administering first aid will be a lot easier for both of you.

Common Injuries and Treatment

The following are some common childhood injuries and simple treatments. Don't hesitate to call your doctor if you feel like the injury is more serious or should be examined.

- **Burns:** Soak the burned area in cool water for at least twenty minutes or until the pain fades. You can hold the burn under cold running water or put ice and cold water in a bowl. Don't use ice alone; it can increase the damage to the skin. Do not put butter or other greases on a burn—they'll trap the heat and make it worse. Simply cover any blisters that develop with a bandage, but don't pop them. Redness and slight swelling are signs of a first-degree burn (the least serious); blistering and significant swelling indicate a second-degree burn; areas that seem white or charred indicate a third-degree burn. If you suspect a second or third degree burn, see a doctor immediately.
- **Poison ingestion:** Take away the poisonous substance, if your child is still holding any, and remove any left in her mouth with your fingers. Keep anything that you remove for later analysis. Check for severe throat irritation, drooling, breathing problems, sleepiness, or convulsions. If you see any of these symptoms, call an ambulance. If not, call your local poison control center.

- **Tick bite:** The faster you get the tick off, the less likely your baby is to get a tick-borne disease. Clean the area with alcohol if it's available, water if it's not. If you have nothing to clean with, skip this step. Pull the tick straight up from the skin using your fingers (tweezers are more likely to break the tick, leaving part embedded). Save the tick in case you need to bring it to a doctor. Mark the area, but not the bite, with a pen, and watch that skin for a few days for a bull's-eye-shaped rash. This rash may indicate Lyme disease, for which your baby will be treated with antibiotics. Depending where you live, you should also watch for signs of Rocky Mountain Spotted Fever (rash on hands and soles of feet, fever).

- **Sand in the eye:** Try to keep your baby from rubbing her eye, but otherwise do nothing, as tears will usually wash out the sand. If not, you can help them by washing the eye with water. If nothing you do seems to work, call your doctor.

- **Bee stings:** If the stinger is visible, try to remove it by scraping across the skin with a credit card. Do not squeeze it. Wash the area with soap and water and apply an ice pack to reduce swelling. You can also counteract some of the effects of the venom by sprinkling it with meat tenderizer (unless it is near the eye) or spreading a paste of baking soda and. water on it. If your baby has a severe reaction—swelling that extends far beyond the site of the sting, a rapid heartbeat, clammy skin, hives, or trouble breathing, call 911. Talk to your doctor once the initial crisis of a severe reaction has passed. Although rare, if your child does have an allergy to bee stings you will need to carry a bee sting kit that includes an epinephrine shot that will dilate the airways and allow your baby to breathe.

- **Sunburn:** If you're like most parents, your first reaction to your baby's sunburn will be guilt. "Oh, how can I have forgotten to put lotion on? Why did we stay at the park all afternoon? Why didn't I go home when I realized I forgot her hat?" After you're done beating yourself up about this, give your baby a bath in cool water or soak some washcloths in water and lay them over the burned area. After she's dry, spread aloe (100 percent) on the burned area.

  You can also soak your baby in a lukewarm bath with either a quarter cup of baking soda or a cup of comfrey tea (comfrey reduces swelling). Give her some ibuprofen. If the sunburn blisters, if your baby gets a fever or chills, or if she seems very sick, call the doctor.

- **Cuts:** Stop the bleeding by applying pressure directly to the cut. If the cut "smiles" (the edges gap apart farther in the middle than on the ends), is deep, or may have dirt or glass stuck inside, see a doctor. Otherwise, wash it thoroughly with soap and water, apply an antibiotic ointment, and put on a bandage. If the cut isn't particularly deep or long, it will probably stay closed on its own. Or you can bring the edges together and fasten with a butterfly bandage or steristrip before covering it with a regular bandage.

- **Splinters:** Wash the area with soap and water. If the splinter protrudes, stick a piece of tape over it and pull the tape off—the splinter may come off with the tape. Still stuck? Move on to the tweezers. If the splinter is embedded, soak the area for ten minutes, wipe with an antiseptic, then numb the skin with ice or a local anesthetic intended for teething—like baby Orajel or Anbesol. Sterilize a sewing needle by holding it in a flame for a few seconds (make sure to wipe off any carbon on the needle) or dipping it in alcohol. Then gently, using the tip of the needle, try to tease the splinter out. If it's still stuck, try again after your baby's bath. Don't poke around for more than five minutes; it's unlikely you'll remove the splinter and you may damage your baby's skin. You can also try gently rubbing the skin over the splinter with a pumice stone—if you take away a thin layer of skin, the splinter may be easier to grab. Call your doctor if it is deeply embedded, is glass or metal and you can't get it all out, or the area becomes infected.

- **Bug bites:** These are not a major deal for most babies and usually look worse than they feel. If your baby seems itchy, put an icepack, cortisone cream, or a paste of baking soda and water on the bite. If the itching doesn't seem to stop or the area keeps swelling, call your doctor, who may prescribe an antihistamine.

- **Scrapes:** Run cold water over the scrape and wash it with soap. Pat it dry with a clean cloth, dab with antiseptic cream, and bandage. Go to the doctor if the scrape is deep, bleeding heavily, embedded with gravel or dirt, or if later you see increasing redness or pus.

- **Choking:** First give your baby a chance to cough and clear her throat herself. If she can't breathe, dial 911 and then place her face down on your arm or lap so that her head is lower than her torso. Support her head and neck. Using the heel of your hand, give five quick thrusts between the shoulder blades. If she's still not breathing, lay her on the floor on her back and, using two fingers, press quickly along the breastbone five times. Keep repeating these two moves. *Do not* use the Heimlich maneuver; a baby's bones and organs are too fragile for this procedure.

ALERT

Do not use baby wipes to clean a cut. They sting and can be irritating to the damaged tissues.

The ER

Sometimes a kiss, a bandage, and an ice pack aren't enough. The following injuries may require immediate medical attention:

- Head injuries:
  - Bleeding that won't stop after ten minutes of direct pressure.
  - Crying for more than ten minutes after he has hit his head
  - A severe fall (down a stairway, for example)
  - He has a seizure
  - He was unconscious, no matter how briefly
  - He vomits afterward
  - His pupils are unequal in size
  - His eyes are crossed
- Cuts: Very deep or present a "smile" (the skin edges in the center of the cut are farther apart than on the ends)
- Burns: blisters, significantly swells, or has white patches or charring

If you take your child to the emergency room, follow these steps to get the help you need.

- **Stay calm.** Your child will pick up on your emotions and may become more upset if he sees you panicking. You need to move quickly, deliberately, rationally. Be sure to take your health insurance card with you. Also take your child's lovey, some books to read, and a quiet toy. Unless your child's injuries or illness is life-threatening there is usually a wait to be seen. Organize in your mind the history of the illness/injury, any pertinent previous illness, and what treatment you've already administered.
- **Choose a child-friendly ER if possible**. Children's hospitals have pediatric specialists available 24/7. Talk to your doctor before your child ever needs an ER about which hospital to use in an emergency.
- **Call your doctor before you go.** She can decide if you need to go to an ER, should come into the office, or can treat the problem at home. She can also call ahead to the ER to alert them that you are coming in.
- **Be your child's advocate.** Speak up and ask to see a doctor immediately if you feel your baby's condition is worsening. Ask questions about diagnosis and treatment and inquire if there are other options if you're not satisfied. Stay with your baby, soothe him in quiet tones.
- **Get clear discharge instructions** and follow up with your own pediatrician.

CHAPTER 18

Travels with Baby

Babies are portable. They are easy to carry, will sleep just about anywhere, and don't beg to stop at McDonald's. Take advantage of it while you can by taking your baby on the road. Go out every day; your baby will thrive on exposure to new sights, sounds, and smells, and you'll keep yourself from going nuts. Go wherever you think your baby might enjoy the new experience. You won't be this mobile again for years to come.

Getting Around Town

Babies don't much care where they're going when they go out, but moms tend to feel a little aimless without a destination. Stores are great places to take babies. Grocery stores, furniture stores, and book stores are all filled with brightly colored objects of various shapes, and people who love to smile at babies. Doors designed for wheelchair access are also stroller-friendly.

Stores and Malls

Go grocery shopping. Your infant car seat may be designed to clip safely to the seat of a shopping cart, or place it inside. Perhaps your local grocery store has special carts with built-in infant seats. (You may want to clean it with a baby wipe.) You can also shop with your baby in a front pack or sling or, if you're only purchasing a few things, leave her in her stroller.

ALERT

Stay away from clothing stores with narrow aisles and tightly packed racks. Your baby will end up with her face shoved into a bunch of clothes, breathing chemicals like formaldehyde (used to protect the fabric), gnawing on sharp-edged tags, and probably drooling on something you can't throw in the washer.

Grocery stores often give free helium balloons to children. Tie it to the car seat, cart, or stroller for instant baby entertainment. If your baby is eating finger foods, try the free samples, or ask for a slice of a soft fruit.

Go to the mall, either indoor or outdoor. Talk to your baby about all the things you see. Admire the fountains and window shop (you don't have to actually buy anything).

See the Sights

Consider a day at a museum. Call ahead and confirm that the museum you are considering visiting allows a baby backpack or a stroller. (Some don't at all, some do on certain days.) Front-carriers and slings can pretty much go anywhere. When your baby is ready to eat, pick a bench in front of a painting you really like; if you're nursing, switch paintings when you switch breasts.

Be a tourist in your hometown. Big or small, your town probably has some tourist destinations locals are usually too busy to visit. If you live in a city, you probably already have your favorite spots to take visitors. Revisit them, and discover a few more.

Gear Up for Traveling

Just as you prepared your home for an infant, travels with baby require very specific equipment. Do some research. Ask other new moms or your pediatrician for their recommendations.

The Equipment

- **Car seat:** Car seat models expire after six years, and technology is constantly changing. Make sure yours is up to date. Today's front-facing car seats include tether straps that attach to anchors that have been installed in all new vehicles since the model year 2001.
- **Stroller:** Strollers for infants should fully recline. If yours doesn't, borrow one that does or use a Snap-N-Go (a metal frame that converts your car seat into a stroller) until your baby can sit upright without slumping.
- **Jogging or off-road stroller:** This is a luxury item unless you're a regular runner, but they are far easier to push on and off sidewalks when you're out for a long walk.
- **Rain cover for your stroller**
- **Sling and/or front carrier**
- **Baby backpack:** Once your baby can sit supported, these are better for long walks with a heavy baby than a frontpack.
- **Diaper bag or diaper backpack**
- **Portable crib or play yard:** Hotels (and sometimes grandparents) will often supply cribs upon request, but these aren't usually in the best condition. If you use one, measure the slats—they shouldn't be more than 2⅜ inches apart. The Graco Pack and Play is a good investment for traveling as it's a crib, bassinet, and play yard in one.

- **Portable highchair:** If your baby is eating finger foods, a highchair will make mealtimes a lot more pleasant for everyone. A clip-on highchair can fit in the bottom of a big duffel bag.
- **Bike seat** or Burley (bike trailer) and helmet

The Accessories

The more comprehensive your diaper bag, the less you'll end up buying on the road. Use your judgment, however. If the majority of your trips are to run errands or pick up older siblings, you may not need everything on this list. Pack the less-used items in a separate bag to keep with you for day trips and overnights. Prepack in advance to prevent last-minute rushing—that's when you forget the essentials.

- Diapers (at least four)
- A refillable pack of baby wipes
- Diaper rash ointment
- Plastic bags
- Light blanket (to cover your baby or use as a play mat)
- Waterproof changing pad or rubberized sheet
- Cloth diaper (for burping and general cleanup)
- Sunscreen (for babies over six months)
- Bottles and formula, unless you're nursing exclusively
- Food for your older baby (Cheerios, etc.)
- A snack for yourself
- Water bottle (for Mom to drink and for cleanups)
- A change of clothes for your baby
- An extra shirt for yourself
- A stain remover stick
- Travel pack of tissues
- A few toys or rattles
- Paperback book or magazine for Mom

Dining Out

Take yourself out to lunch, breakfast, or dinner as often as you can when your baby is in the "luggage" stage (i.e., you can set him down anywhere and he doesn't move). Until your baby is eating solids, you don't even have to worry about selecting a child-friendly restaurant. You actually can eat at a restaurant that has tablecloths (but go early, it'll be less crazy and more fun). Become a regular at a favorite restaurant; you may find your baby "adopted" by the staff who greet him by name. If your baby is sleeping in his car seat, you may be able to safely tuck him under the table for a while. If your baby is hungry and you're nursing, toss a napkin over your shoulder and settle him in to feed; just order a meal that's not too hard to eat with one hand—avoid hot soup or coffee.

Choose a Child-Friendly Restaurant

Once your child can join you in a meal, pick a restaurant that caters to families. If your child is noisy, the other diners won't care as much since you won't be interrupting romantic dates. The restaurant staff will be used to spills, and the other children around will entertain your baby.

FACT

How do you know you've found a kid-friendly restaurant? Well, if your entrance went unremarked by the other diners seated at tables and they didn't turn around and stare, the host or hostess doesn't look panicked when you struggle in, loaded down with baby and gear, it's just noisy enough so you can't hear a spoon drop, the hostess automatically picks up coloring sheets and crayons before leading you to your table, and more than one highchair is stacked in plain view, you've found one.

Other dining tips:

- Bring Cheerios or other finger foods, and dole them out slowly.
- Bring a few small toys in case the finger foods lose their appeal.
- Place your order as quickly as you can, and ask for the check when the food arrives (you may make it through dinner with a contented baby, only to have him melt down during a long wait for the bill).

- Forget about coffee and dessert—if you make it through a salad and main course, consider yourself lucky.
- Tip as heavily as you can; you'll be remembered for that, instead of the mess you left in your wake.

Feeding an Older Baby

If you didn't pack dinner for your older baby, take a creative look at the menu. Do entrees come with vegetables? Maybe you can get a side order of steamed vegetables and cut them small or mash them. (It may take the kitchen two tries to cook the vegetables soft enough for a baby.) Are there eggs on the menu? Ask for scrambled eggs, yolks only. Is there a salad bar? Scavenge it for soft fruits and vegetables you can cut into bite-sized pieces. Are you in an Asian restaurant? Request a dish of cold tofu with a dash of soy sauce. In an Italian restaurant, try a dish of polenta or risotto. And most chefs can quickly prepare a dish of plain pasta.

Two Thumbs Up

Go to the movies. Catch an afternoon matinee, when the theaters are nearly empty, or an evening show on a weeknight. Pick an aisle seat in case you need to bolt—but the odds are that you won't. Theaters are dark, and your baby is likely to go to sleep after nursing or drinking a bottle. If not, she may kick back and watch the show. Or bring quiet cloth toys and teethers (leave the rattles at home). This is not, however, the time to pick an action movie that amplifies tire squeals and gunshots in full digital surround sound. Go for a chick flick—lots of dialog and close-ups of faces (which babies love).

Theaters in some towns even encourage parents to bring babies at special showings where fussing is allowed.

Hit the Trail

If you like to hike, you don't have to give it up now. If you never were a hiker, this may be the time to start (but begin with short, easy trails). Stay out of constant sun (don't forget your baby's hat), and avoid trails with low branches. Use a front pack until your baby is too heavy for one and then switch to a backpack.

You can also just walk around town. Admire your neighbors' gardens and get to know the neighborhood pets by name. Don't limit your walks to balmy spring days. Try rain walks. If your baby is in a frontpack, sling, or backpack, an umbrella will protect both of you and your baby will be fascinated by the sound and smell of rain. Go out for an evening walk and bring a flashlight for extra baby entertainment.

What about parks and playgrounds? They're a great place to meet other moms, but save them for after your baby is sitting or crawling and can take advantage of the swings and sandbox. Until then, pick outings that interest you more; you'll be getting plenty of playground time over the next few years.

ESSENTIAL

After your baby is able to hold up and control his head for extended periods of time (usually at around nine months), he's ready to experience life on a bike. Get a helmet that fits him well (make sure it has a gently rounded, not flared, back, or he won't be able to lean his head back comfortably) and a bike seat (make sure the seat keeps his feet away from the wheels) or a trailer.

Road Warrior

Some babies seem to fall asleep the minute they feel the car's motor start; others scream. The problem with car travel for some babies seems to be boredom. For a very young baby, pictures to look at may help. Prop a book or a plastic picture holder designed for the car on the seat facing your baby, or try hanging a mirror designed for crib use from the back headrest so your baby can admire herself. Company in the back seat or music also keeps your baby content. Bring toys for older babies; hook them to the car seat with plastic links or they'll all end up on the floor in minutes. Stopping to change a diaper or soothe the baby usually doesn't help, unless you're planning a long stop.

If you're going on a long trip, try to plan the trip around your baby's regular sleep schedule. Figure that she might be happily awake in the car seat for as much as an hour—but not much more. If you leave an hour before naptime, she'll be awake for an hour and fall asleep, if you're lucky, for two hours. Then stop to feed her, change her, maybe eat dinner yourself, and get her back in the car for another hour awake and hope that brings you to your destination.

If your baby is hungry, don't remove her from her car seat while the car is in motion. Stop to nurse. The best news about car travel is that children under the age of two rarely suffer from motion sickness. This particular treat may be in your future, but is not something you have to deal with right now.

Packing for Vacation

It may seem like you're moving the fifth army when you pack for vacation with a baby. Besides clothes for your baby, you'll need:

- Car seat
- Stroller
- Food for trip, including powdered formula and water, if you're bottle-feeding
- Diapers and wipes (bring enough for two days; buy the rest at your destination)
- A favorite toy
- "New" toy for trip
- Lovey, if he has one
- Portable crib, sheets, favorite blanket
- Portable highchair
- Tapes of music if you'll be traveling by car
- Baby-proofing gadgets (If your baby is crawling, baby-proof at least one room at your destination or it won't be much of a vacation for you. Bring a pack of outlet covers and a few cabinet locks.)
- Your medical insurance card and doctor's phone number
- First aid kit
- Sunscreen

If Your Baby Gets Sick

Germs and viruses unfortunately can interrupt the most carefully planned vacation. If you are traveling when your baby gets sick, you have a couple of options.

- You've got your first aid kit with you, and you may be able to treat the symptoms and continue the fun.
- You can call your pediatrician and ask for advice—and even a prescription. For example, if you're fairly certain that it's yet another ear infection, your doctor might be willing to call in a prescription for antibiotics. This is more likely if your child has had multiple ear infections and you are fairly certain that this is just another one.
- You can ask the hotel for a recommendation for a local doctor who would be willing to see your baby.
- You can take your baby to the Emergency Room at a local hospital or to a walk-in clinic.

If you are traveling abroad, plan ahead and find the name and location of a children's hospital or English-speaking hospital. You can also call the U.S. embassy and ask for advice in locating medical help and/or a translator.

The Not-So-Friendly Skies

There is nothing that instills panic in the minds of parents—as well as other passengers and flight attendants—as the thought of a baby's first airplane trip. It can be rough. Actually, it can be horrible. Your baby may scream for hours, throw up all over you, and leak through her last dry set of clothes. Or your baby may sleep the whole way and wake only as the plane is coming in for a landing.

While traveling with an infant may be rough on parents, it isn't, under normal circumstances, hazardous to the baby. There is no clear medical reason to forego air travel until an infant is a certain age, although some airlines have restrictions on travel for infants only a few days old. Unless a trip is critical, you might consider holding off until your baby is more than two months old. Airplanes tend to be germ-rich places, and it is a concern when a baby under two months old gets a fever for any reason.

To some extent, whether you spend your flight reading a novel or passing out earplugs is a matter of your baby's temperament and luck, but you can tilt the odds.

When you make your reservations, think about your child's temperament at different times of the day. If she fusses every evening and needs to be walked for hours, a late-day flight is probably not a good idea. If she typically falls asleep easily and sleeps all night, maybe you're a candidate for a red-eye. (This is a risky move, though; fellow passengers who will grin and bear it when a baby is crying on a daytime flight can get downright nasty when their sleep is interrupted by a crying baby.)

A Seat of One's Own

Purchase a seat for your baby. Unfortunately, many airlines have eliminated the reduced-priced tickets for children under two, but your baby might be severely injured if the plane hits turbulence or is in an accident and she isn't strapped in to her car seat. Yes, she can fly free (or for a small fee on international flights) if she sits on your lap, but having a guaranteed spot for your baby's car seat can make the difference between a merely stressful flight and torture. (You can put her down if she falls asleep, for one, and be able to lower your tray table and eat something yourself.)

Make sure that your car seat is FAA-approved and "certified for use in motor vehicles and aircraft."

If you do purchase a seat, make sure to reserve the window for your baby; you won't be allowed to use the car seat in any other seat, as it may block access to the aisle. You can also request a baby meal. Most airlines offer this option, which usually consists of a few jars of baby food.

Know What to Ask For

If you aren't purchasing an extra seat and are traveling with another adult or child, ask for an aisle and a window seat when you make your reservations. If you're lucky, the center seat will remain unoccupied. If not, whoever is assigned that seat will be happy to switch for your aisle or window and may, if your baby starts fussing before takeoff, look for a seat far away.

(Hint: Boarding is not the time to worry about quieting your baby; you want to clear your row.) You may have been advised to ask for a bulkhead row. This tip makes sense, but you can forget about it unless you or your traveling companion is a high-mileage flier. Most airlines award bulkhead seats to good customers, not families with kids.

Try to get a seat in the front third of the airplane. Some airplanes have been remodeled to give front passengers extra leg room, and those few inches may make the difference between whether you can wriggle down to pick up a dropped rattle or not. If the front third is booked, try for one of the last few rows. You'll be close to the bathroom and at least have some floor space to pace with your baby.

Travel Tips

- **Gate-check your stroller.** Tell the person checking boarding passes that you want a gate-check; he'll give you a special tag. Then you can push your baby all the way down the boarding ramp and unload your stroller just outside the door to the airplane. Put on the tag and leave the stroller there. It will be returned to you as you leave the airplane at your destination and will make it a lot easier to get your baby and her gear to the baggage area.
- **Bring a car seat aboard.** (Make sure that it's no wider than fifteen inches—that means it will fit in most coach seats.) You may also have to prove that your car seat is FAA-approved; if it doesn't say so on the label, it may in the instruction manual. Some infant seats will fit in the overhead compartment; if yours does and you don't have a seat reserved for your baby, stash it there as soon as you get it on the plane. You can get it down later if it turns out you have an extra seat. If it doesn't fit, and the plane is full, you'll have to ask the flight attendant to check it for you. If you are using a convertible car seat (the kind that can be strapped in the rear-facing position for infants and switched to front-facing for older children), you may have to strap it in the front-facing position to fit it on the airplane. This isn't ideal, but it's safer than your lap.
- **Bring plenty of extra formula.** Plane travel is dehydrating, and sucking will help protect your baby's ears from pressure problems. Bring plenty of water if you're using powdered formula. Since 9/11, security

rules forbid liquids in sizes over 3 ounces, but formula, breast milk, and juice *can* be brought onboard if you're with a baby. As for water, current security rules don't allow you to bring a bottle of water through the security gates, but you can buy water once you've passed them and then add it to your baby's bottle or sippy cup.

- **Preboarding.** It's easier to get yourself and your gear stowed, strapped in, and settled before hordes of anxious passengers are trying to cram past you. Unfortunately, this courtesy is offered less and less often. If there isn't an announcement, ask if you can preboard, because some airlines will respond to individual requests. If you're traveling as a solo parent with a baby, beg. Groveling is better than being trampled by impatient passengers as you are trying to stow your gear without dropping your baby.

- **Nurse or feed your baby during takeoff and landing.** The sucking and swallowing helps prevent discomfort in her ears from the changes in air pressure. Let her sleep if she's sleeping during takeoff, but wake her up if she's sleeping during landing, as that's when the pressure problems are the worst. If she's not interested in eating, use an eyedropper to put drops of water, juice, or milk in her mouth. She'll swallow them, and the swallowing will clear her ears. (Screaming will clear her ears too, of course.)

- **Drink plenty of fluids yourself.** Bring a sport water bottle, and get it refilled. This will be easier to manage while wrestling a baby than a plastic glass or soda can. This is critical if you are nursing. Again, air travel is extremely dehydrating. If you're not careful your milk supply can be depleted for a day or two.

- **Bring extra clothes.** Your baby is not the only one who is going to get messy if she throws up or has a diaper blow-out. Keep a change of clothes (for yourself) and plastic grocery bags (for the mess) in your carry-on.

- **Bring a favorite toy or two.** Be on the lookout for found toys too. (The laminated card with the picture of emergency exits somehow fascinates babies; you can make puppets out of barf bags or play stacking games with paper cups from the bathroom.)

- **Bring a package of disposable earplugs.** If your baby's screaming is getting you a lot of nasty looks from nearby passengers, stand up and offer the ear plugs around. You'll at least get a laugh, which may win a few people over to your side.

ALERT

Some moms credit over-the-counter antihistamines (usually Benadryl or an equivalent) for insuring that their babies spend most of their plane trips dozing. However, about 10 percent of children react in a paradoxical way to antihistamines and end up speedy instead of drowsy. If you're thinking about trying it, check the dosage with your doctor and do a test run at home.

Other Travel Challenges

One fiction that you need to drop is the idea that the flight attendant is your friend. She may have been your friend when you were traveling on business, carrying a jacket and a briefcase, and quietly sitting in your aisle seat tapping away on your computer. She is probably not your friend when you are pacing the aisle, trying to calm your screaming baby while simultaneously dodging the drink cart. Once in a while, you'll get a wonderful flight attendant who has—or remembers what it is like to have—young children. If the flight isn't too crowded, the attendant may volunteer to hold your baby while you go to the bathroom. (Those of us who have met those flight attendants remember them forever.) Odds are, however, that you won't and you'll be on your own.

Finding a place to change a diaper on an airplane is a challenge. Forget about the bathrooms. Only rarely will you get a plane with a fold-down changing table, and the ones that exist are so small as to be practically useless. The bathrooms themselves have no counter space and the floors are typically wet and sticky.

If you have a row to yourself, change your baby on your seats. Smile apologetically to nearby passengers if it's a smelly diaper and whisk it into the airsick bag as quickly as possible. Speed is important here.

If you don't have a row to yourself, your best bet is to change your baby on the floor at the back of the plane. Try to crouch out of the path of anyone who might walk by, and put a blanket or two on the floor before you spread out your changing pad (again, the floor is likely to be pretty yucky). Or you can punt on the issue by slathering your baby's bottom with diaper cream and putting a superabsorbent diaper or double-diapers on her just before boarding and hope she doesn't poop before landing.

If you're switching planes as a solo parent and can't figure out how you are going to race with your baby, car seat, and diaper bag from gate to gate, try calling the airline. You may be able to arrange for help in the form of a chauffeured electric cart.

International Baby

If you're planning to travel internationally, give yourself plenty of time to get a passport for your baby. Getting a passport photo for an infant can be tricky. The instant cameras used for passport photos in photo shops don't work well with babies because they are designed to focus best at a distance of about four feet, and getting an infant's head to fill the photo requires getting in closer. Some photographers won't even try to produce passport photos of children under two. If you want to try the photo shop, bring a white blanket and an infant seat. Place the baby in her seat because the passport agency does not want your face in the photo with your baby, and the photographer will have a better chance of getting a usable shot if your baby is comfortable, rather than being held in your hands at an awkward distance from your body.

You don't actually have to use an official passport photo. The shot needs to be taken head on, and your baby's eyes should be open. The background should be white or very light. You need two identical photos that are at least two inches square. The face in the picture should measure between 1 and 1⅜ inches from the top of the head to the bottom of the chin.

ESSENTIAL

Don't have an official photo? Get out your ruler and scissors and start measuring photos. If you bought photos from the hospital photographer, try the wallet-sized prints—with some judicious trimming, these very well may work for a passport. Otherwise, lay your baby on a white blanket, and stand over him (you may want to use a stool), taking shots from varying distances in hopes that one will be the right size.

In addition to your passports, bring a copy of your baby's birth certificate and your marriage certificate; they may come in handy. If you are traveling without your spouse, bring a letter from him giving you permission to take your baby out of the country, and have a phone number ready where he can be contacted. Pick a foreign airline if you have the option, as they tend to be more baby-friendly than U.S.-based airlines.

FACT

International flights often accommodate bassinets—special little beds that go on the floor or attach to a bulkhead. Reserve one ahead of time; they are usually free of charge, but may be in limited supply.

If you are packing baby formula, make sure it is unopened. (Pack formula for the plane ride separately). Otherwise, you may not be able to bring it in the country. Be sure to declare it, if asked.

Jet Lag

Babies are not immune to the effects of time zone changes. You may find that traveling east to west is easier on the body than west to east. To help reduce the effects:

- Before you leave, try to gradually move your baby's bedtime up twenty minutes per night until you are on what will be the time at your destination.
- Once there, put your baby to bed at the new location's bedtime.
- If you're feeding on demand, continue to do so regardless of the time differences. If not, adapt to the current time zone.
- Exposure to sunlight and daylight help your baby (and you!) adjust. Try to schedule outdoor activities.

Feeling Adventurous?

Organization is the key to successful outings with your baby. Here's what you need to know to expand your travels with your child.

Into the Woods

You can go camping with an infant, although you may have to pack a few more things than you are used to. Along with your regular camping gear, consider bringing:

- A portable crib
- An inflatable wading pool for use as bathtub
- A large plastic bin to pack your clothes in and use as a tub to wash your baby
- An extra warm sleeper
- A blanket for sitting on when you are outside the tent
- A highchair if your baby is eating finger foods (it will give her a chance to get the food in her mouth before it gets covered with dirt, and can be used to contain her when you don't want to worry about her crawling into the fire)

Check out your campsite completely before letting your baby loose in case previous campers left things behind that you don't want your baby to put in her mouth.

Beach Baby

If you are planning a day—or longer—at the beach with your baby, be sure you protect her from the sun. Pick a sunscreen labeled "broad spectrum," to protect from both UVB and UVA rays, with an SPF of at least 15. For sensitive areas of the body (the nose, cheeks, tops of the ears, and the shoulders) you may want to choose a sunscreen or sunblock with zinc oxide or titanium dioxide. Patch-test any sunscreen before covering your baby with it by putting a dab on the inside of your baby's arm and covering it with an adhesive bandage. Check the skin after twenty minutes and again after twenty-four hours. If you see red blotches or bumps, cross that brand off your list. Babies under six months should only have sunscreen on small areas, such as their faces and the backs of their hands, and should only use sunscreen if protective clothing and shade are unavailable.

Also:

- Even if you are using sunblock, dress your baby in lightweight cotton clothes that cover her arms and legs. Use a hat with a brim that goes all the way around *and* covers the back of her neck, as well as 100 percent ultraviolet filtration sunglasses. She may not keep them on, but she may love them. Do not use play sunglasses to protect her eyes. They can be used as a toy, but, unless they have 100 percent ultraviolet filtration, they can do more harm to her eyes than good when exposed to bright sunlight. If she uses the recommended sunglasses, you'll be protecting her from long-term eye damage and short-term crankiness—bright sun glaring off of water may make her uncomfortable. You can also invest in special UV clothes that are lightweight and sunproof, even when wet.
- Bring or rent an umbrella and keep her in the shade as much as possible. Consider getting off the beach altogether in the middle of the day.
- If she's old enough to hang on to a toy, bring a bucket and shovel. She may not know how to play with them yet, but she'll love it when you demonstrate water dumping and castle building. (Her job at this point is to knock your castles down.)
- Bring lots of regular diapers or swim diapers. (Swim diapers pull on like training pants and, because they don't contain the superabsorbent gels of regular diapers, won't immediately fill up with water and explode. They contain poop pretty well but do less well with pee.) Too much time in a wet diaper can kick off a bout of diaper rash, so you will need to change your baby often.
- Bring extra T-shirts. Leave a shirt on when your baby is splashing in the water to protect her from the sun, and change it when she's done.
- Bring (and remember to drink) extra fluids so you and your baby stay properly hydrated.
- Use cornstarch or cornstarch-based baby powder to remove sand—it works better than water.

Your baby will probably taste the sand and may eat handfuls of it. Don't worry, it will simply go through her digestive system and she'll pass it eventually.

While you'll want to dip your baby's toes in the water, don't take her all the way into the ocean or a pool until she can support her head on her own. The water temperature ought to be fairly warm—above 84°F to prevent hypothermia. You shouldn't keep your baby in the water longer than half an hour; even water that warm will eventually chill your child.

In a pool, go ahead and use a tube specially designed for a baby (with straps between the legs) or a life vest, but don't consider these as replacements for your arms—stay within reach. A baby can slip from a tube or tip face first into the water when wearing a vest.

A Potpourri of Travel Tips

Take that big vacation before your child is crawling or eating solid foods—it will be your last "easy" family vacation for a long time.

- If you're hiking with your baby in a backpack, carry a makeup mirror in your pocket. Pull it out to use as a rear-view mirror to check on your baby.
- For bottle-feeding on a short outing, fill a bottle with hot water before you leave, wrap it in a small towel, and then tuck it into a foam can-holder. The water will stay warm for hours so you can just add pre-measured powdered formula when you're ready to feed your baby.
- Eating in a restaurant? Leave a tip commensurate with the size of the mess you're leaving behind.
- Camping? If you're not nursing and your baby needs a middle-of-the-night feeding, tuck a can of premixed formula into your sleeping bag; it will be warm when your baby wakes up hungry.
- To warm a bottle on an airplane, fill an airsickness bag halfway with hot water (the flight attendants will have the water available for tea). Put the bottle in the water and let it sit.
- If you're staying in a hotel with a minibar, lock it. If it doesn't lock, request that it be emptied.

- When checking into a hotel, mention that your baby wakes at night. You'll probably then be assigned to a room with vacancies around it or at the end of a hall, and you'll be less likely to disturb other guests.
- Struggling with a fussy baby on an airplane? Let Dad handle it; your baby may fuss just as much, but Dad is likely to get more sympathetic looks from the other passengers and help (and sometimes free drinks, as moms report) from the flight attendants. (Sexist, but true.)
- If you can afford it, buy a separate airplane ticket for your baby. Having that extra seat, with a car seat strapped into it, is safer for your baby, and can be the difference between a tolerable trip and a torturous one.
- Hotel crib mattresses sometimes come wrapped in crinkly plastic. Put a towel between the mattress and the sheet to make your baby more comfortable and minimize the noise.
- The wooden highchairs available in some restaurants invert to make stable stands for an infant seat. (Check to make sure that the seat is indeed stable before resting it there.)

CHAPTER 19

Time for Yourself

In the weeks that follow the birth of your baby, the initially constant flow of blood will slow to a trickle and then stop. Your breasts will adjust to nursing—or not nursing—and will cease to feel like foreign objects suddenly attached to your body. You may not be getting much sleep, but you'll get used to surviving on whatever sleep you do get. You will have figured out most of the basic tasks of this new job (even though new things will still be thrown at you regularly.) And you'll begin to think that maybe you should be feeling "normal" and not randomly teary, overwhelmed, or just plain strange.

Life Postpartum

Teary, overwhelmed, and strange is normal in the postpartum weeks and, sometimes, months. You may be irritable and sometimes angry. You may have dramatic mood swings. You may shed tears for no reason and find yourself unable to cope with situations you would normally handle with ease. You may blow up in anger when those around you least expect it.

This is normal. It is normal to have an emotional reaction to a major life change—and a new baby is a major life change. It is normal to be stressed by the demands placed on you as a new mother, to be daunted by the responsibility that is suddenly, literally, in your lap. It is normal to be exhausted when your sleep is constantly interrupted. And it is normal to have a host of physical and emotional reactions to the dramatic postpartum change in your hormone levels. The rapid drop in estrogen levels causes hot flashes, depression, and trouble concentrating. (Like you really need a preview of menopause at this point!) The drop in progesterone can cause anxiety (progesterone, in high doses, has sometimes been prescribed to relieve anxiety). The fall in the level of thyroid function can make you feel sluggish. Mood-controlling hormones, such as serotonin and dopamine, drop as well.

FACT

For some women, the hormonal changes may be too extreme to handle without a doctor's help and/or medication. Accept the help if you fit into that category. You're not being weak, because being better able to control the hormonal changes will help you be a better mom.

What You Can Do

If you feel like you're flipping out, you are. It's not because you can't handle being a mom—it's pure biochemistry. It will probably pass on its own, although you may not believe it at the time. This feeling may be normal, but you don't have to sit there and wait for it to go away. Take a nap or get some exercise. Sunlight helps, so go outside. Eat regularly and well. (If you're a stay-at-home mom, pack yourself a lunch in the morning before your partner leaves or you may miss lunch altogether.) Drink liquids constantly—you need extra for breastfeeding, and fatigue can be a symptom of dehydration. Ask for help from family or friends. Hire a babysitter for a few hours. If you're falling apart and can't get a break immediately, try breastfeeding for a while—the released hormones may be just enough to relax you.

Depression Statistics

If you're feeling overemotional, overwhelmed, and possibly depressed, you are not alone. Consider these statistics:

- Eighty percent of new mothers experience at least a short-term case of the baby blues.
- Ten to fifteen percent of mothers become clinically depressed in the first year after the birth of a child.
- Two in 1,000 new mothers develop postpartum psychosis, which goes beyond depression to hallucinations and delusions, and, sometimes, violent behavior.

Baby Blues Checklist

"I see it coming when a mother is constantly tired and crying," says midwife Jean Rasch. "She isn't enjoying her baby, she hates her husband, and she isn't sleeping. She worries every time she has to deal with the baby—that she didn't get any sleep when he took his last nap; that she won't get any sleep when he takes his next one. And she is really different—chemically different. She is acting other than I know her, than her husband knows her."

How can you tell if you need more help than your best friend, mother, or babysitter can give you? Signs you may need medical help for your baby blues include:

- You can't sleep at night, even when the baby does
- Lack of appetite
- Loss of interest in activities you usually enjoy
- Lack of enthusiasm for anything
- Difficulty making decisions
- Constant anxiety about your baby
- General anxiety
- Recurrent, strong feelings of anger

- Recurrent crying, tearfulness
- Feelings of hopelessness
- Feelings of inadequacy
- Disaster fantasies
- Shaking
- Compulsive behaviors
- Panic attacks (shortness of breath, dizziness)
- Sleeping too little or too much
- Suicidal thoughts*
- Thoughts about harming the baby*

*If you are having suicidal thoughts or thoughts about harming your baby, tell your doctor or a trusted friend immediately.

If you are experiencing an increasing number of these symptoms and they intensify with time, make sure you get all the help you need. Tell the people in your life who are most likely to take action to get you some relief. Include at least one relative or close friend and one health care provider, and enlist some support sooner rather than later.

Professional Help

Only one in several hundred women face postpartum problems that require medication, but get help fast if you think you are one of them because the disease can threaten your life—or your baby's life. Severe postpartum reactions may include depression that goes on for days at a time and gets in the way of your life; mania, including hyperactivity, sleeplessness, and extreme irritability; anxiety, characterized by constant worrying or panic attacks, shortness of breath, or dizziness; or psychosis, in which a mother becomes completely out of touch with reality.

When you bring these problems to your health care provider, she will probably refer you to a psychiatrist who will prescribe antianxiety or antidepressant medications. While women may be told to wean their babies from the breast before starting such medications, the wisdom of this is arguable. As information concerning the use of antianxiety and antidepressant drugs while breastfeeding accumulates, this recommendation is changing. If you think weaning at such an emotionally vulnerable time would add to your trauma, it's possible you may not have to. Ask your doctor for the most up-to-date research on the drug he prescribes. This is an individual decision, so try to weigh the options and come up with the best plan for your situation.

Not for Moms Only

The baby blues can strike dads as well. A recent study in the journal *Pediatrics* suggests that 10 percent of new dads are affected by postpartum depression—and the effect can be long term. Researchers found a doubling of the risk of behavioral problems in the children of fathers who had been depressed eight weeks after the birth. It's important to keep in mind that postpartum depression is not a reflection of his love for either you or the baby.

If you believe that the new father is struggling with depression, insist he seek professional help. Women who are depressed tend to appear sad and in despair. Men's symptoms are often an increase in irritability, aggressiveness, and even hostility. The father may be physically withdrawing from any interaction with the baby and offer little support to the mother. He may work longer, watch more sports, and drink alcohol more. Treatment may include both therapy with a trained professional and medication. The earlier the treatment, the better it is for the family.

About Sex

You will probably be told to hold off having sex until after your six-week checkup. There is nothing magical about six weeks, really. If you had a vaginal delivery, you can safely have intercourse any time after all bleeding stops (bleeding indicates that your cervix is still open and bacteria could easily invade). This usually takes two or three weeks, but it's more important to wait until you actually want to have sex. And you may want to, especially if you've had an easy birth and a baby who sleeps a lot.

Probably, though, you won't want to. Your vaginal area may still be tender, your scar from any episiotomy or tearing may be sensitive. You might feel just fine physically, but the memory of how much the birth hurt may still make you cringe. Your body may feel odd when you are touched, in part because the hormonal effects of breastfeeding change your skin (this can be remedied with lotion or massage oil), and also because you're being touched so much by your baby you just can't take any more.

Starting Over with Sex

Sometime after getting the six-week go-ahead (possibly way after, research shows, if your baby wakes frequently at night) you may find yourself having fond memories of sex, fond enough to contemplate having it again in spite of your exhaustion. Or, more likely, you may want to try it just once to reassure yourself that everything still works, and then have no interest again for months. When you hit this point, think Astroglide.

You will need a lubricant because your vaginal walls postpartum are thinner and produce less natural lubrication thanks to the dramatic drop in estrogen. Gel lubricants are goopy and will remind you of getting a pelvic exam, but Astroglide is barely thicker than water, nearly invisible, and works like magic.

ESSENTIAL

You may find articles that say all you need to solve the lubrication problem is a little extra time for foreplay, starting with dinner out and a bottle of wine. If you're nursing, you really shouldn't have more than a little bit of wine and, in the brief hours your baby gives you between feedings and considering how tired you probably are, how realistic is dedicating hours to foreplay? Go for the lubricant.

If sex hurts, a different position may help. Consider one that puts the least amount of pressure on the scar where you tore or had an episiotomy. That area, typically at the base of the vagina, will become less sensitive eventually, but it may take a year or more. Find a position (use pillows if you have to) that angles your partner away from the scar. If you have very sharp pain, use a mirror to check your scar for a black line like a splinter—you may have a stitch that didn't dissolve and it will need to be removed.

After a C-section the biggest concern is the abdominal scar; any position that puts pressure on it is out.

Talk to you health care provider if dryness is a problem even with the Astroglide. She may recommend an estrogen cream that will make the vaginal tissue softer and more lubricated.

Milk Gets in Your Eyes

Sex can make your milk spray because oxytocin, the hormone that triggers the let-down reflex, is released when you have an orgasm. This can, as you might imagine, be distracting. It's at least good for a laugh, but might make you lose any romantic focus. The best way to handle it, if you don't like cold wet sheets, is to wear a sleep bra with nursing pads. Also, try to feed the baby shortly beforehand (though you may leak anyway).

The optimal time window may take a while for you to figure out. If your baby's been fed recently, he'll be more likely to give you some free time and, if you're nursing, your breasts will be less likely to leak.

Get to Know Yourself Again

Of course, leaking milk effectively makes your breasts off-limits. To be honest, many women find that they can't stand to have their breasts or nipples touched in the first few postpartum months. Your new shape may be a turn-on for your partner, but your bigger breasts may not feel erotic at all to you. This can be frustrating for both of you. The answer, like with any other problem, is to be honest about what's a turn-on and what's not.

There may be other parts of your body that you used to like to have touched and suddenly don't. It might be your stomach—a reminder of how much work you have ahead to tighten it back up again. All these new rules about what can and can't be touched will probably baffle your partner, but your body has been through some huge changes. Why would you expect everything to feel the same?

Timing Is Everything

Complicating the whole sex thing even further is the probability that when you have an orgasm, or are about to, your baby will wake up. Anticipating his cry can ruin the most romantic moment. If you can get away for a few hours, do so.

Don't worry about it if you really, really don't feel like sex, but don't entirely forget about it. Remember there are other ways to be intimate besides sexual intercourse. Start off slow, just touching and cuddling with each other, even if it doesn't lead to intercourse. The goal is not just physical intimacy, but emotional intimacy with your partner. If you continue to have an aversion to sex, after a few months, talk to your healthcare provider to make sure that there are no physical issues. Be honest with your provider about any emotional problems you now feel about having sex.

Birth Control

If you finally find the time, energy, and interest in having sex, you also need to be sure that you use an effective form of birth control. Remember: you can get pregnant while you are breastfeeding. You can even get pregnant before you get your first period.

You have more choices than ever before: a variety of birth control pills, birth control implants, IUDs, diaphragms, condoms, and Natural Family Planning.

You want to choose a method that is effective, easy to use, and comfortable for both you and your partner. The Mayo Clinic website (*www.mayo clinic.com*) has a comprehensive birth control guide that will give you the pros and cons of each form of birth control. Talk to your partner and your health care provider about what will work best for you.

Hair Loss

It can be upsetting to discover that you are losing handfuls of hair every time you shower. This usually starts around three months after delivery, but sometimes occurs later. During pregnancy the typical shedding cycle of hair changes. The good news is that your hair is thicker than ever while you're pregnant. The bad news is that this too shall pass, and you'll lose the normal amount of hair you would have had you not been pregnant—all at once. This may be the time to think about wearing your hair short for a while. Losing short hair is not quite as traumatic somehow, and a lot easier on the shower drain.

The time it takes for your hair to look "normal" again depends on your hair's growth cycle, which can vary dramatically from woman to woman. Get a good haircut or some nice scarves and have faith that it will grow back.

Getting Your Body Back

About six weeks after the birth, your uterus is pretty much back to where it was before delivery in terms of size and position, but keep in mind some things will never be back the way they were. Your uterus will always be a little larger than before, the opening of the cervix wider, and your pelvic muscles and ligaments looser.

Your body may not feel like yours. You just got used to having a huge stomach and now it's relatively flat again, but loose and saggy. Your breasts have very little in common with the ones you were used to. Your waist and hips are wider and will probably stay that way, and don't expect your feet to return to their prepregnancy size. Pregnancy hormones cause your joints to become looser and your feet to become bigger. Many women report that their feet grow a half to a full size larger with each pregnancy.

Body Changes

Even if you've lost all your pregnancy weight, expect your body to look different. This is the normal you, just with a Mommy body. If you've had a C-section, the scar may be permanently numb in spots. Your belly may jut out. Your breasts may sag more. While you may not get your old body back, you can get a body you like.

If you're breastfeeding exclusively, you probably won't get your period for five or six months—and you may not get it for several years. Seems only fair, with all the other messes you've got to deal with, but you shouldn't count on it. Some women get their period back within six weeks, even while breast-feeding their babies every three hours, day and night. Most women get their period back about a month after they stop breastfeeding.

Body Work

If you haven't started exercising regularly before reading this, start now. There are a lot of good reasons to exercise—to stay healthy, to boost your mood, and to fit into your prepregnancy clothes again. But the most important reason is to get back in touch with your body. To put on clothes in which you can't nurse (for an hour anyway), to look in the mirror, and to recognize that the leg you are lifting is actually your own!

Check with your doctor, but start easy exercises for your lower back and abdomen once you have the green light. Keep in mind that you won't have much success even feeling where your abdominal muscles are for a week or two. Make sure, however, that you don't do any exercises that require you to be upside down until all bleeding stops (no shoulder stands, for example, if you're doing yoga) because blood flowing back into the still-open cervix can cause infection. If you've had a cesarean, you may have to wait a full six weeks before starting an exercise program.

ESSENTIAL

Immediately after the birth (or as soon as you have any feeling down in your pelvis) start your Kegel exercises. Squeeze the muscles that control the flow of urine, hold for three seconds, and relax. Do at least twenty a day—and do them for the rest of your life.

Breastfeeding, which uses about 500–1,000 calories a day, will help you lose weight, but plan on dropping the pounds slowly. Focus on eating reasonable portions of healthy foods at regular meals. Dieting should mean controlling eating, if "dieting" means a restrictive fad or starvation diet (living on protein shakes or grapefruit), don't—you'll threaten your baby's health as well as your own.

FACT

Nurse just before you exercise; you'll be more comfortable, and the effect of exercise-induced lactic acid, which can make milk slightly sour, will have dissipated prior to the next feeding.

Exercises with Baby

Here are some activities that are exercise healthy for you and fun for your baby.

- **Fly a kite:** Besides being great for your back and stomach, kite flying can calm a fussy baby. Start out sitting with your knees bent and your feet flat on the floor. Position your baby's body face down against your lower legs and, stabilizing your baby with your hands, roll back, lifting your baby up with your legs. You can stay in that position, pressing the small of your back against the floor, or rock from side to side to help release your back. You can gently lift and lower your baby with your legs to exercise your knee and leg muscles. Or you can do abdominal exercises by lifting your head and shoulders off the ground, reaching toward your baby with a kiss.

- **Straddle stretches:** Sit with your legs in a V and lay or sit your baby in the middle. Stretch to each side and to the middle, holding each stretch at least twenty seconds without bouncing (do go ahead and kiss your baby as much as you want).

- **Baby presses (a.k.a. reverse push-ups):** Lie on your back, knees bent, feet flat on the floor. Put your baby on your chest, holding her under her arms. While pressing your lower back against the floor, lift her slowly in the air above your face until your arms are almost straight.

FIGURE 19-1:
Fly a kite

FIGURE 19-2:
Straddle stretches

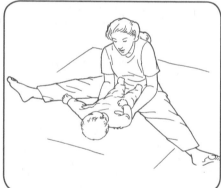

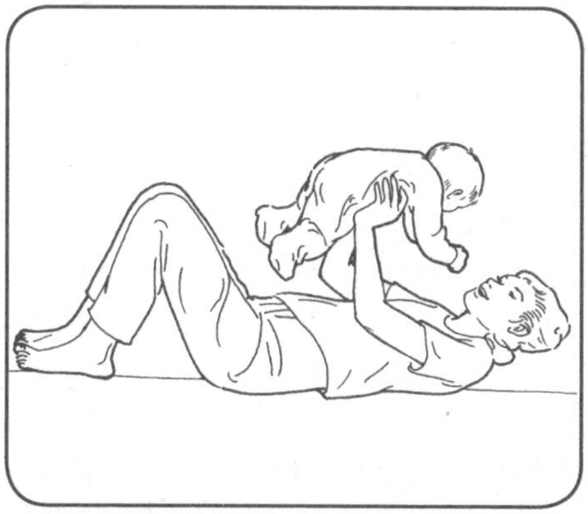

FIGURE 19-3:
Baby Presses

FIGURE 19-4:
Pillow Stretch

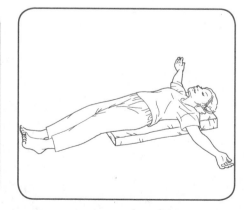

Some Cautions

Hold off any form of impact exercise (running, aerobics) for at least six weeks. Your stretched-out muscles, tendons, and ligaments can't safely support your organs, and your cardiovascular system is still changing back to normal. A few things to keep in mind:

- If your lochia (post-childbirth discharge) turns red after exercising, you're doing too much.
- Don't jog or do any exercises that require bouncing with your baby in a carrier. (You can hold your baby in a front pack, however, while walking or riding a stationary bike.)
- Hold off on a baby jogger until your baby has her head well under control—around six months of age. Younger babies can risk neck injuries.

Great Stretches for Anytime

These exercises are easy to do and require no special equipment.

- **Wall stretch:** Stand facing a wall, about one step (or an arm's length) back from it with your feet shoulder width apart. Put both hands flat against the wall at shoulder height. Bend over, passing your head between your elbows, pressing your back flat, parallel to the ground.
- **Pillow stretch:** Lie on your back, with a pillow or couch bolster under your shoulders. Let your arms and shoulders relax back and tip your head back. This opens your chest, stretches the chest muscles, and counters the curved position you use while holding a baby.

Baby Wrist

Given all the holding, cuddling, and cradling that babies require, it's no surprise that some mothers suffer from a condition sometimes called *baby wrist*. This repetitive stress injury is characterized by pain or tingling in the wrist and can cause long-term damage if not treated. A variation is pain around the thumb or fingers, which doctors used to think came from opening and closing safety pins while diapering, but now associate with lifting and carrying the baby. The pain often increases at night, when the accumulation of fluid increases the pressure on the nerves. Breastfeeding moms may be more vulnerable to this because nursing can cause water retention.

ALERT

Baby wrist often begins with hormonal changes during pregnancy that cause internal swelling in the wrist. It is aggravated by holding the infant with a bent wrist, as well as by diapering, snapping little snaps, pushing a stroller, and lugging a baby carrier. And nursing mothers tend to make the condition worse by curling their hands under their full breasts when they're asleep.

You can head off the condition by stretching your wrists regularly and lifting light hand weights. Make sure you keep your wrists in a "neutral" position (straight, but relaxed), when holding your baby. Big mistakes are cupping your hand around your baby's head while nursing with your wrist at a 90-degree angle and pushing the stroller with your wrists bent. If you've already got a case of baby wrist, ice the area a few times a day and take ibuprofen to reduce inflammation. Wear a wrist brace designed for repetitive stress injuries whenever you can. This may only be when you sleep since you can't pick up your baby while wearing it. (You can get these elastic, metal, and Velcro contraptions at some drugstores.) If the pain persists, talk to your health care provider.

My Aching Back

While you were pregnant, you began to carry yourself differently to balance your growing stomach. Continuing this new posture can strain your back, as can nursing (remember to use a nursing stool and bring your baby to your breast rather than leaning over your baby) and the constant lifting and carrying a new baby needs.

Ice, heat, and massage will help when it gets serious, but it is more important to learn careful lifting, bending, and carrying techniques. To minimize the stress on your back, rediscover your correct posture. Stand in front of a mirror, naked, and close your eyes. Rock from side to side, shrug your shoulders, take a slow, deep breath, and exhale. Then, without opening your eyes, try to find a centered position. Open your eyes and look in the mirror. Are your shoulders even? Is your bottom tipped up? Are your knees tilted in? To adjust your alignment, put your feet just under your hips, then tip your pelvis forward and back until you find its center. Tuck in your bottom, and straighten your shoulders. You may need to do this a few times a day until you get used to your new center.

QUESTION

Why sleep with extra pillows?
Sleep on your back with a pillow under your knees, or on your side with a pillow between your legs to preserve alignment and reduce additional stress.

Become aware of how you hold and handle your baby. When you bend down to pick her up, bend your knees, support her close to your chest, and use your leg muscles to lift—don't lean over. The same goes for the car seat. Climb into the car as far as possible and lift your baby up against you before squirming backward out of the car. Once your baby is too big for the sink or baby tub, think about taking baths with your baby instead of leaning over the tub. When you are on the floor changing a diaper or playing, squat or sit cross-legged to reduce awkward leaning.

Try to carry your baby in the center of your body as much as possible rather than on one hip. Or, if you carry your baby on your hip, switch sides often (the same goes for carrying your baby in a sling). Regularly using your hip as a baby chair can, after a while, cause muscle and nerve damage that can take years to recover from.

CHAPTER 20

Making Memories

You'll want to capture your new baby on film, in still photographs as well as on video. Look to get photos not just of the first steps, but of your daily life with your new baby: the midnight nursings, the hours in a sling, the diaper changes. Your baby's first year is chock-full of memory makers. Here are some ways to catch and preserve those moments—for you and for your baby.

Paparazzi

To have a record of your baby's first year, try some of these suggestions:

- Photograph everything your baby does on a normal day, at regular intervals (three months, six months, nine months). Order double prints (or print out two sets), save one set for the album, and use the other set to make a book for your baby.
- Regularly photograph your rapidly growing child with something that doesn't change in size. For example, use a teddy bear that might tower over your baby at birth, but comes up to his knees at a year. You can also try "baby in a hat," "baby with the cat," or "baby in Mom's rocker."
- Develop a photo series (these work with video as well). For example, you might photograph your baby with a single pumpkin or rose for her first birthday—and add an additional pumpkin or rose in the photo for each additional year of her age. Another photo concept might be "Splish Splash," with pictures from your baby's first bath in the hospital (given by the nurses), and additional ones in the baby tub and then on to the big bathtub.
- Don't put the camera away when your child is crying or screaming. Tears and tantrums are a big part of the first year—and many years to come—and though you may think you'll want to forget them, someday you'll treasure those photos.
- Don't forget to get pictures with each parent. In most couples one person takes on the photographer role, and sometimes finds out when it is too late that he or she is missing from the photographic record.
- Videotape and photograph the significant people in your child's life: grandparents, other relatives, the neighbor's baby that he sees every day at the park, your regular babysitter.
- You don't need to save every work of art once your baby starts scribbling, scrawling, and painting, as you'll quickly be overwhelmed. Instead, save a representative sample and regularly surround your child with his artwork and take a photo.

Keepsakes: Beyond the Photo

Here are some other ways to mark the passage of time of your baby.

- **Proclamations.** In addition to the cards from relatives welcoming your baby to the world, you can keep one from the President of the United States. Just send a birth announcement to the President and Mrs. (Whoever), The White House, 1600 Pennsylvania Ave., Washington, D.C. 20500.
- **The world at large.** You might also want to keep the front page of your local paper on the day your baby was born. It will be a source of fascination to her when she gets older to see what was happening in the world on the day she entered it.
- **The spoken word.** When your baby says her first word—or even babbles regularly—try getting her voice on tape. Introduce each segment by stating the date, place, and activity, and then get her talking or laughing by making silly faces or pointing to pictures in a book. Your computer can be better than a tape recorder (particularly since audio tapes can get lost in a drawer in a muddle of Sesame Street and Raffi tapes). Plug in a microphone (yours may have come with one built in), and use whatever recording software you have on hand. For example, you can access the sound control panel and change the computer's alert sound from a beep to your baby saying "Uh-oh." (Make sure you copy these files whenever you upgrade computers.)
- **Book sense.** Write in the front of your child's favorite books, the ones that you end up reading every night. Put down her name, age, and anything striking about the book (that she always pointed to the lamp in *Good Night Moon* and said "light" for example, or that "moon" was her third word).
- **Journals and diaries.** Keep a journal, recording anything that comes to mind. Keep a pen and journal on your nightstand so it's easily accessible when something special has happened during the day. It's so easy to forget the details of life.
- **Growth Charts.** Start the classic growth chart—the marks on a doorframe—as soon as your baby is standing on her own. Pick a regular time of year to update it, such as your child's birthday, or New Year's, or another date you'll remember.

- **Steps in time.** Make a footprint picture. Buy several extra large sheets of acid-free watercolor paper and a bottle of roll-on stamp pad ink. Fold a paper towel a few times and roll ink onto it. Press your baby's foot first on the inked towel and then firmly onto the paper, starting on one edge and rolling the foot to make the print. Repeat with the other foot. Add a set of footprints every year or so, and by the time your child is in kindergarten you'll be ready to frame these tracks of his growth. If your baby has older siblings, stamp their footprints side by side. (You can try handprints, too, but most babies will clench their hands up; footprints are a lot easier.)

Another great memory maker is on one of your summer outings to the beach, bring along a box of dry plaster and a jug of tap water. When the tide is going out, pick a patch of damp sand, smooth it out, and stamp your baby's feet into it. Mix the plaster in a sand pail according to instructions, and pour it into the footprints. (Be sure and wash out the sand pail immediately or the plaster becomes impossible to remove.) You can pick the "feet" up in about ten minutes; they will dry completely overnight. Tuck a loop of wire or string into each footprint just after you pour the plaster if you plan to hang them on the wall, or use them as is to make a path in your garden.

ESSENTIAL

Keep a birthday journal and write your child a birthday letter in a blank book (available at a stationery store). Start with his birth story and include important family and news events that occurred in the months around his birth. Then update it yearly, with a letter describing his achievements over the year, relating a funny story, detailing major family changes, and reviewing the world news. Keep it a secret, and turn it over to him as a high school graduation present.

First Birthday

The first birthday is not only about your baby, since a one-year-old does not understand the concept of birthdays. This first birthday is also about you; it's a celebration of surviving your first year of parenthood. Yes, you are going to want to sing "Happy Birthday" to your baby, blow out his candle, and then feed him a slice of cake with gooey icing—if only for the photo opportunity—but you can also make this your party.

Think about what would make this celebration meaningful for you. For example, you can have a backyard barbecue for family and friends. It can be a way to reconnect with friends you haven't seen because you've been just too busy and for everyone to see your baby without any pressure on him.

FACT

Don't expect your child to open gifts in any timely manner. You may want to see what's in them, but your one-year-old may happily play with the wrapped boxes for days without losing interest—why push it?

Begin your personal celebration with the moment you went into labor. You'll probably be flashing back to that time anyway, so be conscious of it. Watch the clock, and, no matter how busy your day is, take a few moments to remember what it felt like physically and emotionally when you realized this baby was about to be born. When your child is two or three, you can involve him in this tradition by telling him his birth story on the eve of his birthday. You may find that the "when I was born" bedtime story becomes a favorite.

The Best Part: Baby's First Year

What better way to conclude your first year as a new mom than by sharing these special quotes from your peers? Maybe they'll inspire you to make your own "Best Part" journal entry.

> *"The best part of the first year was . . . everything! Even if, in the moment, it was terrible and I thought I was going to go crazy or burst into tears, when I look back, it was either comical or just wonderful. From Alex's first smile and laugh, to his first steps, and everything in between. I never knew I could love someone so much!"—Kerri*

"Being a mother is the hardest job I have ever loved. I did not know it was possible to love a person in the way and to the depth that I love my daughter. Even when I felt exhausted and frustrated in that first year, I would tiptoe into her room before I went to bed to gaze upon her beautiful, sleeping face, and my heart would overflow with love every time."—Mary

"The best part of the first year was when our kids first recognized us. Picking them up from babysitters and seeing their faces light up because they recognized Mom or Dad. And hearing the babies' first laughs. And having a baby fall asleep on my shoulder was precious. There are so many special moments in the first year, and sometimes you forget how special they are."—Glorianne

"The best part of the first year was looking at the joy and love in my husband's eyes every time he looked at our son."—Kathryn

"The best moment in that first year was holding my newborn twins right after they came out. There hasn't been much in my whole life that has exceeded the incredible feeling of that moment."—Moira

"The best thing about the first year was becoming part of the 'club.' Suddenly I had something in common with all the other women, regardless of where they work or how much money they made. I also took on a different attitude: 'Hey, I gave birth; anything else pales in comparison.'"—Leslie R.

"The best thing was seeing the wonder on my daughter's face over the most ordinary things, like colored lights, a tiny bug on the ground, a beautiful red leaf, or a muddy puddle. She made me slow down to appreciate all the little gifts we come across all day long."—Julie

"The best thing is that after all the sleepless nights and frustration at the beginning about a colicky baby, at the end you get some love back, just a little hug, cuddle, or kiss, that is everything you ever needed."—Esther

"The best part was watching Francis grow from a wailing bundle of reactions and needs into a walking, talking, communicating creature."
—Adrienne

"The best moment of the first year was when my son, Chris, was about a week old. I took him with me to the gas station, and while I was filling the tank, a woman came over and said, 'I see you have a new baby.' I smiled, and she continued, 'Don't you feel like someone turned on the lights and now it's clear to you what life is all about?' She was so right!"—Lynne

"The best part of the first year was learning about this new person in my life, learning about what made my baby smile, cry, laugh, and cuddle."—Lisa

"My best part of the first year was the laughter a baby brings. Before parenthood, it was quiet and settled in my home. There was not so much laughter, not so much to actually smile about. That was the best change."—Ursula

"The best part for me was watching this little being grow from a helpless newborn about which I knew almost nothing into a real little person with her distinct personality, looks, abilities, preferences, and interests."—Cecily

"The best moment came a couple of months after we had Sophia. We visited a friend who had to buzz us in to enter her apartment. When she answered the buzzer, I said, 'It's the Blums.' There was something about that that caught me. We were more of a family. Before that I might have said, 'It's Jodi and Jeff,' but now we were 'the Blums.'"—Jodi

"The best thing about the first year was the incredible love I felt for my son, his first laugh, and the joy of seeing him grow from a newborn baby into a little toddler. What an experience! I wouldn't trade it for anything in the world."—Kim

"The best parts of the first year—all three times—were the gummy smiles just for me."—Julia

"I think the best thing about the first year is realizing the true definition of unconditional love. It is astonishing how fiercely and passionately you fall in love with this tiny creature that can do nothing for you in return, other than need you completely and reciprocate your love in full. You can't remember life without her—or what you remember seems incomplete. Every smile, every gurgle, every coo brings immeasurable joy. There is nothing you wouldn't do for her, no need to say no to any wish she might have (yet), and no feeling of peace quite like the one you get when she falls asleep on your shoulder, blowing her warm baby breath on your neck."—Leslie B.

Charts and Tables

Food Introduction Record

Six months (one meal a day)			
Food	Date of Introduction	Likes/Dislikes?	Allergic Reaction (Describe)
Rice cereal			
Banana			
Avocado			
Applesauce			
Apple juice			
Oat cereal			
Squash			
Pears			
Pear juice			
Sweet potatoes			

Seven months (one to two meals a day)			
Food	Date of Introduction	Likes/Dislikes?	Allergic Reaction (Describe)
Barley cereal			
Peaches			
Carrots			
Plums			
Peas			
Prune juice			

Food Introduction Record—*continued*

Eight months (two to three meals a day)

Food	Date of Introduction	Likes/Dislikes?	Allergic Reaction (Describe)
Chicken			
Green beans			
Grape juice			
Turkey			
Papaya juice			

Nine months (three meals a day)

Food	Date of Introduction	Likes/Dislikes?	Allergic Reaction (Describe)
Beef			

Ten months (three meals a day)

Food	Date of Introduction	Likes/Dislikes?	Allergic Reaction (Describe)
Tofu			
Oranges			
Orange juice			
Wheat cereal			
Lamb			
Broccoli			
Grapefruit			
Beets			

Food Introduction Record—*continued*

Eleven months (three meals a day)			
Food	**Date of Introduction**	**Likes/Dislikes?**	**Allergic Reaction (Describe)**
Egg yolks			
Spinach			
Kiwi			
Potatoes			

Wait until after twelve months:			
Food	**Date of Introduction**	**Likes/Dislikes?**	**Allergic Reaction (Describe)**
Milk			
Whole milk yogurt			
Cottage cheese			
Mild cheese			
Honey			
Egg white			
Peanut butter			
Strawberries			
Raspberries			
Tomatoes			
Pineapple			
Corn			

The most easily digested and least allergenic foods are grouped under the earlier months. The one rule you should follow: Wait at least three days after introducing a new food, adding it in small portions along with foods already allergy tested, before adding another new one.

Health History

Information you and anyone else taking care of the baby will need to have on hand.
Start keeping track of it now.

Date of birth, name of hospital, doctors: _____

_____

Weight, length, head size: _____

Any congenital problems: _____

_____

_____

_____

Complications during pregnancy or delivery: _____

_____

_____

_____

How long breastfed: _____

Food allergies: _____

_____

_____

_____

_____

Drug allergies: _____

_____

_____

_____

_____

Health History—*continued*

Chronic conditions (frequent ear infections, asthma, other): _____

_____

_____

_____

Major medical treatments (surgeries or hospitalizations): _____

_____

_____

_____

Vaccinations: _____

_____

_____

_____

Illnesses: _____

_____

_____

_____

Date of onset: _____   Date of onset: _____

Date of recovery: _____   Date of recovery: _____

Diagnosis: _____   Diagnosis: _____

Medications given: _____   Medications given: _____

Reactions to medication: _____   Reactions to medication: _____

My Baby's Milestones

Claps: _____

Grabs a toy or object: _____ What was it? _____

Rolls over: _____

Sits unsupported: _____

Crawls, creeps, or somehow crosses the room: _____

Pulls up to a stand: _____ On what? _____

Walks: _____ How many steps? _____

Climbs out of crib: _____

Runs: _____

Smiles: _____ At what? _____

Laughs out loud: _____ At what? _____

Shows excitement: _____ At what? _____

Shows anger: _____ At what? _____

Has a favorite toy: _____ What is it? _____

Coos or oohs (vowels): _____ What did it sound like? _____

Babbles (consonants): _____ What sounds are the favorites? _____

Babbles without repeating syllables: _____ What did it sound like? _____

First word: _____ Word? _____

Second word: _____ Word? _____

First animal sound: _____ What animal? _____

List all the words your baby can say on his or her first birthday: _____

_____

New Mom Milestones

Record (and celebrate!) these stellar events in your new life as a mom.

First time you have sex: _____

First time you like it: _____

First postpartum menstrual period: _____

First outing without your baby: _____

_____

_____

How long? _____ Baby stayed with whom? _____

First outing without worrying about your baby: _____

_____

_____

First evening date with your partner: _____

_____

Five consecutive hours of sleep: _____

Seven consecutive hours of sleep: _____

First overnight away from baby: _____

_____

Returning to work: _____

First weekend away: _____

_____

_____

Vaccinations

Your doctor's vaccination recommendations may vary,
and typically these schedules change regularly.
Here is a typical first year vaccination schedule:

Hepatitis B	Birth, one month, six months
Diphtheria, Tetanus, Pertussis	Two months, four months, six months
H. Influenza type B	Two months, four months, twelve months
Polio	Two months, four months, twelve months
Measles, Mumps, Rubella	Twelve months
PCV	Two months, four months, six months

Exercise Primer

Just after the Birth

- **Kegels:** Tighten your vaginal and pelvic muscles (as if stopping a stream of urine), hold for three seconds, and relax. Do five repetitions every hour or so for the first few days to increase blood circulation to the area and promote healing.
- **Tummy Tighteners:** Lie on the bed, inhale, and slowly exhale through pursed lips while you tighten your abdominal muscles as much as you can. Repeat five times.
- **Chin to Chests:** Lie flat on the bed (without a pillow) and slowly lift your head and touch your chin to your chest; you should feel your lower abdominal muscles tighten. Repeat five times.
- **Pelvic Rocks:** Lie on the floor with yours knees bent and feet flat. Tighten your abs while tucking your bottom under your pelvis, pressing your lower back into the floor. Then relax, letting your back curve. Repeat five times.

Abdominal Exercises

After a C-section, don't do any abdominal exercises until your doctor approves and the incision has healed completely. (The incision may, however, still feel numb.)

Before starting any abdominal exercises, check for diastasis, or separation of the recti abdominis muscles. Lie down with your knees bent and feet on the floor. With the finger of one hand, feel just below your navel for the soft indentation between the two bands of stomach muscles. Exhale as you lift your head and shoulders and see how many fingers fit into the indentation—if it's more than two and a half, do only the first three exercises.

- **Diastasis Corrector:** Lie on your back, knees bent, feet flat on floor. Push the muscles in center of abdomen together while you exhale and slowly lift your head.
- **Leg Slides:** Lie on back with bent knees, feet flat. Slowly slide legs out until straight while pressing the lower back to the floor, then return to bent position.
- **Shoulder Lifts:** Lie down with your knees bent. With your fingers stretching toward your toes, raise your head and shoulders off of the bed. Repeat five times.
- **Curl-ups:** Start with shoulder lifts, but come a little further, reaching between your knees, until your back begins to lift. Repeat five times.
- **Side Reaches:** Just like curl-ups, but reach to the outside of one knee for five reps, and then to the outside of the other knee for five more.

FIGURE APP-1:
Curl-ups

FIGURE APP-2:
Side reaches

Hand and Wrist Exercises

- **Wrist Rolls:** Stretch your arms forward and rotate wrists in one direction and then the other. Repeat ten times.
- **Wrist Lifts:** Place your forearm on a table, palm up, and wrist and hand hanging over the edge (first position). Hold a light weight (or can of soup) in your hand, and curl your wrist slowly up toward your arm (second position), and then slowly down. Repeat ten times.
- **Wrist Twists:** Again, with your forearm on a flat surface, palm up, wrist and hand hanging over the edge (first position), hold one end of the weight or can and turn your hand slowly until your palm faces down (second position); then rotate back. Repeat ten times.

FIGURE APP-3(A):
Wrist lift
(first position)

FIGURE APP-3(B):
Wrist lift
(second position)

FIGURE APP-4(A):
Wrist roll
(first position)

FIGURE APP-4(B):
Wrist roll
(second position)

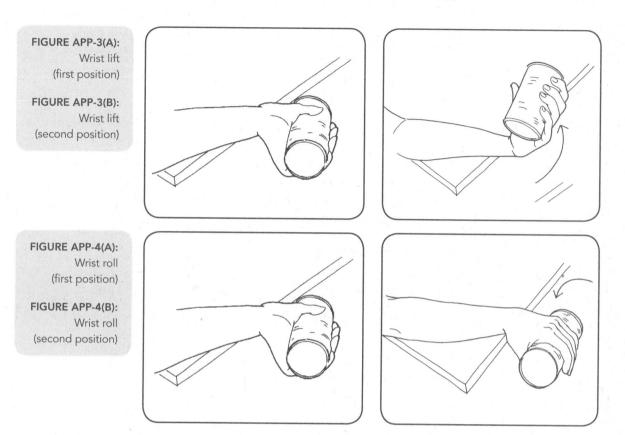

Back Exercises

- **Cat Back:** Position yourself on your hands and knees, arms directly below your shoulders, knees directly below your hips. Drop the center of your back toward the floor, inhaling. On the exhale, arch your back up. Repeat ten times slowly. Remember to breathe.

FIGURE APP-5(A):
Cat back
(first position)

FIGURE APP-5(B):
Cat back
(second position)

- **Wall Sits:** With feet shoulder-width apart and knees slightly bent, stand with your back against the wall, pressing the small of your back into the wall. Slowly lower yourself until your thighs are parallel to the floor, keeping your back pressed against the wall.
- **Crocodile:** Another yoga position. Start on your back, legs straight. Bend your right leg and rest the sole of that foot on the left knee, and scoot your hips slightly toward the right. Roll over to the left, your right knee dropping on the floor, arms reaching straight out in front of your face. Holding the right knee down with the left leg, turn the upper body and reach the right arm around in the opposite direction.

FIGURE APP-6:
Wall sits

FIGURE APP-7:
Crocodile

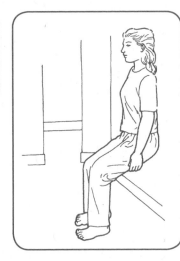
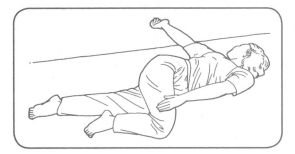

- **Knee Hug:** Lying on your back, pull your knees into your chest and wrap your arms around your legs. Rock from side to side.
- **Child's Pose:** For this yoga position, rest on your knees, in the "cat back" position. Slowly bring your hips back and down toward your heels, folding your stomach across your thighs and knees, until your forehead touches the ground. Depending on your flexibility, you can slowly bring your arms to the side, or bend them at the elbows and stack your hands under your head. Stay, breathing slowly, as long as the position feels comfortable.

Resources

Websites

www.aap.org
This is the website of the American Academy of Pediatrics, with a comprehensive section for parents.

www.americanbaby.com
This is the website of the magazine *American Baby* and has articles of interest to new parents.

www.babycenter.com
This online resource has a range of articles of interest to parents, with information from experts as well as advice from other moms.

www.cdc.gov
This website for the Centers for Disease Control and Prevention is an excellent resource for health information for all ages.

www.cpsc.gov
The U.S. Consumer Product Safety Commission website provides information on product safety standards. You can subscribe to free e-mail announcements of safety news and product recalls.

www.naeyc.org
The National Association for the Education of Young Children promotes excellence in early childhood education. It has a comprehensive section for parents.

www.parenting.com
This comprehensive site for *Parenting* and *Baby Talk* magazines has articles and forums for parents.

www.parenting.ivillage.com
Part of iVillage, this website has information and message boards for parents.

Books

Borden, Marian Edelman. *The Pocket Idiot's Guide to Play Groups*. New York: Alpha, 2008.

Huggins, Kathleen. *The Nursing Mother's Companion: Revised Edition*. Boston: Harvard Common Press, 2005.

La Leche League International. *The Womanly Art of Breastfeeding: Seventh Revised Edition*. New York: Penquin, 2004.

Meek, Joan Younger, and Sherill Tippins. *The American Academy of Pediatrics New Mother's Guide to Breastfeeding*. New York: Bantam, 2005.

Pantley, Elizabeth. *The No-Cry Sleep Solution: Gentle Ways to Help Your Baby Sleep Through the Night*. New York: McGraw-Hill, 2002.

Sears, Martha. *The Breastfeeding Book: Everything You Need to Know about Nursing Your Child from Birth Through Weaning*. Boston: Little, Brown, 2000.

Sears, William, and Martha Sears. *The Baby Book: Everything You Need to Know about Your Baby from Birth to Age Two*. Boston: Little, Brown, 2003.

Index

The EVERYTHING Series!

BUSINESS & PERSONAL FINANCE

Everything® Accounting Book
Everything® Budgeting Book, 2nd Ed.
Everything® Business Planning Book
Everything® Coaching and Mentoring Book, 2nd Ed.
Everything® Fundraising Book
Everything® Get Out of Debt Book
Everything® Grant Writing Book, 2nd Ed.
Everything® Guide to Buying Foreclosures
Everything® Guide to Fundraising, $15.95
Everything® Guide to Mortgages
Everything® Guide to Personal Finance for Single Mothers
Everything® Home-Based Business Book, 2nd Ed.
Everything® Homebuying Book, 3rd Ed., $15.95
Everything® Homeselling Book, 2nd Ed.
Everything® Human Resource Management Book
Everything® Improve Your Credit Book
Everything® Investing Book, 2nd Ed.
Everything® Landlording Book
Everything® Leadership Book, 2nd Ed.
Everything® Managing People Book, 2nd Ed.
Everything® Negotiating Book
Everything® Online Auctions Book
Everything® Online Business Book
Everything® Personal Finance Book
Everything® Personal Finance in Your 20s & 30s Book, 2nd Ed.
Everything® Personal Finance in Your 40s & 50s Book, $15.95
Everything® Project Management Book, 2nd Ed.
Everything® Real Estate Investing Book
Everything® Retirement Planning Book
Everything® Robert's Rules Book, $7.95
Everything® Selling Book
Everything® Start Your Own Business Book, 2nd Ed.
Everything® Wills & Estate Planning Book

COOKING

Everything® Barbecue Cookbook
Everything® Bartender's Book, 2nd Ed., $9.95
Everything® Calorie Counting Cookbook
Everything® Cheese Book
Everything® Chinese Cookbook
Everything® Classic Recipes Book
Everything® Cocktail Parties & Drinks Book
Everything® College Cookbook
Everything® Cooking for Baby and Toddler Book
Everything® Diabetes Cookbook
Everything® Easy Gourmet Cookbook
Everything® Fondue Cookbook
Everything® Food Allergy Cookbook, $15.95
Everything® Fondue Party Book
Everything® Gluten-Free Cookbook
Everything® Glycemic Index Cookbook
Everything® Grilling Cookbook
Everything® Healthy Cooking for Parties Book, $15.95
Everything® Holiday Cookbook
Everything® Indian Cookbook
Everything® Lactose-Free Cookbook
Everything® Low-Cholesterol Cookbook

Everything® Low-Fat High-Flavor Cookbook, 2nd Ed., $15.95
Everything® Low-Salt Cookbook
Everything® Meals for a Month Cookbook
Everything® Meals on a Budget Cookbook
Everything® Mediterranean Cookbook
Everything® Mexican Cookbook
Everything® No Trans Fat Cookbook
Everything® One-Pot Cookbook, 2nd Ed., $15.95
Everything® Organic Cooking for Baby & Toddler Book, $15.95
Everything® Pizza Cookbook
Everything® Quick Meals Cookbook, 2nd Ed., $15.95
Everything® Slow Cooker Cookbook
Everything® Slow Cooking for a Crowd Cookbook
Everything® Soup Cookbook
Everything® Stir-Fry Cookbook
Everything® Sugar-Free Cookbook
Everything® Tapas and Small Plates Cookbook
Everything® Tex-Mex Cookbook
Everything® Thai Cookbook
Everything® Vegetarian Cookbook
Everything® Whole-Grain, High-Fiber Cookbook
Everything® Wild Game Cookbook
Everything® Wine Book, 2nd Ed.

GAMES

Everything® 15-Minute Sudoku Book, $9.95
Everything® 30-Minute Sudoku Book, $9.95
Everything® Bible Crosswords Book, $9.95
Everything® Blackjack Strategy Book
Everything® Brain Strain Book, $9.95
Everything® Bridge Book
Everything® Card Games Book
Everything® Card Tricks Book, $9.95
Everything® Casino Gambling Book, 2nd Ed.
Everything® Chess Basics Book
Everything® Christmas Crosswords Book, $9.95
Everything® Craps Strategy Book
Everything® Crossword and Puzzle Book
Everything® Crosswords and Puzzles for Quote Lovers Book, $9.95
Everything® Crossword Challenge Book
Everything® Crosswords for the Beach Book, $9.95
Everything® Cryptic Crosswords Book, $9.95
Everything® Cryptograms Book, $9.95
Everything® Easy Crosswords Book
Everything® Easy Kakuro Book, $9.95
Everything® Easy Large-Print Crosswords Book
Everything® Games Book, 2nd Ed.
Everything® Giant Book of Crosswords
Everything® Giant Sudoku Book, $9.95
Everything® Giant Word Search Book
Everything® Kakuro Challenge Book, $9.95
Everything® Large-Print Crossword Challenge Book
Everything® Large-Print Crosswords Book
Everything® Large-Print Travel Crosswords Book
Everything® Lateral Thinking Puzzles Book, $9.95
Everything® Literary Crosswords Book, $9.95
Everything® Mazes Book
Everything® Memory Booster Puzzles Book, $9.95

Everything® Movie Crosswords Book, $9.95
Everything® Music Crosswords Book, $9.95
Everything® Online Poker Book
Everything® Pencil Puzzles Book, $9.95
Everything® Poker Strategy Book
Everything® Pool & Billiards Book
Everything® Puzzles for Commuters Book, $9.95
Everything® Puzzles for Dog Lovers Book, $9.95
Everything® Sports Crosswords Book, $9.95
Everything® Test Your IQ Book, $9.95
Everything® Texas Hold 'Em Book, $9.95
Everything® Travel Crosswords Book, $9.95
Everything® Travel Mazes Book, $9.95
Everything® Travel Word Search Book, $9.95
Everything® TV Crosswords Book, $9.95
Everything® Word Games Challenge Book
Everything® Word Scramble Book
Everything® Word Search Book

HEALTH

Everything® Alzheimer's Book
Everything® Diabetes Book
Everything® First Aid Book, $9.95
Everything® Green Living Book
Everything® Health Guide to Addiction and Recovery
Everything® Health Guide to Adult Bipolar Disorder
Everything® Health Guide to Arthritis
Everything® Health Guide to Controlling Anxiety
Everything® Health Guide to Depression
Everything® Health Guide to Diabetes, 2nd Ed.
Everything® Health Guide to Fibromyalgia
Everything® Health Guide to Menopause, 2nd Ed.
Everything® Health Guide to Migraines
Everything® Health Guide to Multiple Sclerosis
Everything® Health Guide to OCD
Everything® Health Guide to PMS
Everything® Health Guide to Postpartum Care
Everything® Health Guide to Thyroid Disease
Everything® Hypnosis Book
Everything® Low Cholesterol Book
Everything® Menopause Book
Everything® Nutrition Book
Everything® Reflexology Book
Everything® Stress Management Book
Everything® Superfoods Book, $15.95

HISTORY

Everything® American Government Book
Everything® American History Book, 2nd Ed.
Everything® American Revolution Book, $15.95
Everything® Civil War Book
Everything® Freemasons Book
Everything® Irish History & Heritage Book
Everything® World War II Book, 2nd Ed.

HOBBIES

Everything® Candlemaking Book
Everything® Cartooning Book
Everything® Coin Collecting Book
Everything® Digital Photography Book, 2nd Ed.

Everything® Drawing Book
Everything® Family Tree Book, 2nd Ed.
Everything® Guide to Online Genealogy, $15.95
Everything® Knitting Book
Everything® Knots Book
Everything® Photography Book
Everything® Quilting Book
Everything® Sewing Book
Everything® Soapmaking Book, 2nd Ed.
Everything® Woodworking Book

HOME IMPROVEMENT

Everything® Feng Shui Book
Everything® Feng Shui Decluttering Book, $9.95
Everything® Fix-It Book
Everything® Green Living Book
Everything® Home Decorating Book
Everything® Home Storage Solutions Book
Everything® Homebuilding Book
Everything® Organize Your Home Book, 2nd Ed.

KIDS' BOOKS

All titles are $7.95

Everything® Fairy Tales Book, $14.95
Everything® Kids' Animal Puzzle & Activity Book
Everything® Kids' Astronomy Book
Everything® Kids' Baseball Book, 5th Ed.
Everything® Kids' Bible Trivia Book
Everything® Kids' Bugs Book
Everything® Kids' Cars and Trucks Puzzle and Activity Book
Everything® Kids' Christmas Puzzle & Activity Book
Everything® Kids' Connect the Dots
    Puzzle and Activity Book
Everything® Kids' Cookbook, 2nd Ed.
Everything® Kids' Crazy Puzzles Book
Everything® Kids' Dinosaurs Book
Everything® Kids' Dragons Puzzle and Activity Book
Everything® Kids' Environment Book $7.95
Everything® Kids' Fairies Puzzle and Activity Book
Everything® Kids' First Spanish Puzzle and Activity Book
Everything® Kids' Football Book
Everything® Kids' Geography Book
Everything® Kids' Gross Cookbook
Everything® Kids' Gross Hidden Pictures Book
Everything® Kids' Gross Jokes Book
Everything® Kids' Gross Mazes Book
Everything® Kids' Gross Puzzle & Activity Book
Everything® Kids' Halloween Puzzle & Activity Book
Everything® Kids' Hanukkah Puzzle and Activity Book
Everything® Kids' Hidden Pictures Book
Everything® Kids' Horses Book
Everything® Kids' Joke Book
Everything® Kids' Knock Knock Book
Everything® Kids' Learning French Book
Everything® Kids' Learning Spanish Book
Everything® Kids' Magical Science Experiments Book
Everything® Kids' Math Puzzles Book
Everything® Kids' Mazes Book
Everything® Kids' Money Book, 2nd Ed.
Everything® Kids' Mummies, Pharaoh's, and Pyramids
    Puzzle and Activity Book
Everything® Kids' Nature Book
Everything® Kids' Pirates Puzzle and Activity Book
Everything® Kids' Presidents Book
Everything® Kids' Princess Puzzle and Activity Book
Everything® Kids' Puzzle Book

Everything® Kids' Racecars Puzzle and Activity Book
Everything® Kids' Riddles & Brain Teasers Book
Everything® Kids' Science Experiments Book
Everything® Kids' Sharks Book
Everything® Kids' Soccer Book
Everything® Kids' Spelling Book
Everything® Kids' Spies Puzzle and Activity Book
Everything® Kids' States Book
Everything® Kids' Travel Activity Book
Everything® Kids' Word Search Puzzle and Activity Book

LANGUAGE

Everything® Conversational Japanese Book with CD, $19.95
Everything® French Grammar Book
Everything® French Phrase Book, $9.95
Everything® French Verb Book, $9.95
Everything® German Phrase Book, $9.95
Everything® German Practice Book with CD, $19.95
Everything® Inglés Book
Everything® Intermediate Spanish Book with CD, $19.95
Everything® Italian Phrase Book, $9.95
Everything® Italian Practice Book with CD, $19.95
Everything® Learning Brazilian Portuguese Book with CD, $19.95
Everything® Learning French Book with CD, 2nd Ed., $19.95
Everything® Learning German Book
Everything® Learning Italian Book
Everything® Learning Latin Book
Everything® Learning Russian Book with CD, $19.95
Everything® Learning Spanish Book
Everything® Learning Spanish Book with CD, 2nd Ed., $19.95
Everything® Russian Practice Book with CD, $19.95
Everything® Sign Language Book, $15.95
Everything® Spanish Grammar Book
Everything® Spanish Phrase Book, $9.95
Everything® Spanish Practice Book with CD, $19.95
Everything® Spanish Verb Book, $9.95
Everything® Speaking Mandarin Chinese Book with CD, $19.95

MUSIC

Everything® Bass Guitar Book with CD, $19.95
Everything® Drums Book with CD, $19.95
Everything® Guitar Book with CD, 2nd Ed., $19.95
Everything® Guitar Chords Book with CD, $19.95
Everything® Guitar Scales Book with CD, $19.95
Everything® Harmonica Book with CD, $15.95
Everything® Home Recording Book
Everything® Music Theory Book with CD, $19.95
Everything® Reading Music Book with CD, $19.95
Everything® Rock & Blues Guitar Book with CD, $19.95
Everything® Rock & Blues Piano Book with CD, $19.95
Everything® Rock Drums Book with CD, $19.95
Everything® Singing Book with CD, $19.95
Everything® Songwriting Book

NEW AGE

Everything® Astrology Book, 2nd Ed.
Everything® Birthday Personology Book
Everything® Celtic Wisdom Book, $15.95
Everything® Dreams Book, 2nd Ed.
Everything® Law of Attraction Book, $15.95
Everything® Love Signs Book, $9.95
Everything® Love Spells Book, $9.95
Everything® Palmistry Book
Everything® Psychic Book
Everything® Reiki Book

Everything® Sex Signs Book, $9.95
Everything® Spells & Charms Book, 2nd Ed.
Everything® Tarot Book, 2nd Ed.
Everything® Toltec Wisdom Book
Everything® Wicca & Witchcraft Book, 2nd Ed.

PARENTING

Everything® Baby Names Book, 2nd Ed.
Everything® Baby Shower Book, 2nd Ed.
Everything® Baby Sign Language Book with DVD
Everything® Baby's First Year Book
Everything® Birthing Book
Everything® Breastfeeding Book
Everything® Father-to-Be Book
Everything® Father's First Year Book
Everything® Get Ready for Baby Book, 2nd Ed.
Everything® Get Your Baby to Sleep Book, $9.95
Everything® Getting Pregnant Book
Everything® Guide to Pregnancy Over 35
Everything® Guide to Raising a One-Year-Old
Everything® Guide to Raising a Two-Year-Old
Everything® Guide to Raising Adolescent Boys
Everything® Guide to Raising Adolescent Girls
Everything® Mother's First Year Book
Everything® Parent's Guide to Childhood Illnesses
Everything® Parent's Guide to Children and Divorce
Everything® Parent's Guide to Children with ADD/ADHD
Everything® Parent's Guide to Children with Asperger's
    Syndrome
Everything® Parent's Guide to Children with Anxiety
Everything® Parent's Guide to Children with Asthma
Everything® Parent's Guide to Children with Autism
Everything® Parent's Guide to Children with Bipolar Disorder
Everything® Parent's Guide to Children with Depression
Everything® Parent's Guide to Children with Dyslexia
Everything® Parent's Guide to Children with Juvenile Diabetes
Everything® Parent's Guide to Children with OCD
Everything® Parent's Guide to Positive Discipline
Everything® Parent's Guide to Raising Boys
Everything® Parent's Guide to Raising Girls
Everything® Parent's Guide to Raising Siblings
Everything® Parent's Guide to Raising Your
    Adopted Child
Everything® Parent's Guide to Sensory Integration Disorder
Everything® Parent's Guide to Tantrums
Everything® Parent's Guide to the Strong-Willed Child
Everything® Parenting a Teenager Book
Everything® Potty Training Book, $9.95
Everything® Pregnancy Book, 3rd Ed.
Everything® Pregnancy Fitness Book
Everything® Pregnancy Nutrition Book
Everything® Pregnancy Organizer, 2nd Ed., $16.95
Everything® Toddler Activities Book
Everything® Toddler Book
Everything® Tween Book
Everything® Twins, Triplets, and More Book

PETS

Everything® Aquarium Book
Everything® Boxer Book
Everything® Cat Book, 2nd Ed.
Everything® Chihuahua Book
Everything® Cooking for Dogs Book
Everything® Dachshund Book
Everything® Dog Book, 2nd Ed.
Everything® Dog Grooming Book

Everything® Dog Obedience Book
Everything® Dog Owner's Organizer, $16.95
Everything® Dog Training and Tricks Book
Everything® German Shepherd Book
Everything® Golden Retriever Book
Everything® Horse Book, 2nd Ed., $15.95
Everything® Horse Care Book
Everything® Horseback Riding Book
Everything® Labrador Retriever Book
Everything® Poodle Book
Everything® Pug Book
Everything® Puppy Book
Everything® Small Dogs Book
Everything® Tropical Fish Book
Everything® Yorkshire Terrier Book

REFERENCE

Everything® American Presidents Book
Everything® Blogging Book
Everything® Build Your Vocabulary Book, $9.95
Everything® Car Care Book
Everything® Classical Mythology Book
Everything® Da Vinci Book
Everything® Einstein Book
Everything® Enneagram Book
Everything® Etiquette Book, 2nd Ed.
Everything® Family Christmas Book, $15.95
Everything® Guide to C. S. Lewis & Narnia
Everything® Guide to Divorce, 2nd Ed., $15.95
Everything® Guide to Edgar Allan Poe
Everything® Guide to Understanding Philosophy
Everything® Inventions and Patents Book
Everything® Jacqueline Kennedy Onassis Book
Everything® John F. Kennedy Book
Everything® Mafia Book
Everything® Martin Luther King Jr. Book
Everything® Pirates Book
Everything® Private Investigation Book
Everything® Psychology Book
Everything® Public Speaking Book, $9.95
Everything® Shakespeare Book, 2nd Ed.

RELIGION

Everything® Angels Book
Everything® Bible Book
Everything® Bible Study Book with CD, $19.95
Everything® Buddhism Book
Everything® Catholicism Book
Everything® Christianity Book
Everything® Gnostic Gospels Book
Everything® Hinduism Book, $15.95
Everything® History of the Bible Book
Everything® Jesus Book
Everything® Jewish History & Heritage Book
Everything® Judaism Book
Everything® Kabbalah Book
Everything® Koran Book
Everything® Mary Book
Everything® Mary Magdalene Book
Everything® Prayer Book

Everything® Saints Book, 2nd Ed.
Everything® Torah Book
Everything® Understanding Islam Book
Everything® Women of the Bible Book
Everything® World's Religions Book

SCHOOL & CAREERS

Everything® Career Tests Book
Everything® College Major Test Book
Everything® College Survival Book, 2nd Ed.
Everything® Cover Letter Book, 2nd Ed.
Everything® Filmmaking Book
Everything® Get-a-Job Book, 2nd Ed.
Everything® Guide to Being a Paralegal
Everything® Guide to Being a Personal Trainer
Everything® Guide to Being a Real Estate Agent
Everything® Guide to Being a Sales Rep
Everything® Guide to Being an Event Planner
Everything® Guide to Careers in Health Care
Everything® Guide to Careers in Law Enforcement
Everything® Guide to Government Jobs
Everything® Guide to Starting and Running a Catering
    Business
Everything® Guide to Starting and Running a Restaurant
**Everything® Guide to Starting and Running
    a Retail Store**
Everything® Job Interview Book, 2nd Ed.
Everything® New Nurse Book
Everything® New Teacher Book
Everything® Paying for College Book
Everything® Practice Interview Book
Everything® Resume Book, 3rd Ed.
Everything® Study Book

SELF-HELP

Everything® Body Language Book
Everything® Dating Book, 2nd Ed.
Everything® Great Sex Book
**Everything® Guide to Caring for Aging Parents,
    $15.95**
Everything® Self-Esteem Book
Everything® Self-Hypnosis Book, $9.95
Everything® Tantric Sex Book

SPORTS & FITNESS

Everything® Easy Fitness Book
Everything® Fishing Book
Everything® Guide to Weight Training, $15.95
Everything® Krav Maga for Fitness Book
Everything® Running Book, 2nd Ed.
Everything® Triathlon Training Book, $15.95

TRAVEL

Everything® Family Guide to Coastal Florida
Everything® Family Guide to Cruise Vacations
Everything® Family Guide to Hawaii
Everything® Family Guide to Las Vegas, 2nd Ed.
Everything® Family Guide to Mexico
Everything® Family Guide to New England, 2nd Ed.

Everything® Family Guide to New York City, 3rd Ed.
**Everything® Family Guide to Northern California
    and Lake Tahoe**
Everything® Family Guide to RV Travel & Campgrounds
Everything® Family Guide to the Caribbean
Everything® Family Guide to the Disneyland® Resort, California
    Adventure®, Universal Studios®, and the Anaheim
    Area, 2nd Ed.
Everything® Family Guide to the Walt Disney World Resort®,
    Universal Studios®, and Greater Orlando, 5th Ed.
Everything® Family Guide to Timeshares
Everything® Family Guide to Washington D.C., 2nd Ed.

WEDDINGS

Everything® Bachelorette Party Book, $9.95
Everything® Bridesmaid Book, $9.95
Everything® Destination Wedding Book
Everything® Father of the Bride Book, $9.95
Everything® Green Wedding Book, $15.95
Everything® Groom Book, $9.95
Everything® Jewish Wedding Book, 2nd Ed., $15.95
Everything® Mother of the Bride Book, $9.95
Everything® Outdoor Wedding Book
Everything® Wedding Book, 3rd Ed.
Everything® Wedding Checklist, $9.95
Everything® Wedding Etiquette Book, $9.95
Everything® Wedding Organizer, 2nd Ed., $16.95
Everything® Wedding Shower Book, $9.95
Everything® Wedding Vows Book, 3rd Ed., $9.95
Everything® Wedding Workout Book
Everything® Weddings on a Budget Book, 2nd Ed., $9.95

WRITING

Everything® Creative Writing Book
Everything® Get Published Book, 2nd Ed.
Everything® Grammar and Style Book, 2nd Ed.
Everything® Guide to Magazine Writing
Everything® Guide to Writing a Book Proposal
Everything® Guide to Writing a Novel
Everything® Guide to Writing Children's Books
Everything® Guide to Writing Copy
Everything® Guide to Writing Graphic Novels
Everything® Guide to Writing Research Papers
Everything® Guide to Writing a Romance Novel, $15.95
Everything® Improve Your Writing Book, 2nd Ed.
Everything® Writing Poetry Book
